Development on Purpose

Faith and Human Behavior in the Social Environment

Lisa Hosack

ISBN: 978-0-9897581-5-4

*Dedicated to my mother, Shirley Coffman,
who did not live to see this book completed,
but whose impact is felt throughout its pages.*

*And to my sister, Lori, who faithfully prayed
for this book and its writer.*

Contents

Acknowledgments

Many individuals played a role in the completion of this book. Sincere thanks to Rick Chamiec-Case for his wisdom and unfailing support and to Sandy Bauer, Jane Hoyt-Oliver, Rebecca Rine, and Seulgi Byun for their excellent and helpful feedback. I am indebted to several classes of students who read rough drafts and provided input and inspiration. Finally, my greatest cheerleader, Robert N. Hosack, provided countless words of encouragement, not to mention, editorial support. My thanks to you all.

Preface

One of the things I learned quickly in my roles as a student, social worker, parent, and eventually social work professor, is that while human nature and development is fascinating, it's also incredibly complex and multifaceted. You don't have to work very long in the social work field to encounter head-scratching examples such as siblings raised in the same home environment who turn out as entirely different adults. Or children taught in identical educational environments who wind up learning completely different things. Or the way in which some adults who have experienced trauma recover and grow from suffering while others get trapped in resentment, hopelessness, and despair.

Social workers have long believed that individuals cannot be understood without a careful examination of the person *and* their environment—their families, schools, neighborhoods, ethnic groups, workplaces, and so on. Most social workers are also familiar with the need to do a micro and macro examination of a case in order to understand the immediate context of the individuals as well as the broader forces that impact their lives. That means that studying the health of a depressed client's marriage is no more important than studying the nature of the neighborhood in which the couple rents an apartment. Those forces work together, along with many other important variables, to impact the daily realities experienced by those we serve.

What social workers know (or perhaps intuitively sense) is that there is a complex interplay of nature, nurture, and environmental influences that intertwine to inform and shape individuals. In fact, we could safely say that development takes a uniquely different form in each person on the planet. Indeed, while there are indeed quantifiable aspects of the ways in which humans grow and develop, the particulars of each person and the context in which they live come together uniquely, creating an infinite number of variables and outcomes. And that infinite number of variables, while frustrating for those who wish to accurately describe and predict human behavior, meld in altogether unique and individualized ways. This is the wonder and mystery of human development. No two stories are the same.

Taking into account both the person and the environment is also important because social workers want to help clients to actually change and accomplish their goals and, therefore, need to know where obstacles to progress actually lie. To do this, social workers naturally want to locate the heart of the problem. But a problem may have multiple different underlying causes. Take a depressed male client, for example. He may be depressed because his marriage and family are functioning poorly. In this case, his sense of hopelessness about relationships in his *micro* environment surfaces as the primary factor behind his depression. Another plausible option is that his depression is rooted in pessimism about the future, an obstacle linked to his *macro* environment. The client may have marketable job skills but live in an economically depressed community with bleak vocational prospects. We might also conclude that the man's depression is the result of unresolved psychological issues from his past. He could be depressed because current stresses have overwhelmed his ability to cope or because past emotional wounds have been triggered by his current circumstances. Alternatively, the source of the client's struggle may be neither his interpersonal relationships, setting, nor psychological history, but an illness within his physical body. Finally, we might suggest that, like dominoes, these areas have *each* been activated, one after another, in rapid succession. Indeed in many cases, there isn't a singular cause to a problem such as depression, but a combination of factors working together.

Whenever social workers attempt to help, they face the challenge of holding elements of the unique person in one hand along with elements of the unique environment in the other hand. Social workers are trained to value an understanding of both the person and their environment, a concept often referred to as *person-in-environment*. Historically, social workers have looked to theories for help in explaining this tension. As we will see in later chapters, theories typically emphasize the things held in one hand or the other. *Psychodynamic theory*, for example, locates the problem within the "person" hand. In our depressed male case, it encourages us to look to unresolved past psychological issues as primary sources of his depression. *Cognitive-behavioral theory* also locates the problem within the person hand and suggests that the client has unproductive thought patterns that make and keep him depressed. This theory may connect, for example, his inability to find work with a view of himself as inherently flawed. Other approaches, such as *social learning theory,* look to the "environment" hand, explaining our client's problem on the basis of what he has learned from various social groups, especially those modeling harmful behaviors.

Persons and environments are both divine priorities. Consider, for example, how God interacts with us as separate and unique persons, demonstrating the importance of our individuality. Our unique emotions, concerns, and circumstances are never outside of God's concern. The Psalm writers speak often of God's tender and watchful care for their needs as individuals. On the other hand, God desires just environments where people can flourish as persons, families, and communities. The Old Testament prophets write about our responsibility to work toward policies and practices that are characterized by mercy and justice. We are called to fight injustice and its consequences in our local and global communities. Indeed, Scripture speaks of the ways in which God attends to both the "person" and "environment" hands by attending to us individually while simultaneously shepherding all of humanity, not to mention the entirety of the natural world. Imagine God holding you and the entire universe in His hands. Colossians 1:17 indicates that indeed God is holding all things together through the work of Jesus Christ.

Adding to the complexity of our person and environment challenge is the reality that development is constantly in flux. This is true because nature, nurture, and environmental influences themselves are constantly changing. Human development is not only unique in the way it plays out within each individual; it's an ever-moving target. Children get older and grow up, poverty increases or decreases, physical bodies decline, and religious beliefs strengthen and weaken.

What does this mean for social workers seeking to understand their clients well in order to help them well? Among other things, it means that while most of us like simple answers to problems, categories do not sufficiently capture or explain human development. Grouping individuals by things such as age, ethnicity, and socioeconomic status gives us helpful parameters, but never the complete picture. Theories are also useful, but also fall short. Instead, what is consistently required from each of us is a posture of humility and curiosity toward the persons we serve. The complexity of these persons and their environments necessitates carefully listening to their stories and the particular ways they have been shaped by their places and experiences. Ultimately, this is what makes social work so fascinating — no story is the same.

This book reaches farther than most by incorporating faith-based themes with our understanding of persons and environments. This is an important gap in social work literature as the Christian faith offers insights about persons and environments that add remarkable depth and wisdom. As persons of faith in social work, we draw upon rich theological themes related to God, our roles in relationship to God, and the world we inhabit. For example, biblical themes related to our individuality, relationality, and embodiment provide the appropriate context for accurately understanding human behavior and development.

Our faith has much to say about human nature. For example, the Bible highlights the fallen, sinful nature of humans, a stark reality for each of us. Christian theology also highlights the ways that sin extends to all of creation and, therefore, leaves its indelible mark on every social institution—families, workplaces, schools, neighborhoods, and even churches. Every conceivable environment has been tainted by sin. We see its destructive consequences in our own actions, the actions of others toward us, and the large-scale actions of nations. As social workers, we see the marks of sin all over the cases in which we work.

But the Christian story is ultimately one of redemption and hope. Though sin is destructive and the world deeply broken, God has hardly abandoned His creation. Jesus Himself comes to us like a physician to the sick, offering grace, mercy, and healing. As Christians in social work, we act as God's hands and feet, his tangible, earthly representatives. But we must never imagine ourselves as those who are first on the scene. God is always there before us, calling forth light from darkness.

The Bible also reveals the deeply relational nature of humans, that is, the way in which we are created and hardwired for connection with God and other people. Healthy and life-giving relationships form the rich context—the environment—by which we experience divine and human love. Relationships enable us to grow into the persons we were originally created to be and to fulfill the purposes for which we were created.

We will explore each of these points later, but for now we can conclude that Christianity provides particular insights that should not be minimized or ignored. Yes, the study of persons and their environments is complex, but we're also given foundational parameters by which to ground our exploration. Anchoring our study of Human Behavior in the Social Environment [HBSE] in these theological truths enhances our ability to understand persons and their environments.

I want to note at the start that a Christian perspective does not negate the importance of the many theories of human behavior or development offered by social work or sister disciplines. A Christian understanding can, however, prompt us to question, enthusiastically adopt, or soundly reject some of the presuppositions underlying commonly-held theories. By examining theories in light of biblical themes, we are better equipped to understand and serve. Additionally, I am not suggesting that there is necessarily a qualitative difference between the work done by Christians in social work and social workers from other backgrounds. That is not my argument here.

Instead, I outline a perspective I believe to be helpful and important to Christians in social work. We cannot fully understand ourselves and one another without grasping, for example, the ways we were created. Or appreciate the power of sin to deceive and tempt, drawing us toward activities that ultimately bring harm. How often do we as social workers become exasperated when we coach our clients about the right thing to do, yet they still choose the wrong direction. An understanding of biblical themes can lead us to more accurately understand the dynamics surrounding our clients and their struggles. By this I do not imply just an *intellectual* grasp of the situation, but an understanding that translates into empathy, grace, and accountability. I believe that a more accurate assessment of persons and their situations, one that accounts for biblical themes of human nature, also facilitates responses that more closely reflect those to which we are called.

Accounting for biblical themes is also important because it can sustain us during times of discouragement. Working with people is less predictable than working with, say, computers. Both entail flexibility and trouble-shooting, but our clients cannot be programmed to act in the ways we wish they would. At times they make destructive and harmful decisions. When you care about people and their environments, setbacks are disheartening. Grounding ourselves in realities such as human agency, fallenness, and promise of redemption can sustain us when we feel ineffective or even angry. Understanding the nature of persons can, for example, allow us to be faithful in our work while remembering that ultimately persons make their own choices. In complex situations where we play only a small role, an understanding of God's redemptive heart allows us to trust that He is always present and working.

At this point, I want to briefly explain the organization of the text. The book is divided into two parts. Part 1 explores the frameworks and theories of HBSE from a faith-based perspective. Part 2 covers six stages of the lifespan, using case studies to apply some of the theories and frameworks from Part 1. In this sense, Part 1 is designed to be more theoretical and Part 2 to be more applied.

The book is further divided into twelve chapters. Five key biblical themes are briefly identified in the beginning of the book and further discussed in Chapter 1. These themes are not intended to be inclusive, but were chosen because of their application to HBSE. Chapter 2 discusses a theological perspective for HBSE. The biological, psychological, and social realms—the biopsychosocial perspective—was used to organize Chapters 3–6. Chapters 7–12 examine cases across the lifespan using some of the principles described in Part 1. In sum, this book pulls together three streams by examining: (1) biblical themes and a theological model in Chapters 1–2, (2) the intersection of biblical themes and biological, social, and psychological theories in Chapters 3–6, and (3) the practical application of biblical themes to various stages of the lifespan in Chapters 7–12.

Like every author who comes from a particular vantage point, I want to be transparent about the theological and denominational perspective from which I am writing. My point in doing so is not to suggest my denominational tradition as the preferable one, but simply to identify my roots for the sake of reader understanding. During the majority of my adult years, I have been discipled within the Reformed tradition, and careful readers may hear this denominational "accent" throughout. But each of us speaks with our own accent and must listen carefully to one another's core message. That type of listening is cultivated and intentional, a gift to the speaker.

I have written this text for Christians in social work, while acknowledging this as a wonderfully diverse group. While we likely will not agree on every matter, I write with hopes that this text may be helpful to a group with many common core beliefs. Related to this point, please note that I have chosen to refer to God with male pronouns throughout this book, more for ease in reading than as a specific theological statement.

Readers should also note that this book takes an intentionally micro HBSE focus. Due to space limitations, many critically important macro issues, including groups, communities, social welfare politics and policies, and economic forces will not be significantly addressed. Understand that in no way does this lessen their importance, however, to fully grasping the complexity of human behavior and development.

I wish to acknowledge two excellent texts which greatly influenced this work. *The Reciprocal Self* by Jack O. Balswick, Pamela Ebstyne King, and Kevin S. Reimer informed my thinking around relational reciprocity and Trinitarian anthropology. *Exploring Psychology and Christian Faith* by Donald J. Tellinghuisen and Paul Moes was equally influential. Their delineation of biblical themes and their general tone influenced my approach in this text. To each of these authors, my sincere gratitude.

This text is designed to accompany standard HBSE textbooks. It has self-contained chapters that may be read and used interchangeably. It is for students and social workers on the frontlines who wish to better understand the remarkable persons you serve. Those on the frontlines also include those working to improve the world by setting and impacting public policy and filling critical leadership roles within the field. This book is also for you, because ultimately persons and environments form the basis of all social work practice.

My hope is that God may guide us in better understanding how and why He has made us. May we all grow and develop in the right direction.

Balswick, J.O., King, P.E., & Reimer, K.S. (2016). *The reciprocating self: Human development in theological perspective* (2nd edition). Downers Grove, IL: InterVarsity Press.

Tellinguisen, D.J. & Moes, P. (2014). *Exploring psychology and Christian faith: An introductory guide*. Grand Rapids, MI: Baker Academic.

Chapter One

Biblical Themes
to Ground Us

U nderstanding human behavior in its social environments is a
complex, yet fascinating, endeavor. Many developmental theories offer explanations that guide social work practitioners in
understanding the behaviors of their clients. However, while
social work as a discipline draws primarily upon scientifically-proven explanations of human behavior, Christians in social work draw not only
upon those knowledge sources, but also on Biblical revelation. Believing
the Bible to be divinely communicated truth, we rightly look to the Scrip-
tures for guidance in understanding God's intentions in our formation. As
we will see, the Bible provides us with an understanding of human behavior and development that requires our careful attention. While social scientists, including many Christians in social work, are expanding the current knowledge base through research, the Bible provides another form
of revelation from which to understand persons and their development.

In this chapter, we will look more closely at the biblical themes that
were identified in the previous pages. There are also many other important biblical themes, but these have been chosen for their relevance to the
study of HBSE. The themes will additionally be revisited throughout the
book as they provide a foundation for critiquing the theories and cases we
will explore later.

Social Work: Humans are Relational

*If the divine Trinity shows a community of Father, Son, and Holy
Spirit bonded by love, then humans created in God's image find
their truest life and fulfillment in human community and not in
isolation.*

Donald K. McKim (2001)

9

Here is the good news: the living God is not a solitary God. The living God is not a lonely God...from all eternity, the living God has existed as Father, Son, and Holy Spirit. From all eternity, God has been able to speak of himself of "we," "us," and "our."

Darrell Johnson (2015)

One does not live alone. Living is a communal act, whether or not its communality is acknowledged.

Wendell Berry (1990)

We begin with the theme that we are formed as deeply relational persons. We often think of relationships as interpersonal connections we choose or reject throughout life. Indeed, relationships are demonstrations of our relationality, but the concept goes beyond that. Relationality—being *characterized by relationships*—is a part of our DNA, part of the substance that makes us human. To be human *means* to be relational, whatever the specific number of friends, enemies, or acquaintances one may hold at a point in time.

Human relationality may seem obvious, even intuitive, to social workers who typically appreciate the value of relationships. The name of our discipline—social work—even suggests that there's something inherently *social* about the work we do. However, it is instructive to take a closer look at the nature of relationality. What does it mean that we are formed for relationships? And related to this, if God formed us as inherently relational, what *type* of relationships does God intend for us? Relationships vary significantly in purpose, degrees of closeness, and health. These questions will be addressed more fully as we consider cases across the lifespan. But we first need to consider some foundational truths about our relationality or the ways that we are characterized by relationships.

Human relationality is demonstrated through our relationship with God. We are related to God because we share some of His characteristics. We are created with characteristics that resemble God who "created mankind in His image" (Genesis 1:27, NIV) or as His image-bearers. *Imago Dei* is the theological term that characterizes this truth. Image-bearing is a critical starting point for understanding human development (Grenz, 1994). It means that we can look to the nature of God for clues about ourselves.

Familial metaphors prove somewhat useful here. Like a child who shares his mother's calm temperament or a teenager with musical aptitude like her grandfather, we see resemblance within family relationships. *Imago Dei* goes farther, however, to indicate that core characteristics of God's nature are actually imprinted on us; among others, these include our moral, spiritual, and intellectual natures (Moes & Tellinghuisen, 2014) and our own creative abilities (Crouch, 2013).

We can take *Imago Dei* a step farther because it forms the basis of understanding ourselves as relational. A core tenet of the Christian theology of most believers is understanding God as a Trinity or, in other words, believing in the triune (three-part) nature of God. The Trinity itself is a picture of God as relational. The three persons of the Trinity—God, Son, and Holy Spirit—share a relationship with one another. This means that within His very being, God is relational. And if God is relational at His core and we are formed like him, we can conclude that our core is relational as well.

We can also look at God's actions as a means of understanding our own relational nature. God interacts with us in ways that *assume* our relationality. Consider the manner in which a relationship is formed. What actions are involved? It depends on the type of relationship, of course, but often an act of initiation and communication between different persons is involved. Relationships also entail the exchange of things such as information, services, or support.

God's actions toward us include each of these aspects. There is divine initiation, communication, and the exchange of resources. But the relationship isn't entirely one-sided. When we examine the nature of God's actions—the way He pursues a relationship with us—we can infer that we have the ability to *respond* to Him (Balswick, King, & Reimer, 2016). It seems improbable that God would reach out to us if we lacked the ability to respond to him and to form a connection. It is true that the divine-human relationship is much different than our relationships with one another, but it has the characteristics of a relationship nonetheless. We can affirm our relationality because we resemble a God whose very being is comprised of three related parts. Beyond this, the Triune God pursues a relationship with us and invites us to respond to His extraordinary invitation. His very pursuit of a connection bears witness to our relational nature.

While theologians debate the meaning of *Imago Dei* or our image-bearing nature, we might further suggest that our formation in God's image creates a foundation for our value, dignity, and rights as persons (Wolterstorff, 2010). In other words, if we bear aspects of God in our nature, then we also carry a measure of the worth and value that is connected *to* God. Like the paintings of a well-known and respected artist, we have value simply because we were formed by Him. Like the son of a famous politician, we have status because of our connection to him.

Human value and worth is extended even farther by God's love. God's love for the persons he has created assigns them additional value and worth. Our status as His beloved makes us valuable. In the same way that the unconditional love of a parent validates the worth of their child, even when that child does not act lovingly in return, God's love for humanity is a demonstration of the worth and value of all persons. A parent's unconditional love for their child elevates the youngster as one worthy of love, despite the presence of any actions that might suggest otherwise. In the same manner, God's love, demonstrated through his actions toward us, gives each person significance. This point is all the more poignant when we consider the imbalance in the relationship, as what we give back to God pales in comparison to what He offers.

Our core relationality and connectedness to God also provides a foundation for our relationships with one another. As fellow image-bearers, we are fundamentally similar. While on the surface there are many things about one another we do not share or even understand, we all carry the unique marks of humanness. We all bear the marks of our Creator. Remarkably, God's glory is displayed in us, His creation, however dimly that glory may appear at times. Importantly, our shared status as image-bearers should inform our posture toward relationships with those with whom we differ. We hold more in common than we often realize.

Our experiences also testify to our relationality. Each of us has a wide range of relational experiences. We are indebted to people in our lives who have come close and offered healing, encouragement, instruction, and guidance. We can also recall the pain and disappointment of relationships that have lacked critical ingredients such as faithfulness, trustworthiness, or consistency. Undoubtedly, our relationships have been both deeply meaningful and deeply problematic. But despite their qualities, our experiences tacitly affirm our relational nature, that we are interdependent beings, connected to God and each other.

Social workers around the world rightly prioritize the importance of relationships. As people of faith, we affirm this priority. A difference is, however, that we tie our relationality *first* to God who created us to be in relationship with Him and other people. We ground our relational nature in Him, the one we resemble. Beyond this, we desire to use the characteristics of His relationship with us as a model for our relationships with others.

In sum, we may conclude that if the Triune God is relational and created us in His image, we share His relational nature. In other words, we are relational because God is. Our relational nature is further confirmed by the ways that He interacts with us, reaching out and inviting a relationship. Our relatedness to God is the ultimate foundation for our shared value and worth as persons. We can also look to our shared humanity as the basis for forming relationships, especially with those with whom we differ. Our relational nature informs innumerable aspects of our lives and, as we will see, is a critical force in development.

All have Sinned and Fallen Short: Humans Sin and are in Need of Redemption

> *If only there were evil people somewhere, insidiously committing evil deeds, and it were necessary only to separate them from the rest of us and destroy them. But the line dividing good and evil cuts through the heart of every human being. And who is willing to destroy a piece of their heart?*
>
> *Aleksandr Solzhenitsyn (1973)*

> *Grace remits sin, and peace quiets the conscience. Sin and conscience torment us, but Christ has overcome these fiends now and forever.*
>
> *Martin Luther (1529)*

Christians in social work have, perhaps, a keen sense of the effects of the fall. In many respects, the very existence of social work is a manifestation of the fall. Our work presupposes that something is wrong and needs fixing. Our efforts to act as agents of redemption within places of darkness reflect this core biblical theme.

Most Christians are familiar with the concept of sin as a violation against God and His laws for the world. The Bible speaks not about God's laws as arbitrary or despotic restrictions of our freedom, but as loving means of our protection. Sin violates God's laws or protections and therefore is harmful for us. Sin, in all its tempting forms, keeps us trapped in unproductive or harmful patterns; ultimately, it inhibits our freedom. Freedom is experienced when we work in tandem with God's purposes for the world and for us as individuals. We experience freedom when we are for what God is for and against what God is against. Cornelius Plantinga, Jr. (2002) writes:

> ...the real human predicament, as Scripture reveals, is that inexplicably, irrationally, we all keep placing our lives against what's good for us. In what can only be called the mystery of antiquity, human beings from the time of Adam and Eve... have so often chosen to live against God, against each other, and against God's world (p. 50).

Placing ourselves under the authority of God and His commands has the paradoxical effect of making us the most free as human beings because we are living in alignment with God's purposes for us. In other words, living in accordance with God's good intentions for us facilitates our flourishing as persons. The problem is that in our sinfulness, we have the inherent sense that *we* know what is best for us—that *we* have the ability to act as God. From our skewed vantage point, we perceive God's path as anything but freedom. At times, submitting to God seems more like a burden than the "light and easy yoke" that Jesus spoke about. We fight the same temptation as Adam and Eve, the impulse to act as our own god.

To complicate things more, our sin and rebellion against God often takes on highly subtle forms. Martin Luther famously wrote, "Your gods are whatever your heart clings to (as cited in Lenker, 1908)." The problem is that we are often drawn to things that appeal to our hearts, yet are ultimately *false* gods—things that imitate God. Because they are imitations of God, they lack the ability to deliver on their promises and quickly disappoint.

Beyond this, we struggle to see ourselves as we actually are, rationalizing bad behavior, blaming other people for our actions, and minimizing the depth of our sinfulness. The fall penetrates our own thinking and our own desires. Many followers of Christ have experienced the sense of frustration that Paul writes of in Romans 7:18, "For I know that good itself does not dwell in me, that is, in my sinful nature. For I have the desire to do what is good, but I cannot carry it out."

But God has not abandoned His creation. Desiring a continued relationship with us, he offers redemption through the work of Jesus Christ. Though we are "dead in our sin," we can be "alive in Christ" and no longer the "slaves" of sin. The word redemption implies "paying off," something like what we do with a mortgage or a student loan. Sin created a hefty debt that only an enormous redemptive act could pay. The cross and resurrection of Jesus Christ—the most pivotal events in human history—provided the basis for redemption from sin as Christ paid the penalty for sin and its deadly consequences once and for all.

It might be difficult to find another biblical theme with as much application to social work because sin forms the backdrop and the basis for much of our work. While God's good creation has not been entirely destroyed by sin, it has been significantly damaged. In essence, sin forms the foundation for a multitude of problems that harm and place our clients (not to mention ourselves) at risk such as poverty, abuse, racism, disease, environmental damage, and human trafficking.

Sin negatively affects persons as well as the environments around those persons. In fact, the Bible reveals sin as so extensive that it invades individuals, families, institutions, organizations, governments, and every conceivable part of the world. The words of confession from The Book of Common Prayer (1960) describe well our individual and corporate predicament related to sin,

> We have erred and strayed from thy ways, like lost sheep…we have followed too much the devices and desires of our own hearts…we have left undone those things which we ought to have done, and we have done those things which we ought not to have done (pp. 41-42).

In our current context, as people of faith, we live with a tension that some refer to as the "already, but not yet." Christ's redemptive work has already occurred, but the world continues to suffer under the effects of sin. We are waiting for the destructive effects of sin to be eliminated for good. But we don't wait passively. As Christians in social work, we are invited into the holy work of co-laboring with God. Our small acts of daily obedience contribute to His grand purposes. The call is to work in ways that are redemptive and restorative, whatever the precise nature of our jobs. Plantinga (2002) writes:

> Proclamation of the resurrection of Jesus isn't nearly everything Christians have to offer the world, but it's the platform for everything they have to offer. Every Christian hospital, college, orphanage, media ministry, counseling service, political party, relief agency, and AIDS clinic builds on this platform (p. 80).

Within the "not yet," the consequences of sin remain great for both individuals and institutions. People get snared by sin, both through their own intentional acts and through the macro-level effects of the fall. Our clients experience this when they struggle with issues far outside their control such as disease, poverty, and death.

But Christians in social work operate from a platform of redemption. It is from this firm and hopeful place that we serve in the myriad places we are called. Because of redemption, there can be no situation or person beyond hope. We do not work alone, however, as the Holy Spirit ultimately leads and guides this divine labor. As co-laborers and Christians in social work, it is critical that we understand that God is the one doing the work and we are simply responsible to respond to Him in obedience and submission. Even in our roles as helping professionals, we are easily tempted to see ourselves as self-important saviors rather than humble servants.

While sin is the core problem, it is helpful for Christians in social work to understand the different ways that sin is manifested. For example, we need to differentiate between sin on the micro level, such as parents who make the choice to abuse their children, and sin on the macro level, such as unjust social welfare policies. While sin has affected everything, the primary sources of client problems may lie primarily in one place or another. In many situations, we assist clients in dealing with micro-level sins (for example, substance abuse) that may partly be related to systemic injustice.

Often, the more complex the problem, the more numerous are the ways in which sin is manifested. Sin in one situation may spread to another. A person who is unjustly fired from a job, for example, and does not find forgiveness or peacefulness may project unresolved anger and a need for revenge onto other people. Corruption within a government may limit economic opportunities for those in poverty, contributing to negative behaviors such as theft or drug sales. In these ways, the negative effects of sin move across micro and macro levels and from person to person.

Christians in social work are wise to understand that sin undergirds most of the situations we encounter. The goal is not to identify the presence of sin for the purpose of condemnation, but to assist people in finding freedom from its destructive effects. At times, calling dysfunctional situations what they are and identifying sin as a powerful influence provides much-needed clarification. It can also lead to what is often needed—repentance, a turn from what is destructive toward what is instead life-giving.

Applying a theology of sin to social work practice requires careful and thoughtful application. It must be balanced with an understanding of grace, compassion, and redemption. If we, for example, do not remember ourselves as sinful, we will adopt a posture of superiority and impatience with our clients. We must closely monitor our own tendencies toward judgement. We have to pair an understanding of sin with a working knowledge of human development. Some childhood behaviors, for example, are less willful forms of disobedience than normal developmental responses. Above all, we must hold the tension between identifying sin and its effects while also holding grace, compassion, and the hope of redemption.

Finally, Christians in social work may wonder about situations in which clients are not persons of faith. Many clients, groups, and organizations obviously do not endorse a theology of sin. It is still the case that identifying sin is important, whether it is acknowledged by clients and organizations or not. Regardless of the mission and values of one's employer, Christians in social work can internally acknowledge the presence of sin and work to lead others toward freedom. While it is inappropriate to use the language of faith within secular settings, by tacitly acknowledging the role of sin and the need for redemption, we rightly understand the scenario and our roles within it.

A Messy World: Creation is in Need of Restoration

For the creation was subjected to frustration...

Romans 8:20

In the biblical narrative, what begins in the Garden of Eden finds its completion at the consummation of history, when God establishes the new creation, the realm in which humans enjoy perfect fellowship with each other, creation, and the Creator.

Stanley J. Grenz & John R. Franke (2001)

The wolf will live with the lamb, the leopard will lie down with the goat, the calf and the lion and the yearling together, and a little child will lead them. The cow will feed with the bear, their young will lie down together; and the lion will eat straw like the ox. The infant will put its hand into the viper's nest. They will neither harm nor destroy on all my holy mountain; for the earth will be full of the knowledge of the Lord as the waters cover the sea.

Isaiah 11:6-9 (NIV)

It has been said that a big view of fallenness necessitates a big view of redemption and restoration (Plantinga, 2002). God's restoration project is a massive one indeed. He is steadily renewing all of creation to its original, unblemished state. God is not passively waiting for His perfect kingdom to come; He is working in the present to restore a fallen world. In the language of social work, His restoration project is micro, mezzo, and macro. He is renewing relationships within individuals, within organizations, and within governments.

As we stated in the previous section, the fall introduced many obstacles, notably shame, into our relationships. Relationships lost their inherently life-giving qualities and instead became vehicles for selfish purposes. Like Adam and Eve, humankind learned to hide its sinfulness behind rationalizations and blame. The natural world became something to exploit for self-centered ends versus a treasure to tenderly steward.

The original, unblemished creation, however, provides a model for human flourishing and arguably the ultimate model for the work of Christians in social work. While it is hard to visualize the world without sin, we can try to imagine completely healthy and life-giving relationships. We can try to envision relationships of every sort—micro, mezzo, and macro—that lead to the flourishing of participants of every age, race, and ethnicity.

Our world scarcely resembles Eden though. Humans, for example, exploit the natural world, have violent conflicts with each other, and experience feelings of shame and self-loathing. How is God restoring our presently broken world? In a big picture sense, God is doing so by *restoring* broken relationships between Himself, us, and the natural world. Not only is He doing this work, but He is employing us as agents of restoration. Ultimately, tangible activities such as facilitating reconciliation between parents and children or enforcing policies that protect the poor are examples of divine restoration in action.

If restored relationships between God, us, and creation represent an ideal context where persons flourish, we do well to pursue this ideal in our work with persons and their environments. In a practical sense, we ought to ponder what restoration would look like in the lives of our clients. We might ask ourselves what it would look like for our clients to have restored relationships with God, that is, to see themselves as His beloved. We may ponder how they might have restored relationships internally, seeing themselves more honestly and accurately. We might ponder how they could experience restored relationships with other people, actively pursuing forgiveness or setting appropriate boundaries. We will thoughtfully contemplate what truly restorative institutions and communities look like and work toward that vision.

An expansive view of restoration can be applied to all aspects of our work. Indeed, restoration is a broad concept that can entail constructive movement of any size in any area—healing in one's relationship with God, one's self, or with other people, for example. These areas are also interconnected. For example, individual psychotherapy may lead someone to better understand how the affirmation that was absent in their background results in their unrealistic expectations of others. This insight can lead to them changing their behavior and considerably improving their relationships with others. The reality is that healthier relationships *of any type* more closely mirror the relationships God intends. In other words, growth and healing in *any* of the God-creation-self dimensions reflects God's intentions and facilitates human flourishing.

Many aspects of the way God is bringing restoration to the world lie outside of our comprehension. We have limited vision and often find it difficult to see the possibility of restoration and hope within the darkest of places. Here is where we as Christians in social work must hold the tension between the gravity of sin and God's redemptive and restorative purposes.

Our responsibility is listening for God's leading and faithfully responding in ways that *facilitate* redemption and restoration, whether in individuals or systems. In doing so, we also leave the outcomes in God's hands.

Seeing our work through this perspective requires faith, imagination, and, at times, the ability to find meaning in mundane tasks that appear to hold little restorative value. Sometimes work bears little restorative "fruit," forcing us to hold out hope for the change that is needed. At times, we must see our work as seed planting, with hope that others will faithfully nurture what we have started. Other times, we have the privilege of seeing restoration clearly in the form of a reconciled marriage or the reversal of an unjust policy. However incremental the progress seems, we engage the holy work of restoration whenever we work toward restored relationships between persons, themselves, and God.

Our daily work is couched within the knowledge that the restoration of all things will eventually be complete. Grenz (1994) sums up the marvelous reality of the ultimate restoration,

> ...the entire biblical panorama may be read as presenting the purpose of God as that of bringing into being a people who reflect the divine character and thus are the *imago dei*. At the eschaton [end of the world], God will complete what was the divine intention from the beginning and has from the beginning been set before us as our human destiny. On that day, we will reflect fully the divine image as God's representatives after the pattern of Christ (p. 200).

Dust of the Earth: Humans are Embodied

> *We talk about the need to deal with the real, the material, this worldly stuff...the Christian faith is a this worldly faith. In a sense, the very core of it is the notion that God himself became flesh. That's, I think, what puts us in a different position in the way we view the world. It should at least.*
>
> Brian Dijkema (2015)

> *We are made in God's image and have a unique relationship with him, so we occupy a special place in his creation, yet we are made from the "dust of the earth" and have much in common with the rest of creation. God created us to be physical in order to care for a physical creation—to tend the garden.*
>
> Paul Moes & Paul Tellinghuisen (2014)

Why emphasize the biblical theme of embodiment—the idea that we have been created with a physical body, that we are made of tangible, physical material? Aren't bodies just unimportant containers for holding more important things like souls and minds? On the contrary, we are wise to carefully consider our embodiment as the Bible emphasizes the importance of the physical body. As Brian Dijkema (2015) writes, our faith is "this worldly." It has a true, earthly dimension. In His incarnation, for example, Jesus took on a physical body with all of the accompanying needs that bodies entail. Many of his earthly miracles involved the physical body as he healed diseases and multiplied food for hungry crowds. Importantly, the cross included real physical suffering with blood, bruises, and broken bones. The resurrection was not solely a "spiritual" one as the living Jesus, bearing the scars of His ordeal, was witnessed by many (Setran & Kiesling, 2013).

Our physical selves matter. This point is important because we are prone to both over- and under-emphasize our physical nature. At various points in history, the physical body has been deemphasized in ways that have distorted views of human development. This was true when, for example, portions of the early church emphasized the nonmaterial aspects of our humanness—the soul and spirit—over the physical body (Plantinga, Thompson, & Lundberg (2010). If we deemphasize our physical selves, we run the risk of overemphasizing "spiritual" solutions that can prove shortsighted and even damaging. In some streams of modern Christianity, there has been a lack of emphasis on our embodied selves, a perspective which can contribute to an unhealthy detachment from the body or a shallow understanding of components such as sexuality.

Conversely, the scientific revolution has contributed to overemphasizing our material selves by seeking biological origins to nearly any observable phenomenon (Moes & Tellinghuisen, 2014). Scientific advances in understanding human behavior and development have been remarkably helpful. Significant biochemical breakthroughs in understanding psychiatric disorders, for example, have led to significant relief for those who suffer. But as we will discuss in a later chapter, this view can go too far by deemphasizing free will and our responsibility in decision-making.

Philosophers and scientists have historically disagreed about this issue. While Plato and other ancient Greeks advocated a mind-body distinction, *dualism*, that persisted for centuries, many people now lean toward a form of *monism* which assumes the mind and body are one entity. In this view, the mind is part of the brain, not external to the brain (Myers and Jeeves, 1987). Within the monistic perspective, human components or qualities identified as "spiritual" (e.g., the soul), are believed to operate *through* the physical. This view subscribes to a "holistic duality" of body and soul. Plantinga and colleagues (2010) provide this helpful reframing of the issue:

In dualism, there are two eternal principles—spirit (the divine) and matter. In monism there is only the first of these principles, the divine, which possesses true reality...The Christian [view]...is neither dualistic nor monistic...Rather, it is best characterized as a duality that embraces two sorts of things: Creator and creature (p. 168).

A full exploration of the issue is beyond this book, but a proper understanding of embodiment provides guidance in understanding HBSE. The physical world was created and declared "good," highlighting the value of all that God made. As part of the creation, our bodies are good—in fact, they are holy and sacred. Therefore, they must be carefully nurtured and protected. Far from just a container, our bodies are critical to our growth and development as humans. The needs of our physical body are not tangential, but central to our very existence. They are also central to our flourishing.

The implications of embodiment for Christians in social work are profound. We uphold the importance of embodiment when we attend to the basic physical needs of our clients such as safety from physical harm. When we attempt to help families impacted by disease or illness. When we assist poor clients in signing up for food stamps. And when we advocate for policies that protect the physically vulnerable, such as persons with disabilities and older adults. Myers and Jeeves (1987) summarize this section well:

The human part of you and me is not a ghost in a body but rather the whole, unified system of brain and mind...we may indeed have been created from dust...but the end result is a priceless creature, one rich with potential beyond our imagining (p. 23).

Choices, Choices, Choices: Humans have Agency

"It is our choices, Harry, that show what we truly are, far more than our abilities."

Professor Dumbledore in Harry Potter and the Chamber of Secrets (1998)

"Every day brings new choices."

Martha Beck (2011)

"Agency" refers to the ability of a person to make choices and to act within a particular environment. Often, agency is contrasted with "structure" or those elements of an environment that limit someone's choices, such as their socioeconomic status, job skills, or geographical location. As persons, we are agents who are free to make regular decisions about our lives including what to eat and where to go. At the same time, our choices are bounded by a whole host of structures. We are free to make choices about the type of job to pursue, for example, but the range of our vocational options will be limited by our qualifications and skills. Our agency is limited by many factors, such as our physical nature, our individual abilities, and our specific environments.

In a different sense, social psychology highlights other limits on agency by describing conditions under which we are highly influenced, almost hard-wired, to respond as social beings. These tendencies regularly play out in our lives, often completely outside of our awareness. For example, we are prone to defend what we believe by paying careful attention to data that reinforce our beliefs or to use *confirmation bias*. Or we are prone to credit successes to our individual abilities, but blame failure on things outside of our control or to use *self-serving bias*. We often view our own groups as superior and other groups as inferior, using *in-group bias*. If responses such as these are automated, predictable patterns, one could argue that agency is also limited in these ways, many of which we are unaware.

Additionally, neuroscientists increasingly locate genetic origins for human behaviors, indicating that what appear to be choices may actually represent involuntary responses that are partly or entirely automated. The search, for example, for the genetic sources of personality traits such as empathy and compassion is well underway. The same is true for religious beliefs.

Holding the possibilities of agency with the realities of structure—in the form of environmental elements, unconscious behavioral tendencies, and biological forces—social workers may wonder, "just how free are we?" With time and further research, learning about agency and structure will continue to evolve. Research into aspects of the environment that trigger particular biological or behavioral responses also continues to grow.

Despite many unknowns, however, Christians in social work can affirm the fact that God has formed humans with agency. Many biblical concepts imply the presence of human agency, such as obedience and submission. These imperatives suggest that we have actual choices. God's commands throughout the Old and New Testaments infer an ability to follow or to deviate from His standards. Some may argue that human responsiveness to

God actually originates with Him who does the prompting, but some level of human agency is still implicated, even when considering the role of the Holy Spirit.

Agency plays an important role in our faith lives. Some have questioned why God does not function as a dictator, creating persons with no choice but to follow Him. In response, we can infer that while God wants a connection with us, He wants us to choose that connection rather than to have it forced upon us (Grenz, 1998). Refusing to control our actions, He instead draws us through acts of love that capture our hearts and minds. Even acts of discipline are entirely undergirded by love and a desire to draw us. God does call us to obedience, but not like a tyrannical boss or an oppressive slave master. Instead, he wants willing submission as we trust His goodness.

Agency implies many things, perhaps most importantly, responsibility. Choices carry consequences. Because agency implies the freedom to make choices and choices involve consequences, we are "responsible agents" (Moes & Tellinghuisen, 2014). Our responsibility extends to our individual choices, but also to the choices of groups of which we are a part, such as our families, churches, and neighborhoods. For Christians, this responsibility extends to our most important group, the body of Christ. As community members and members of the Church, we are responsible, for example, to advocate against local government policies that unjustly impact the poor. At times, we are responsible to lovingly confront friends who are making destructive choices. In our various roles, we have responsibility for choices that are made.

Because agency is a part of how we were formed, relationships require adequate opportunity for freedom and choice. In fact, at times we can pinpoint problems in relationships by assessing the levels of freedom and autonomy they allow the participants. Relationships that overly control an individual's choices restrict the room necessary for healthy growth, development, and creativity. We see this principle illustrated clearly in authoritarian families where agency is minimized. We also see this principle among people who suffer under corrupt governments where their rights and free speech are thwarted.

Agency is an important biblical theme for social workers to consider. As a part of our created nature, human agency must be carefully protected. The nature of human agency varies greatly depending on the developing stage and maturity of a person or group, but all persons, even those with highly limited capacity, benefit from appropriate agency. Restricted agency can be harmful as it ignores a core component of our created nature; in this respect, it can inhibit human flourishing. At the same time, people must be held responsible for the choices they freely make, even choices that prove misguided. We rightly respect agency by giving others choices when possible, holding them responsible for their choices, and fighting for their opportunities to have a voice.

Chapter Summary

Biblical themes of relationality, fallenness and the need for redemption, the need for restoration, embodiment, and agency provide considerable insight into understanding HBSE. When we frame our understanding of HBSE through these themes, we better grasp the ways that our created nature directly impacts our clients and our world.

Discussion Questions

1. How does an understanding of the universal nature of sin impact the way we interact with those who are suffering?

2. How does the concept of embodiment impact our work with clients? What examples of prioritizing embodiment can you identify in various areas of social work practice?

3. Many Christians in social work are employed in secular settings. How can one incorporate these biblical themes in settings where they cannot be explicitly discussed or referenced?

4. Do you think scientists will eventually discover a biological origin for every human response? If so, how will this change your understanding of agency?

References

Balswick J.O., King, P.E., Reimer, K.S. (2016). *The reciprocating self: human development in theological perspective.* Downers Grove, IL: IVP Academic.

Beck, M. (2011). *Expecting adam: a true story of birth, rebirth, and everyday magic.* New York: Three Rivers Press.

Berry, W. (1990). *What are people for?* Berkeley, CA: Counterpoint.

Church of England (1960). *The Book of common prayer with the additions and deviations   proposed in 1928.* Cambridge: University Press.

Crouch, A. (2013). Playing god: redeeming the gift of power. Downers Grove, IL: InterVarsity Press.

Dijkema, B. (2015). The work of our hands. *Comment Magazine,* March, 2-4.

Grenz, S.J. (1994). *Theology for the community of god.* Nashville, TN: Broadman & Holman Publishers.

Grenz, S.J. (1998). *Created for community*. Grand Rapids, MI: Baker Academic.

Grenz, S.J. & Franke, J. (2001). *Beyond fundamentalism: shaping theology in a postmodern context*. Louisville, KY: Westminster John Knox Press.

Johnson, D. (2015). Entering the trinity: living in the circle of "us." *Conversations*, *13*(1), 5-8.

McKim, D.K. (2001). *Introducing the reformed faith*. Louisville, KY: Westminster John Knox Press.

Meyers, D.G. & Jeeves, M.A. (1987). *Psychology through the eyes of faith*. Washington, D.C.: Christian College Coalition.

Moes, P. & Tellinghuisen, D.J. (2014). *Exploring psychology and christian faith: an introductory guide*. Grand Rapids, MI: Baker Academic.

Plantinga, C. (2002). *Engaging god's world: a christian vision of faith, learning, and living*. Grand Rapids: Eerdmans.

Plantinga, R.J., Thompson, T.R., Lundberg, M.D. (2010). *An introduction to christian theology*. Cambridge: Cambridge University Press.

Rowling, J.K. (1998). *Harry potter and the chamber of secrets*. New York: Scholastic, Inc.

Setran, D.P. & Kiesling, C.A. (2013). *Spiritual formation in emerging adulthood: a practical theology for college and young adult ministry*. Grand Rapids, MI: Baker Academic.

Solzhenitsyn, A. (1973). *The gulag archipelago 1918-1956*. New York: HarperCollins.

Wolterstorff, N. (2010). *Justice: rights and wrongs*. Princeton, NJ: Princeton University Press.

Chapter Two

A Theological Model for Understanding Human Behavior in the Social Environment (HBSE)

In this chapter, we will build upon the biblical themes identified in Chapter 1 by exploring a model for the understanding of HBSE.

Theories are principles that attempt to explain various phenomena. Theories can be categorized according to their primary emphases. To explain human behavior and development, we usually look to theories whose primary emphases are in biological, psychological, or social realms. Social workers seek to apply theories from each of these realms in light of an individual's context or environment. Someone's context or environment includes variables such as their age, the quality of their relationships, socioeconomic status, or geographical setting. For example, attachment theory is a psychological theory that attempts to explain the quality of a person's current relationships in light of the quality of their early relationships with their primary caregivers. Social learning theory is a social theory which is used to explain a person's behavior, such as their parenting style, in light of the models of parenting the individual has learned and observed.

Theories are enormously helpful in understanding human behavior, but they also present challenges for Christians in social work. As indicated in the previous chapter, the challenge for practitioners of faith is understanding theories and all of human behavior and development in light of biblical revelation. This is not only a challenge, but an opportunity. The richness of the biblical narrative—in its movement from creation to fall to redemption to restoration—provides a context for understanding persons and the world they inhabit. Our call is to consider our work with individuals, families, groups, organizations, and communities within that narrative. Therefore, we strive to contemplate human behavior, growth, and development, and the vast number of environments within the perspective of that grand, unfolding narrative.

Some of the primary limitations with current HBSE theories (considering them collectively) relate to their lack of a unified purpose and their shallow picture of relationality. We will first consider purpose. What do various theories explicitly or implicitly suggest as their *purpose* for human development? Toward what ultimate goals do they encourage us? As persons of faith, we will ponder those goals and purposes and ask ourselves how they interact with God's design. Theories emphasize many different aspects of development, but in doing so, they fail to provide a singular, unified sense of the direction we ought to be moving in our growth and development. As indicated in a previous chapter, the discipline of social work emphasizes the importance of relationships, but does so within a limited perspective. We will additionally consider a fuller model of relationality by viewing the nature of relationships intended by God—relationships of shalom.

Development for a Purpose

A shortcoming for Christians in social work relates to the lack of a unifying and singular *purpose* for human development within available theories and perspectives. While available theories aim to explain behavior, they contribute little to identifying an overall purpose for human development, what Balswick and colleagues (2016) have described as a *teleology*. Teleology refers to a branch of philosophy that deals with ultimate ends and refers to the idea that there is purpose or finality in the world, a *telos* (Dubray, 1912). Teleology suggests that there is an overarching *divine* purpose that provides guidance and meaning for life. It implies that there is a "why," a reason or ultimate aim behind our behavior, development, and the environments in which we operate. In the study of HBSE, it suggests that we exist and develop *for* something, *toward* something. That *something* is so life-giving and glorious that we risk missing something important if we bypass it.

Each category of HBSE theories implicitly points to different goals for human development. For example, biological theories highlight the goal of biological maturation and adaptation. From a strictly biological point of view, the goal is for our bodies, especially our brains, to grow and mature properly. Psychological theories point to the goal of normative (versus abnormal) psychological development. The goal, for example, is for us to learn the right things or to have the right kind of attachments to people. The goal of many social theories is for us to have a rich and available network of supportive relationships.

We readily affirm these goals as well as the goals of all biological, psychological, and social theories. However, these theories do not go far enough in outlining an *overarching* goal and purpose for human development, nor do they account for God's intent in forming us. Our model provides a telos and draws upon God's creational purposes by identifying **the ultimate goal of human development as secure relationships with God, ourselves, other people, and all of creation.** It suggests that we develop for a purpose greater than biological maturation, normative psychological development, or even a robust social network. As important as those goals are, we ultimately grow and develop well when we grow in loving connections with God, other people, ourselves, and the world.

With this as our ultimate goal, our telos, we identify a singular, unified purpose for human development. Having an ultimate aim suggests that we can assess different theories in light of this overarching goal. The full range of our activities can be evaluated in light of this supreme purpose. We can ponder ways to nurture this telos within every age group and every imaginable environment. We will certainly look to strong attachments, social networks, and biological protective factors in pursuing the right relationships for which we strive. But ultimately, the goals of these theories ought to support God's goals for our development.

"All of creation" is an important component of this model. By this we include, among other things, social institutions, communities, and the natural world. The emphasis on creation (which could also be known as "environment" in HBSE terms) fits well within social work. Social work as a discipline has been characterized by a commitment to highlighting two aspects—the person and their environment—when understanding human behavior and development. Indeed, a significant amount of social work research and practice focuses on better understanding person-environment intersections, especially for at-risk populations.

As Christians in social work, we strongly affirm our discipline's understanding of human development as occurring within the context of physical environments and networks of relationships. The prioritization of assessing these across micro, mezzo, and macro levels is important. However, acknowledging that persons have dynamic, interactive relationships with the whole of their environment does not go far enough as, again, it fails to identify a telos or ultimate goal for these interactions. Instead, it primarily explores the *nature* of the intersections, identifying optimal (or harmful) aspects for various groups of people. This is highly useful information that often directly contributes to our understanding and practice as Christians in social work. Nonetheless, it falls short of intentionally pointing us toward the ultimate aims that are outlined here.

Christians in social work have much to contribute to the HBSE discussion. Because the books of the Bible were set in specific historical times and places, they do not explicitly address every issue faced by our contemporary world. We must apply principles to our specific contexts. They do provide, however, communication about God's intended purposes for creation from the beginning of the world until the end of time. In doing so, it provides a unified vision for the way things *ought to be* in our world and how persons ought to relate to each other. The Biblical narrative underscores a telos or ultimate purpose which provides guidance about human development and the contexts in which this best occurs.

Relationships of Shalom

You may recall the previous chapter's discussion of relationality as a biblical theme. We already know this is a part of how we were created. But if the goal of the development throughout our lives is secure or "right" relationships between God, ourselves, others, and the world, you may be wondering what those relationship ought to look like. HBSE theories offer many excellent ideas about healthy relationships. For example, attachment theory emphasizes consistent, loving relationships between primary caregivers and children. Social learning theory emphasizes appropriate modeling. These theories identify many important relational traits, but again, are fragmented. There is not necessarily one unifying direction for the relationships we are called to foster, nor one idea about what makes a relationship "healthy" or not.

The Bible offers a robust vision of healthy relationships. This vision could be (and has been) fleshed out by authors who seek to understand, for example, how to apply a biblical vision of love to marriage. Or how to lead an organization well in light of Jesus' example and his teaching on servanthood. The goal here, however, is to provide a broad model for the secure divine and human relationships we are to be pursuing throughout our lives. In considering this model, we will draw upon two areas—creation and the nature of the Trinity.

Creation

We can learn more about the secure relationships that represent our telos or purpose in development by looking at the world before the fall. The Garden of Eden presented a picture of full and untarnished relationships between God, man and woman, and the natural world. Before sin, there was complete harmony between God and all of creation, a dynamic which is referred to as *shalom*, a Hebrew world without a clear English equivalent, but often translated as "peace." Shalom, however, is a rich concept that goes far beyond peace or the absence of conflict. Shalom implies completely right relationships with a holistic sense of completeness, harmony, and fullness. "Shalom" relationships are mutually beneficial, enhancing the well-being of all involved. The concept of shalom is also woven throughout the biblical narrative as the arc of scripture, including creation, the exodus, the life of Jesus, atonement, the church, and the consummation of the world, bends towards shalom—relationships that are right, restored, and complete (Yoder, 1987).

Many developmental theories emphasize the need to grow and develop as an individual, family, or community through maturation or self-actualization. These are certainly healthy goals, but the creational design suggests that growth, individually and collectively, is important *because it serves to facilitate shalom in our relationships*. Growth and development serve a larger goal than simply benefiting ourselves. For example, it is important for adolescents to develop well because doing so facilitates relationships of shalom in their lives. This entails many things, including understanding aspects of developmental risk in the young person's life, such as living in a high-crime, transient neighborhood. The problem is that such a context can work against relationships of shalom in the young person's life by forming an environment in which a general spirit of anxiety and distrust thwarts healthy relational connections.

In our therapeutic culture, often more emphasis is placed upon personal growth for the sake of one's own happiness than for the positive impact it has on their broader relationships. At times, an emphasis on our clients' personal happiness, fulfillment, and independence dominates our efforts as social workers. These traits have value, but must be understood in proper context. Emphasizing individual independence, for example, without a rich understanding of our need for *dependence* on God and others veers from a healthy view of God's design.

In light of this model, what do relationships of shalom actually look like? Answering this question will require carefully examining individual situations, but in general, they should affirm individuals as image-bearers and therefore as beloved by God. They should resemble the relationship of God toward us. This relationship is characterized by many things, including unconditional love, a respect for individual agency, mutual giving and taking, communication of expectations, and honesty. Relationships of shalom honor our need for agency as well as our need to depend upon one another and God. Finally, because God consistently relates to us in ways that are redemptive and restorative, relationships of shalom entail honest confession, the promise of forgiveness, and reconciliation.

Consider the example of a family. A family of shalom is characterized by unconditional love and a binding commitment to one another. Such a family has enough connectivity to make the members feel they are part of something larger than themselves (Van Hook, 2008). On the other hand, such families allow each individual to be unique, bearing particular gifts, abilities, and roles. Families characterized by shalom communicate expectations honestly and openly, but also hold members responsible for their actions as "responsible agents."

Families have the ability to nurture relationships with God, self, others, and creation in multiple ways. A secure sense of self is more likely to result in children who come from families where they are valued and seen as adding something unique and necessary to the family unit. Viewed another way, the secure sense of self that can be facilitated by a family has been shown to facilitate a healthier relationship with others and with God. Those who see themselves as worthy of love because they have experienced it unconditionally from their families often have less difficulty believing and accepting love from other sources.

Environments ought to facilitate God's shalom also. A national government ought to be one in which, for example, there is enough individual freedom and autonomy to facilitate growth. Ideally, there is also mutuality in the relationship, clear communication, honesty, fair expectations, and a binding commitment. The same could be said of a workplace or a school or a church.

The goal of relationships of shalom provide considerable direction in our assessment and work within micro and macro environments. We can evaluate the health of a family environment, for example, by assessing the *degree to which it contributes* to relationships of shalom within and between each of the individuals. In doing so, we may examine the cohesiveness of the family unit. We also consider the relationship between the family and the community around them, including their school, neighborhood, and church. We ponder whether each of these relationships increases shalom for the family, and we structure our interventions accordingly.

We can evaluate a child welfare agency by considering, among other things, the degree to which the work of the agency contributes to right relationships between children and birth parents, children and foster parents, sibling groups, and among employees and administration. Social workers know well that this type of movement is often incremental, even undetectable at times. Change of any sort involves a multitude of variables that ultimately are outside of our control. What remains within our control, however, is purposeful social work that strives to impact humans and their environments for good by aligning them with the types of relationships that God intends.

The Trinity

We draw additional insight into right relationships, those of shalom, by examining the model of the Trinity—Father, Son, and Holy Spirit. The Trinity aids us in understanding the *nature* of relationships of shalom by providing a model of individuality and connectivity (Balswick, King, & Reimer, 2016). Within the Trinity, the individual and corporate aspects of God are represented (Grenz, 1994). God is both three independent persons and one interdependent whole. Another way of viewing this is that God has the qualities of an individual and of a fully-connected, relational being. This is similar to our own human experience as both independent individuals and interdependent persons. We can infer that growing as an individual—meaning gaining better understanding of our gifts, abilities, temperaments, and personalities—is a critical part of our development. At the same time, the relational aspect of the Trinity suggests that growing in relationships is equally critical to our development. Growth in both respects is integral to our development.

Interestingly, both aspects work hand-in-hand. We do not lessen our individuality by drawing closer to God and others. We actually *gain* it because such relationships teach us the good and bad about ourselves— our gifts, personalities, weaknesses, and sinful patterns. Characterized by mutuality and give-and-take, healthy relationships provide the room to openly encounter ourselves. They allow us to grow in the deep knowledge that we are loved in spite of our flaws.

Drawing near to God has the additional effect of healing our relationships with ourselves. Unlike human relationships which may serve to diminish or shame us, drawing closer to God bolsters our inherent sense of worth as His beloved. Growth in God's love also serves to lessen our reliance on false ways of being in the world, such as validating self-worth through good deeds, physical appearance, or performance.

A wise friend reminded me recently that "all things are spiritual." She meant by this, I believe, that God is working all around us, whether we see and recognize his subtle movements or not. In the process of assisting people—with their family conflict, their poverty, or their internal shame—we are actually facilitating relationships of shalom in their lives. What is important to recognize, though, is that movement toward healing in these areas is also movement toward God. Like the Trinity, we are interconnected persons, meaning that growth in one aspect of our lives can create benefit in another. Development in right direction, toward relationships of shalom in any and all aspects of our lives, ultimately draws us closer to our Creator and to places of flourishing.

As social workers, we know that many formative relationships fall short. Many people with whom we work have not been loved well and therefore believe they are unlovable. Many have had their shortcomings held against them and have not experienced the dynamic of grace. We will learn more about the characteristics of relationships that facilitate healthy growth and development in Part Two. Understanding an ideal model for development, however, allows us to better assist others who suffer from the lack of shalom in their relationships. This is how we join with God in His restoration project, by working to restore shalom in relationships where sin has introduced havoc.

Chapter Summary

We are developing *for* something, namely relationships of shalom between God, ourselves, other people, and creation. This is the purpose for which we are formed. This is relevant for social workers because persons ultimately flourish when they are aligned with God's purposes (Volf, 2011). God's intention that we be in right relationships with Him, ourselves, and creation forms the ideal *by which we can evaluate all human behavior and development*. It forms the critical basis by which we make assessments, in our own lives and in those with whom we work.

Grounding human development in a theological purpose does not remove the potential for subjectivity nor guarantee "success" in our interactions with persons and their environments, however. Sometimes we are unable to accurately assess a situation from our vantage point. We intervene in ways we believe will facilitate shalom in a person's life, yet misread or overlook a critical component of the situation. We advocate for social welfare policies which are characterized by justice and shalom, only to later discover inconsistent administration that has benefited some and not others. We work toward true racial reconciliation in our organizations only to find that lasting change is characterized by one step forward and two steps back.

The path toward relationships of shalom is often a challenging one. While we are inherently relational beings, forming relationships of shalom is an ongoing work-in-progress. Nonetheless, it can be remarkably clarifying to regularly consider how the situations in our client's lives contribute or detract from the ideals presented by God's purposes and design. Doing so allows us to make healthy adjustments, repositioning ourselves and encouraging others toward our loving Creator.

Discussion Questions

1. Make a list of characteristics of relationships of shalom within an organization. Think about the rationale for each of your choices; consider how would each of your characteristics help employees to flourish?

2. Imagine that you are the director of a psychiatric group home for adolescents. What characteristics would you encourage within the facility so that all of the members have opportunities for flourishing? What policies would you adopt to support your goals?

3. The chapter indicated that individual and corporate growth are both important. How does this principle apply to the local church? Does your local church emphasize growth in one dimension more than the other? If so, ponder why this is the case.

4. How do we actually grow in our relationship with God? What actions are required on our part?

References

Balswick, J. O., King, P. E., & Reimer, K. S. (2016). *The reciprocating self: human development in theological perspective*. Downers Grove, IL: Intervarsity Press.

Dubray, C. A. (1912). *Introductory philosophy; a text-book for colleges and high schools*. New York: Longmans, Green, and Co.

Grenz, S. J. (1994). *Theology for the community of God*. Grand Rapids, MI: Broadman and Holman.

Van Hook, M. P. (2008). *Social work practice with families, second edition: a resiliency-based approach*. Chicago, IL: Lyceum Books.

Volf, M. (2011). *Public faith: how followers of Christ should serve the common good*. Grand Rapids, MI: Brazos Baker.

Yoder, P. (1987). *Shalom: the bible's word for salvation, justice and peace*. Newton, KS: Faith and Life Press.

Chapter Three

The Perspectives of Social Work from the Lens of Faith

N ow that we have looked at some important biblical themes and outlined an overarching model that delineates the purposes for development, we will spend the next few chapters looking at some of the specific perspectives and theories utilized in the study of HBSE. This chapter examines the correlation between the Christian faith and the biopsychosocial perspective, developmental psychology, lifespan theory, and risk and resiliency theory. Each topic is first described, followed by a discussion of its intersection with the biblical themes discussed in Chapter 1 and the model for development described in Chapter 2.

The Biopsychosocial Perspective Described

One of the strengths of social work as a discipline is its determination to assess clients and situations holistically, not relying on simplistic analyses that omit important aspects of the person or their environment. To accomplish this purpose, social workers frequently use the *biopsychosocial perspective* which explains human behavior through examination of the biological, psychological, and social dimensions of the person. The perspective further accounts for the multitude of ways in which persons differ, for example, by gender, race, and ethnicity. The biopsychosocial perspective was first described by psychiatrist, George L. Engel (1977), who defined "health" as a complex reciprocal interaction between biological, psychological, and social influences, a contrast to the primarily biological view of health that had been dominant for decades.

Importantly, in 1984, the World Health Organization (WHO) suggested a fourth dimension, the spiritual. WHO later expanded the definition of health to "*a dynamic state of complete physical, mental, spiritual and social well-being and not merely the absence of disease or infirmity*" (1998,

p. 1). Wright, Watson, and Bell (1996) advocated for the inclusion of spirituality in all aspects of the healing process, a change that has gained widespread favor in the last two decades.

The inclusion of spirituality contrasted a longstanding approach in helping professions from viewing individuals as detached objects to exploring the full dimension of the person under examination. The spiritual needs of the individual, instead of viewed as peripheral, began to be seen as integral to health and well-being. Widespread acceptance of the biopsychosocial model and the more recent attention to spirituality have led many to now view a strictly scientific approach to health as significantly lacking.

A large body of research has further underscored the importance of the spiritual dimension by documenting the positive relationship between spirituality and health (Koenig, King, & Carson, 2012). Spirituality (one's internal belief system) and religion (the outward manifestations of one's internal beliefs) are now well-defined (Hill & Pargament, 2003) and reliable assessment instruments have been developed (see Hill & Maltby, 2009). In fact, current research has moved beyond simply documenting the positive impact of religion and spirituality to studying the pathways themselves, learning exactly how religion and spirituality proves beneficial.

To better understand the biopsychosocial perspective, we will review two case examples. In each case, put yourself in the role of the social worker and consider how you would respond to the given situations. To illustrate the perspective, the biological, psychological, sociological, and spiritual dimensions are identified separately in Answers A-D and jointly in Answer E.

Case One

A twenty-year old male enters the college counseling center of the large public university where he is enrolled as a student. Upon meeting with you, the next available intake social worker, he reports classic symptoms of depression that have increased over the past three months including insomnia, constant fatigue, depressed mood, and poor appetite. You additionally note the client's flat affect and hopelessness about his future. He denies active suicidal thinking or a concrete plan, but does acknowledge occasionally thinking that death would be preferable to the pain of his current experience. As the intake social worker, you must summarize the presenting problems of this client and make a recommendation related to the next step of his treatment. You decide:

   a. That the client's presenting symptoms are the manifestation of a biochemical problem situated within his brain chemistry. You reason that the client has no previous symptoms of depression in his own medical history, but does have depression in his family history, therefore is likely genetically predisposed to the problem. You refer the client to the campus doctor for a psychiatric evaluation.

b. That the client's presenting symptoms are the manifestation of an internal struggle to prove himself worthy to his parents and peers through his academic performance. The rigor of academics, in addition to a relentless need to validate himself through achievement, has placed the client on an unsustainable path. You refer him to the psychotherapeutic staff at the counseling center.

c. That the client's presenting symptoms are a manifestation of the difficulties he is having adapting to the college environment. Struggling to form meaningful relationships, the student has only superficial peer relationships which are characterized by drinking and partying. He finds himself deeply lonely, geographically far from family and high school friends and shallowly connected to the people around him. You refer him to the Student Development and Campus Activities departments for help with forming social connections.

d. That the client's presenting symptoms are the manifestation of his confusion about the overarching purpose of life and the nature of a higher power and religiosity. Beyond his own current struggle, the student questions how a higher power or God could allow the suffering and injustices of the world to occur without intervening. While he wants to believe that there is a grand purpose for his existence, he is discouraged and angered by a deity that seems detached. You refer him to a ministry group on campus for assistance with his deep spiritual questions.

e. That the client's presenting symptoms are the likely manifestation of a combination of factors that include his biological predisposition to depression, unhealthy psychological drives, unsupportive social relationships, and unanswered spiritual questions and longings. While it is impossible to determine the precise extent to which each factor impacts his current depression, his symptoms are concerning enough to warrant interventions in all four areas. Your plan is to refer him for a psychiatric evaluation, to a therapist at the counseling center, to the student development and campus activities offices, and to a student ministry.

In this case example, the biopsychosocial perspective avoids an overly simplistic assessment of the situation, providing a more holistic assessment of our client's problems. While one dimension may be the most influential or represent the highest priority for intervention, each of the dimensions contributes to the student's struggle.

Case Two

The public school district of the city in which you live has hired you, a social worker, to develop and direct a new program targeted to reduce school absenteeism. The district knows that absenteeism is a significant factor in academic underperformance and believes it is critical to address this problem. The purpose of your program is to increase school attendance in each school in the district by addressing the core issues underlying chronic absenteeism. Your staffing and funding are limited and you must determine where to focus your interventions. After studying the problem, you decide:

a. That the primary problem is related to families simply not waking up on time and children coming to school late or not at all. Many of the students in your district are from single-parent homes where the parent works third-shift hours, making it difficult to get children to bed on time and ready for school in the morning. You decide to focus your program on educating children and their parents about the importance of taking responsibility for themselves by going to bed at a consistent time, setting multiple alarms, and preparing for school the night before. You work to educate parents about how more structure in the home holds benefits both for children and overworked parents.

b. That the primary problem is related to families not seeing the importance of regular school attendance because they have a sense of hopelessness about education in general. You launch a media campaign for parents about the relationship of school attendance to academic performance and their future prospects. You talk with discouraged and hopeless parents and work to build hopefulness and optimism toward the future.

c. That the primary problem is related to the lack of social support for families struggling with aspects of parenting. Because it is difficult to schedule meetings with single parents, you utilize avenues such as school orientations and parent-teacher conferences to inform parents of chronically absent children that the school and the district is "on their side." You want parents to feel that the school, your program, and they themselves are working as a team to achieve the same goals. You create a buddy system by which an adult in the school building commits to warmly greet each at-risk child each morning and to personally connect with them by phone if they are absent.

d. That the primary problem is related to the lack of an overall pur-pose and framework of meaning in the lives of families with chron-ically absent children, a framework that comes from the practice and teachings of religion. Such a framework provides guidance and meaning, particularly in times of struggle and difficulty, and keeps families moving in healthy directions. In this case, the work is aimed toward goals such as strengthening the parental hierar-chy and increasing parental engagement and responsibility. You communicate with local churches, promoting church-school-fam-ily partnerships that provide support as well as education about spirituality and religion.

e. That the primary problem is complex and difficult to summarize in a singular way. You determine that children are absent for a variety of reasons, including families being disorganized and per-missive, having little psychosocial support, seeing little value in school attendance, experiencing hopefulness about education and the future, and lacking any divine or overarching purpose and guidance. You develop a multi-pronged approach that serves to educate, support, and empower parents of chronically absent children. You emphasize a team-based approach by which schools and families work together to tackle the problem. Because your program is new, you carefully track attendance across the district. You personally meet with families that have extreme cases of ab-senteeism and individually problem-solve with them. You com-pile and analyze data on an ongoing basis to determine which interventions are effective with which types of cases.

In these case examples, we see the ways in which the different di-mensions—biological, psychological, and social, and spiritual—lead to different conclusions about the cause of the problem. Examples "A" locate the source of the problem in biology. Individuals are depressed because of their biochemistry. Examples "B" suggest the problem as rooted in psy-chology with absenteeism linked to hopelessness about the future. The depressed student is plagued internally by expectations he cannot meet. Examples "C" identify the problem as social in nature, pointing to the depressed student's isolation and loneliness. Examples "D" identify the problem as spiritual in nature, meaning rooted in the relationship with life's larger purposes. Examples "E" illustrate a biopsychosocial approach in which multiple perspectives are taken into account. This type of multi-level analysis is necessary for any social worker attempting to understand human complexity and seeking to intervene accordingly.

Using the biopsychosocial perspective means that you draw from *multiple* dimensions when forming hypotheses about a case or situation. At times, we are not sure where the precise source(s) of a problem lies, but the biopsychosocial perspective encourages us to cast a large net and to carefully monitor progress in order to accurately tailor our interventions. The biopsychosocial perspective rightly understands the holistic nature of persons and systems, asking us to think broadly and analytically about problems and potential solutions. The broad nature of the approach is particularly important as cases and problems become increasingly complex. A complex problem involving many different constituents, such as school absenteeism, for example, rarely has a singular cause or solution. In reality, the more complex the problem, the more we are required to view it from multiple angles.

The Biopsychosocial Perspective, Biblical Themes, and the Model for Development

Because of its widespread usage in social work, it is important to examine the biopsychosocial perspective in light of our biblical themes and our model for development. The biopsychosocial perspective captures well biblical themes of relationality and embodiment, but minimally highlights human agency, sinfulness, and the need for redemption and restoration. The perspective is not clear on its purpose as it is more of a means of evaluating persons.

Relationality is an integral part of the social dimension of the biopsychosocial assessment. Assessing the quality and nature of relationships in individuals, groups, or communities is strongly emphasized by this approach. In this respect, the perspective mirrors the biblical emphasis on relationships as vital to well-being and growth throughout the lifespan. Similarly, the biological dimension of the biopsychosocial perspective captures well the biblical emphasis on embodiment and the importance of our physical nature. The perspective neither views biology as all that matters, nor underestimates its significance.

The more recent addition of spirituality into the biopsychosocial perspective adds a critical dimension that is central to biblical emphasis. Most Christians in social work strongly affirm the recent focus on spirituality and religion as it legitimizes spiritual assessments which can facilitate valuable conversations and interventions in this area. The emphasis appropriately validates a part of our humanness that warrants careful assessment and inclusion in treatment planning. Furthermore, the overwhelming indication that religion and spirituality (with some minor exceptions) are positive factors in a person's biology, psychology, and social life confirms its importance and inclusion in the biopsychosocial perspective.

Overall, in its breadth, the biopsychosocial perspective matches the Bible's holistic emphasis on the physical body, emotions, relationships, and spirituality. By creating humanity and calling all of creation "good," every component of ourselves has importance and value. Each dimension is part of the good creation. In this respect, the biopsychosocial perspective appropriately captures the importance of each component of personhood, highlighting them all as areas that God has formed in His likeness.

The biopsychosocial perspective, however, also has limitations. Because it is not a theory (i.e., an explanation for a phenomenon such as human behavior), it is important to keep in mind that its emphasis is simply pointing to the multidimensional nature of human behavior and development. It does not suggest a *purpose* for our development or point us toward a particular telos. It does not answer questions about "why," but simply points practitioners to the various dimensions. For example, the perspective does not point to sin—individual or societal—as the primary source of suffering. Expectedly, it does not consider the need for redemption or restoration. The perspective indirectly draws our attention to harmful dynamics within the environment, such as racism, poverty, and abuse, but these dynamics are conceptualized solely as social problems and not as the manifestations and consequences of a fallen world.

The biopsychosocial perspective also focuses minimally on human agency—the ability of persons to respond in various ways to the biological, psychological, social, or spiritual realities around them. The biblical theme of agency emphasizes the range of choices God has given us. This includes the ways we respond to adversity and suffering. For example, we can choose to situate the darkest of circumstances in the light of biblical hope. We can draw upon the resources within and around us—physical, emotional, relational—to survive situations beyond our control. Human agency allows us to choose resurrection hope when encountering seemingly hopeless situations, such as those involving disease, racism, natural disaster, and abuse. Remarkably, human agency makes it possible to hold on to Christ, our ultimate hope, in a world filled with scenarios beyond our control.

Emphasizing human agency and resurrection hope in light of suffering does not dismiss other parts of ourselves such as our emotions, bodies, or relationships. The biopsychosocial perspective is accurate in emphasizing our holistic nature. Because we encounter situations with our whole selves, suffering is experienced in our bodies, emotions, and minds. Our holistic nature implies that when working with suffering persons, we will need to attend to their physical, emotional, spiritual, and intellectual selves.

For Christians in social work, the biopsychosocial perspective provides a helpful, holistic means of assessment and intervention planning. Gaining a truly holistic view of persons and environments, however, will require more from us. It will require consideration of the ways sin creates destruction in the scenario, places where redemption is needed, and the ways in which agency can facilitate hope in the face of suffering. The biopsychosocial perspective is *descriptive*; it tells us where to look for the sources of problems and encourages us to do so in a holistic fashion. But it is not *prescriptive*, pointing us toward our ultimate Source.

Developmental Psychology Described

You may wonder why there is a section on developmental psychology in a book for social workers. It is important to include this area because HBSE shares some of its knowledge base with developmental psychology. While social work as a discipline does not focus on persons in precisely the same manner, several principles from developmental psychology influence and enhance the study of HBSE.

Similarly to HBSE, developmental psychology looks at the "interplay among the biological, psychological, and social-contextual aspects of normal and abnormal human development" (Cicchetti & Toth, 2009, p.16). Developmental psychology also views human development as being malleable and interdependent with its context (Flanagan & Hall, 2014). Growth and development are viewed as processes that continue throughout the entire lifespan.

Developmental psychology also focuses on concepts of normalcy and abnormality within persons. Speaking about this, Flanagan and Hall (2014) write:

> Health and disorder are viewed as existing along a continuum, with individuals ranging from more to less healthy in a particular realm rather than in the clearly distinguishable categories of "disordered" or "nondisordered." All points along the continuum are significant, not merely cut-off points or the end points as (1) the line between adaptation and maladaptation is often unclear, and (2) all degrees of competence offer value to researchers exploring the interplay of development and (mal)adaptation (p. 19).

In other words, there is benefit to studying both normality and ab-normality within persons and all points in-between. Rather than focus-ing solely on disordered categories, studying manifestations all along the continuum sheds light on the ways that persons differ. Social work shares this interest in studying the development and contexts of *all* persons, re-gardless whether they fall into a "disordered" category or exhibit healthy adaptive behaviors. We care deeply about both health and disorder be-cause they help us to better understand and support the range of persons with which we work.

Social work and developmental psychology also share a commitment to understanding behavior within its context as represented by the *ecolog-ical approach* (Bronfenbrenner, 1979). This approach examines persons in light of their position within five different systems—the microsystem, mesosystem, exosystem, macrosystem, and chronosystem. The concept of *reciprocal determinism*—which states that the environment and person have a back and forth relationship in which each is changed by the other (Bandura, 1989)—is also central to both approaches. Unlike *determinism*, which implies that outcomes are simply a response to things that have already occurred, reciprocal determinism suggests a fluid, sometimes unpredictable, interaction between persons and their environment. The person's thoughts, feelings, and behaviors impact the environment and similarly, the environment impacts the person's feelings, thoughts, and behaviors, forming an ongoing feedback loop. Another way of referring to the type of relationship is *transactional* because there are continual mod-ifications between a person and their environment that work to produce change in both entities (Flanagan & Hall, 2014).

Consider the example of a parent and child who are members of each other's microsystem. A parent with a quick temper may elicit a strong emotional response from their child with a similarly short temper. If the parent's angry outbursts increase over time, the child's outbursts may es-calate as well, leading to more intense levels of conflict. If the parent re-sponds with calmness, however, the child may more quickly deescalate their anger or similarly stay calm. Over time, the child may even gain greater self-control and emotional regulation. The parent and child there-fore have a transactional relationship in the sense that they are continual-ly changed by each other. Reciprocal determinism describes the ongoing processes between the parent and child.

Developmental psychologists have identified the concept of *develop-mental pathways*. Such pathways are the product of the interaction be-tween the person and their environment (Loeber & Burke, 2011). Like a literal path through a forest or neighborhood, developmental pathways indicate the orderly, general direction that a person is moving. For example, based on particular pathways, a young person may be heading toward increasingly problematic behaviors or steadily moving in the direction of healthy choices. Their choices, while not consistently positive or negative, tend to fall along a trajectory. The study of developmental pathways can be helpful as we try to understand how small choices accumulate and contribute to positive or harmful pathways. Developmental pathways also point to the importance of making healthy "small" choices as they contribute to substantive, longstanding patterns.

The concepts of *equifinality* and *multifinality* are additionally helpful in understanding and qualifying developmental pathways. Equifinality suggests that different environmental inputs can lead to the same outcome. For example, persons from both high-income and high-poverty homes can each achieve the same vocational goal. Multifinality says that persons may start out in similar environments, but end up in entirely different places. Two children, for example, raised in similar faith-based homes, may end up with entirely different views on faith as adults.

These concepts indicate that while development does occur along pathways, those pathways are also variable and unique. They point to a trajectory along which a person seems to be developing, but numerous variables continue to play roles. Equifinality and multifinality suggest that we must be careful to avoid assumptions about particular environmental inputs. Development is not formulaic. Negative inputs do not necessarily lead to the same outcomes. In the same way, positive inputs do not necessarily result in positive outcomes. We can see trends and identify behaviors that enhance or detract from developmental pathways, but there must be room for variation in individual responses to environmental inputs.

Another helpful process stemming from developmental psychology is *developmental cascades.* These refer to "the cumulative consequences for development of the many interactions and transactions occurring in developing systems that result in spreading effects across levels, among domains at the same level, and across different systems or generations" (Masten & Ciccetti, 2010, p. 491). Developmental cascades are like chain reactions or snowball effects. They indicate that environmental inputs and developmental pathways not only impact a person's life in the present, but can alter the entire course of their life. Masten & Ciccetti (2010) write further, "Cascade effects could explain why some problems in childhood predict widespread difficulties in adulthood, whereas others do not" (p. 491).

Developmental cascades refer to a wide variety of phenomena. They can refer to physical changes at the gene-environment interaction level which subsequently impact behavior and social adaptation (Hanson & Gottesman,

2007). The "biological embedding of experience" (Masten & Ciccetti, 2010, p. 492), such as what occurs when an infant experiences sustained trauma, can lead to cascading effects. The imprinting of trauma on the child's brain and body can contribute to a decline in the child's social and psychological functioning which can lead to lasting future effects in their life. Cascades can "snowball" in a positive direction also. The consistent affirmation and support of a child's musical gifts can encourage the young person to hone their skills which can ultimately lead to a rewarding musical career.

Developmental cascades can also be identified within each level of the ecological perspective. Relationships in which positive or negative behavioral patterns are transmitted (mediated by genes and environment) can cascade in microsystems such as families. Those cascades can be transmitted across generations (Meaney, 2010). In the broadest sense, we can conceptualize the ways that cascades impact social institutions, such as churches and schools, and even governments and nations.

Developmental Psychology, the Biblical Themes, and the Model for Development

It is important to examine concepts from developmental psychology in light of our biblical themes and our model for development. While developmental psychology is a broad area and we have only highlighted some core concepts, it points toward a purpose which varies from our model. Ultimately, the purpose of the concepts described is maturation. While maturation of all types (emotional, intellectual, physical) is obviously a healthy and appropriate purpose, our ultimate goal is to be maturing toward God and in our status as His beloved.

Developmental psychology helpfully emphasizes the fluid, unpredictable nature of human development as typified in the concepts of *equifinality* and *multifinality*. The approach rightly implies that one's biological, psychological, and social factors explain part of their story, but not the whole story. Furthermore, while these dimensions may be predictive of someone's future at some level, they are never foolproof means of predicting the course of someone's life.

In its call for our obedience and repentance, the Bible implies an ability to make choices that significantly alter the course of our lives. Our future is not determined in the sense that we are active participants in our own lives. In this respect, developmental psychology rightly upholds the concept of human agency. Humans, regardless of their situations, have been given agency. Our choices frequently have limits, but some degree of agency remains.

Belief in the ability of *anyone* to change, regardless of their circumstances, is an important biblical concept which is echoed well in both developmental psychology and social work. A belief in the ability of persons to change is underscored by the work of the Holy Spirit who initiates and produces change. In some cases, God produces dramatic and unexpected change within persons that defies the direction of developmental pathways and reverses longstanding developmental cascades. At other times, the Holy Spirit produces slow, but steady change as we regularly choose submission and obedience.

Christians in social work also affirm the role of developmental pathways and cascades. Daily choices, even the smallest ones, in the right direction are important, for example, to forming regular patterns of obedience. One faith-based student ministry group uses the slogan, "Everything Matters." We can affirm the importance of all behavioral choices as mattering; they contribute to both life-giving and soul-crushing habits and rituals. Because we are largely formed by patterns, attending to patterns of behavior is critically important at all stages of the lifespan.

Perhaps most importantly, developmental psychology emphasizes the back and forth nature of relationships through reciprocal determinism, a dynamic mirrored in the biblical theme of relationality. Relationships *do* change us as reciprocal determinism suggests. Furthermore, the emphasis on our interdependent nature—that we need one another for our own growth and well-being—is a beautiful biblical concept. This concept is illustrated by the metaphor of the Church as a physical body, implying that the functioning of the whole is entirely dependent on the contributions of its various components. In Christ, we indeed function as one, working together for the flourishing of each individual member.

Lifespan Developmental Theory

Lifespan developmental theory is highly important in HBSE as it is a common structure used in studying the various life stages. The theory provides an overarching framework for studying individual development from conception to old age (a process also known as *ontogenesis*). It also serves as an organizing framework for a vast amount of information about lifelong development.

Unlike some theories which are very specific, lifespan developmental theory includes many areas of study that share a focus on development across all of its ages and stages. The theory's assumption is that development occurs throughout one's entire life and that every stage (infancy, childhood, adolescence, adulthood, and older adulthood) contains tasks that contribute to ontogenetic development. From the perspective of this theory, development is lifelong, multidimensional, multidirectional, multidisciplinary, characterized by plasticity (capable of being molded), and contextual (Baltes, Reese, & Lipsitt, 1980).

The goals of the theory are multiple. They include organizing the nature and sequence of development across the lifespan, identifying the connections between various developmental events, and delineating the biological, psychological, social, and environmental factors which relate to lifespan development. An additional goal is to specify the opportunities and limitations that impact lifespan development, including an individual's range of plasticity (Baltes, Lindenberger, & Staudinger, 2007).

Lifespan developmental theory also focuses on normative and non-normative age-related influences. Determining the characteristics of normative development permits generalization across persons of similar ages or stages. At its most basic level, it implies that we can understand much about a person's behavior by examining their stage of life. For example, research in this area might explore the expected social responses of infants. It might examine typical personality development among late adolescents or the effect of aging on one's self-esteem (Chibocus, Leite, & Weis, 2005). Within lifespan developmental theory, we might also look at the impact of the stage of life on events or circumstances that are non-normative, such as the effect of early-stage dementia on middle-aged adults. Or the effects of pregnancy on the development of early adolescents.

According to lifespan developmental theory, individuals organize their own development *and* contribute to the development of others. Throughout development, they are impacted by many interdependent environmental influences. They, in turn, influence the environment around them (Chibucos, Leite, & Weis, 2005). It is in these rich intersections that we learn about the normative and non-normative ways that persons develop from conception to old age.

Lifespan Developmental Theory, the Biblical Themes, and the Model for Development

It is important to consider lifespan developmental theory in light of our biblical themes and model for development. While the theory relates minimally to sin, redemption, and restoration, it beautifully captures the natural chronology illustrated throughout creation. Humans enter the world as infants, but immediately begin the process of biological maturation, one that continues throughout their lives. The wonder of human growth is perhaps seen most clearly in periods of accelerated biological growth, such as the first year of life. Older adults often experience wonder when they reflect on how, over the relatively short span of a lifetime, change occurs so dramatically. God could have created us as fully developed persons, but instead designed a remarkably dynamic process by which we are continually evolving and changing.

In its current fallen state, however, creation is subject to the natural processes of age-related decline and eventually to death. We are mortal creatures with bodies that are finite, not infinite. To state it bluntly, we have an expiration date. We share this quality with other parts of creation—animals and plants which are also subject to eventual decline and death. The temporal nature of our bodies and all of creation is evident in the words of Solomon, "There is a time for everything, and a season for every activity under the heavens: a time to be born and a time to die, a time to plant and a time to uproot" (Ecclesiastes 3:1-2). Lifespan developmental theory captures important aspects of our God-given design, highlighting how we grow across all dimensions, but at the same time, are earthly and mortal.

In examining its purpose, lifespan developmental theory creates a helpful organizational framework for evaluating how each stage of the lifespan contributes to growth toward our telos. Particular stages, such as infancy, adolescence, and older adulthood, can be examined in light of our ultimate goals. Lifespan developmental theory provides a useful *framework* for studying each stage in order to understand God's overall purposes within them. But in and of itself, it does not suggest a *purpose* other than moving smoothly through the various stages of life.

Risk and Resiliency Framework

The concepts of risk and resiliency have a rich history in social work, a discipline which has long been interested in building client and system strengths. As helping professions have transitioned from a dominant focus on pathology to the additional focus on positive assets, increased attention has been paid to factors that promote or endanger health and flourishing. Four concepts are important to the risk and resiliency framework—risk, risk factors, resiliency, and protective factors.

Resiliency is defined as "the ability to overcome adverse conditions and to function normatively in the face of risk" (Jenson & Frasier, 2006, p 5). Therefore, a *risk factor* is defined as "any event, condition, or experience that increases the probability that a problem will be formed, maintained, or exacerbated" (Fraser & Terzian, 2005, p. 51). Cumulative risk factors imply significantly higher risk because they involve multiple risk factors (Wright & Masten, 2005).

The identification of risk factors originated in the 1970s when researchers began questioning why the outcomes for people from similar backgrounds varied so considerably (Garmezy, 1991). Environmental factors such as poverty, unsafe neighborhoods, substandard schools, and abusive homes quickly surfaced, among others, as factors that increased the probability of negative developmental outcomes. The identification of at-risk groups later developed as researchers identified groups with particularly high or chronic exposure to risk. Solely focusing on risk factors proved unsatisfying for practitioners wanting to bring about positive change and avoid stigmatizing already-struggling groups, however. Research expanded to study ways to offset the probability of negative outcomes through resilience and protective factors (Benard, 1991; Garmezy, 1985).

Resilience is the capacity to adapt successfully in spite of the presence of adversity or high levels of risk (Luthar, 2003; Olsson, Bond, Burns, Vella-Brodrick, & Sawyer, 2003). Related to the formation of resilience, protective factors are conditions or attributes of individuals, families, communities, or societies that either mitigate or eliminate risk. *Protective factors* work to facilitate the building of resiliency. Cumulative protective factors imply significant protection from risk due to the presence of multiple positive influences (Browne, 2014).

Interestingly, research indicates that a small part of resiliency relates to inherent traits in the individual (meaning traits they are born with) and a large part can be learned (Moore, 2013). Resiliency can be strengthened in advance of risk. Children, for example, can learn resiliency during their growing up years. Resiliency can also be strengthened after a traumatic event occurs. It refers to the ability to not merely *survive*, but to find ways to *thrive* in spite of traumatic experiences.

The risk and resiliency framework is highly useful in social work. While it is a framework that organizes, not a theory that explains, the concepts are extremely helpful. First, the framework identifies the at-risk populations which are the core focus of social work. Secondly, it identifies places where individuals and systems are already resilient and places where resiliency needs strengthening. This point is especially salient for social workers who frequently work with clients who face complex and intractable risks. Therefore at times, placing emphasis on strengthening resiliency versus reducing risk factors is needed. Sometimes it is the only option available to us. For example, in practice with immigrant children, increasing resiliency in the face of loss and trauma is a more attainable goal than changing the scenario in their originating country or the policies of the receiving country. Both goals are relevant, but changing policies and systems is a significantly more complex problem, requiring significantly more time and intervention.

For social workers, the practical findings of resilience research are particularly helpful. The Search Institute—a group that researches risk and resilience—for example, has identified what they term developmental assets, relationships, and communities. *Developmental assets* are characteristics of individuals and environments that offset risk and optimize development, such as clear boundaries and expectations in families, internal social competencies such as decision-making and interpersonal skills, and safe and supportive schools and neighborhoods. *Developmental relationships* are those that facilitate growth through support and empowerment for each individual involved. *Developmental communities* are those that embody developmental assets and relationships, creating a rich context for the potential flourishing of all its members, particularly children and adolescence (see www.search-institute.org/).

The risk and resiliency framework fits well with the strengths-based perspective of social work. The strengths-based perspective identifies assets within every individual and system. The perspective calls us to identify, but also to build upon, inherent strengths. The risk and resiliency framework expands the approach by identifying risks, but emphasizes finding ways to offset risks through protective or preventive efforts. At their core, these two approaches share the belief that individuals are not victims of their circumstances, but persons whose internal and external resources may be harnessed to help them thrive in the face of adversity.

Risk and Resiliency Framework, the Biblical Themes, and the Model for Development

The risk and resiliency framework intersects indirectly with several biblical themes, particularly those of relationality, the harmful effects of sin, and the hope of redemption. In its emphasis on the importance of relationships, the potential harm represented by risk factors, and the power of protective factors, the risk and resiliency framework beautifully echoes several biblical themes.

A large and growing body of research into resilience and protective factors points to the importance of healthy interpersonal relationships, whether those are in families, peer groups, schools, or communities. Relationships have the power to positively shape one's identity and create a foundation for thriving in the face of challenges (Walsh, 2003; Walsh, 2007). The link between strong, healthy relationships and high resiliency is a clear one. In this manner, risk and resiliency research supports the biblical emphasis on relationships as key to our growth and flourishing as human beings.

Previously, we discussed how persons thrive most when they have healthy and growing connections with God and other people. These types of relationships are similar in nature to the developmental relationships described in the previous section. Resiliency research indicates that developmental relationships facilitate growth between persons. They also facilitate growth *within* persons by supporting one's individual self-identity and self-esteem. Importantly, they can also facilitate growth toward God—whether God is a conscious part of a person's life or not. Human relationships characterized by love and commitment mirror, even in small ways, the unconditional love and commitment of God. Through loving, developmental relationships, people are indeed drawn closer to the love of God. In this way, developmental relationships and communities form an extraordinarily rich context for the growth that God intends.

While sin is not discussed within this framework, risk factors often represent individual or systemic sin, such as in cases of abuse, racism, and poverty. We know that sin interferes with relationships and can curtail human growth and development. In a similar way, risk factors can hinder growth in the relationships between ourselves, others, and God. While these concepts are not the same, they share considerable overlap in their nature and outcomes. Whether we speak of risk factors or of sinful effects (or both), the power of agency still comes into play, however. We have the ability to respond to sin through confession and repentance and to make positive choices in spite of the presence of risk. We are not victims and remain free agents regardless of our circumstances.

The risk and resiliency framework points to the need to mediate risk by bolstering resiliency and protective factors. In this sense, it resembles the biblical theme of redemption which also points to the possibility of hope beyond the immediate situation. Indeed, the Bible points to hope and peace that extend beyond human comprehension. These concepts are not identical, though, as redemption never comes from us, but from God. As important as risk and resiliency are, the most resilient individual still needs redemption. The human spirit can be resilient, remarkably so, but even the most admirable human qualities only carry us so far.

Risk factors can produce negative outcomes, even despair and hopelessness, but not when countered with life-giving relationships and resurrection hope. The risk and resiliency framework suggests that people, even those in dire circumstances, are never without hope. This is a helpful and appropriate emphasis, but the Bible offers the same message on a far grander scale—that God has intervened in our fallen creation to provide a redemptive pathway to true freedom and hope.

The Bible is also clear about the possibility of hope and the ability to experience peace amidst suffering. Like resiliency, the ability to experience "peace that passes understanding" in situations that defy comprehension is counterintuitive. They share this point in common, but a biblical view of suffering entails another dimension, which is trust in a God who is good, loving, and present in spite of circumstances that suggest otherwise. Resiliency is admirable and, as social workers, we are wise to facilitate it in our clients whenever and wherever we can. But persons of faith who endure great suffering often speak less about themselves as heroic and more about "coming to the end of themselves" and finding God to be present in the darkest moments of their lives. Are they resilient? Perhaps, but in the end, they often testify that it is God who is holding them together and providing the hope they need to go forward.

In terms of purpose, a risk and resiliency framework doesn't point to a particular purpose beyond building resiliency and avoiding or mitigating risk. As with other theories, these are highly worthwhile pursuits, but do not necessarily point us toward God and His purposes. Ultimately, mitigating risk and building resiliency are important for their roles in moving us closer to the relationships with God, self, and others for which we were formed.

Chapter Summary

A review of the biopsychosocial perspective, developmental psychology, lifespan theory, and risk and resiliency theory indicates the many ways they contribute to our understanding of HBSE. Christians in social work enhance their understanding of each of the theories by considering their intersections with important biblical themes.

Discussion Questions

1. How does the biopsychosocial perspective form a useful tool in social work? What are its limitations?

2. What is the relationship between risk factors and individual and systemic sin?

3. Discuss the concept of human resiliency in light of biblical concepts such as the need to depend on God and our human frailty?

4. How is lifespan theory helpful in the study of HBSE? Are there ways the theory limits our understanding of persons?

References

Baltes, P.B., Lindenberger, U., Staudinger, U. (2007). Life span theory in developmental psychology: Theoretical models of human development. In W. Damon & R. M. Lerner (Eds.), *Handbook of child psychology: Theoretical models of human development* (pp. 1029–1143). New York: Wiley.

Baltes, P., Reese, H., & Lipsitt, L. (1980). Life-span developmental psychology. In M.

Rosenzweig, & L. Porter (Eds.), *Annual Review of Psychology, 31*, 65-110.

Bandura, A. (1989). Social cognitive theory. In R. Vasta (Ed.), Annals of child development. *Six theories of child development* (pp. 1-60). Greenwich, CT: JAI Press.

Benard, B. (1991). *Fostering resiliency in kids: Protective factors in the family, school and community.* Portland, OR: Western Center for Drug-Free Schools and Communities.

Bronfenbrenner, U. (1979). *The ecology of human development.* Boston: Harvard University Press.

Browne, C. (2014). The strengthening families approach and protective factors framework: branching out and reaching deeper. *Center for the Study of Social Policy,* 1-51.

Chibucos, T. R., Leite, R. W., & Weis, D. L. (2005). Life-span developmental theory. In *Readings in family theory* (pp. 39-68). Thousand Oaks, CA: Sage Publications.

Cicchetti, D., & Toth, S. L. (2009). The past achievements and future promises of developmental psychopathology: The coming of age of a discipline. *Journal of Child Psychology and Psychiatry, and Allied Disciplines, 50*(1-2), 16–25.

Engel, G. L. (1977). The need for a new medical model: A challenge for biomedicine. *American Association for the Advancement of Science, 196,* 129-136.

Executive Board, 101.(1998) *Review of the constitution of the World Health Organization: Report of the executive board special group.* Retrieved at World Health Organization website: http://www.who.int/iris/handle/10665/79503

Fraser, M.W., & Terzian, M.A. (2005). Risk and resilience in child development: Practice principles and strategies. In G. P. Mallon & P. McCartt Hess (Eds.), *Handbook of children, youth, and family services: Practice, policies, and programs* (pp. 55–71). New York: Columbia University Press.

Flanagan, K. S., and Hall, S. E. (2014). Overview of developmental psychopathology and integrative themes. In K.S. Flannigan & S.E. Hall (Eds.), *Christianity and developmental psychopathology* (pp. 13-42). Downers Grove, IL: InterVarsity Press.

Garmezy, N. (1985). Stress-resistant children: The search for protective factors. In J. E. Stevenson (Ed.), Recent research in developmental psychopathology *Journal of Child Psychology and Psychiatry Book Suppl. 4,* 213-233, Oxford: Pergamon.

Garmezy, N. (1991). Resiliency and vulnerability to diverse developmental outcomes associated with poverty. *American Behavioural Scientist.* 34, 416-430.

Hanson, D. R., & Gottesman, I. I. (2007). Choreographing genetic, epigenetic, and stochastic steps in the dances of developmental psychopathology. In A. S. Masten (Ed.), *Multilevel dynamics in developmental psychopathology: Pathways to the future.* Minnesota Symposia on Child Psychology (pp. 27–43). Mahwah, NJ: Erlbaum.

Hill, P.C. & Maltby, L.E. (2009). Measuring religiousness and spirituality: Issues, existing measures, and the implications for education and wellbeing. In M. de Souza, L.J. Francis,, J. O'Higgins-Norman,, & D. Scott. (Eds.) *International handbook of education for spirituality, care and wellbeing* (pp. 33-50). Dordrecht: Springer.

Hill, P. C., & Pargament. K. I. (2003). Advances in the conceptualization and measurement of religion and spirituality. Implications for physical and mental health research. *The American Psychologist, 58*, 64–74.

Jenson, J. M., & Fraser, M. W. (2006). *Social policy for children and families: A risk and resilience perspective.* Thousand Oaks, CA: SAGE Publications.

Loeber, R., & Burke, J. D. (2011). Developmental pathways in juvenile externalizing and internalizing problems. *Journal of Research in Adolescence, 21*, 34-46.

Luthar, S. S. (2003). *Resilience and vulnerability: Adaptation in the context of childhood adversities.* Cambridge University Press.

Masten, A.S., & Cicchetti, D. (2010). Developmental cascades. *Development and Psychopathology, 22*(3), 491-495.

Meaney, M. J. (2010). Epigenetics and the biological definition of gene environment interactions. *Child Development, 81*, 41–79.

Moore, E. (2013). *Research summary: Resilience and at-risk children and youth.* Retrieved from National Center for Homeless Education website: https://nche.ed.gov/downloads/resilience.pdf.

Olsson, C. A., Bond, L., Burns, J. M., Vella-Brodrick, D. A., & Sawyer, S. M. (2003). Adolescent Resilience: A Concept Analysis. *Journal of Adolescence, 26*, 1-11.

Search Institute (2019). *The power of relationships.* Retrieved at https://www.search-institute.org/.

Walsh, F. (2003). Family resilience: A framework for clinical practice. Family Process, 42, 1-18.

Walsh, F. (2007). Traumatic loss and major disasters: Strengthening family and community resilience. Family Process, 46, 207-227.

Wright, M. O. D., & Masten, A. S. (2005). Resilience processes in development: Fostering positive adaptation in the context of adversity. In S. Goldstein, & R. Brooks (Eds.), *Handbook of resilience in children* (pp. 17-37). New York: Kluwer Academic/Plenum.

Wright, L.M., Watson, W.L. & Bell, J.M. (1996). *Belief: The heart of healing in families and illness.* New York, NY: Basic Books.

Chapter Four

The Biological Dimension

I n this chapter, we will explore the biological dimension of HBSE. We will ponder big questions, such as, "How much impact does your biology or, more specifically, your brain, have on your personality and behavior?" and "How do we uphold a proper emphasis on our embodiment while not *over*emphasizing our physical selves?" While information is continually being added to our understanding in this area, there are principles and theories that can guide our work. We will first review some foundational biological principles and then explore key themes within neuroscience, determinism, and the medical model. These areas will additionally be considered in light of our biblical themes and model for development. The chapter concludes with some theological principles related to this area.

Foundational Principles from Biology

Historically, there has been a long debate between viewing behaviors as originating in "nature"— that is, from biology—and viewing them as originating in "nurture"—that is, from experiences. We now have a healthy respect for both phenomena and focus our energies on the fascinating and complex ways they intersect with one another (Ashford, LeCroy, & Lortie, 2006; Matto, Strolin-Goltzman, & Ballan, 2014). We may look at, for example, the relationship of environmental inputs, such as child neglect, on the neurological development of an abused child's brain.

The best explanations of human behavior focus on the *intersections* of genetics and environment. Someone may have genetic predisposition to substance abuse, for instance, but never be introduced to harmful substances. Someone may be mildly biologically wired to be anxious, but be spared from the major life stressors that would trigger their underlying vulnerability. In other cases, a genetic predisposition to depression may be easily activated by the stressors of a person's life. Indeed, environmental inputs and biology come together in altogether unique ways in lives of our clients. Maintaining an intersectional approach matches social work's holistic emphasis, because even in persons with high biological risk, every situation is different and the outcomes of cases therefore vary greatly.

Despite the need to focus on person-environment intersectionality, biology plays an inestimable role in human behavior and development. Growth in the understanding of biological mechanisms can be largely attributed to advances in genetics—the study of hereditary characteristics carried from one generation to the next (Dick, 2011). For example, the 2003 *Human Genome Project*—which sequenced the DNA of every gene in the human body—laid a foundation for the subsequent study of the genetic linkages of both normative physical development (such as aging) and physical problems (such as schizophrenia) (https://www.genome.gov). The study of *epigenetics*, the changes in organisms caused by modifications of gene expression, has led to further understanding. The exploration of *epigenomes*, the collections of chemical compounds that instruct the actions of genomes, have led to remarkable advances in health and disease. In 2012, the EN-CODE project—which described the functional elements encoded in the human genome through the mapping of epigenetic modifications—was published (http://www.nature.com/encode/#/threads). Insights into how epigenomes affect gene expression, changes during normal development, and changes during disease, continue to evolve.

Remarkably, the cells throughout our bodies contain genes possessing tiny units of inheritance. A copy of the entire *genome*—more than three billion DNA base pairs—is contained in each cell that contains a nucleus (Annunziato, 2008). This means that down to the cellular level, the smallest components of our physical selves, we are both uniquely individual, yet undeniably similar. Biologically, we are each a distinct creation, formed from the collective genetic material of our parents. But though we are each separately formed, we are made from the same earthly material. Even our biology testifies of our individual and communal nature.

Principle 1: We are Hardwired for Growth through Relationships

A specific application of biology of importance to social workers lies in the area of neuropsychology, the study of the brain as it relates to psychological behaviors. A full review of neuropsychology exceeds the parameters of this book, but it is important to understand some fundamental terms and themes with relevance for HBSE and Christians in social work.

First, we are biologically hardwired for growth. Our predisposition toward growth is perhaps most evident during the earliest years of our lives. **Ontogeny**—the period of the development of an organism which includes the prenatal and early childhood stages—is marked by a heightened ability to adapt to changes in the environment. It represents a critical period when the nervous system has particularly heightened sensitivity to environmental stimuli. At birth, for example, each neuron in the brain has approximately 2,500 **synapses** or connections with other neurons. By age three, there are 15,000 synapses per neuron, six times the number at birth (Institute of Medicine and National Research Council, 2015).

During its first years of life, the brain grows rapidly due to **neurogenesis**, the process of new neurons being generated from neural stem cells. Each neuron sends out branches, increasing the number of synaptic contacts through a process known as **mylenation** (also known as **synaptogenesis**). So, although the total number of neurons remains the same, the exponential growth of synaptic connections between neurons and the myelination of nerve fibers—the process of coating the axon with myelin which protects the neuron and allows it to conduct signals more efficiently—contributes to dramatic brain growth. Related to this is the process of **synaptic pruning**, during which unused neural connections are eliminated to permit the growth of more powerful ones (Fuchs & Flugge, 2014; Kolb, Gibb, & Robinson, 2003).

Brain development hardly concludes in early childhood, however. **Neuroplasticity** refers to the lifelong ability of the brain to reorganize neural pathways in response to new experiences.

This process occurs under two conditions—during normative development as the brain matures and as an adaptive mechanism to compensate for lost functioning and maximize remaining functioning after injury. Within limits, the brain is able to change, modify, and repair itself throughout the lifespan. Neuroplasticity occurs in response to environmental and experiential inputs. In other words, we are biologically wired for learning, growth, and adaptation throughout our entire lifespan (Garland & Howard, 2009).

There are limits to our neuroplasticity, however. Such limits are often referred to as **ceiling effects**. Learning disabilities provide an example. About 85 percent of learning disabilities in America are considered biologically-based. However, neither biology nor environment can fully predict the trajectory of an individual with a learning disability. With specific training, the brain's left hemisphere, where most learning disabilities are centered, can form and develop new neural pathways. Inputs such as a highly structured daily schedule or specialized educational assistance can facilitate neuroplasticity (Haight & Taylor, 2013). Biology is being altered by environment, producing important changes in the life of the individual with the learning disability. There are limits to the effects of such environmental inputs as, often, these cannot alter the brain in such a substantial way that the problem is eliminated. But a proper understanding of ceiling effects means that we never know precisely where they lie. Instead, we consistently and repetitively introduce healthy environmental inputs, systematically evaluating their impact in the life of the individual. But even in situations where the potential for learning seems harshly limited, neurogenesis continues to highlight our God-given capacity for growth.

Neuroplasticity also has age-dependent determinants (Dennis, Spiegler, Juranek, Bigler, Snead, & Fletcher, 2013). A newborn does not have the neurological capacity, for example, to skip, speak in full sentences, or perform calculus problems. Age-appropriate ranges are frequently used to identify normative physical and psychological development including gross and fine motor skills, language development, vision, and hearing. Interestingly, there are developmental milestones such as learning to talk, walk, and interact socially that are universal and independent of their cultural context. These are referred to as **experience-expectant** developmental processes as they are the result of neural growth that results from experiences that are present in any environment (with the exception of situations of severe deprivation) (Haight & Taylor, 2013). Conversely, **experience-dependent** developmental processes vary considerably according to the individual's cultural context and environmental inputs (Lourenco & Casey, 2013). Whether or not a child learns to speak Spanish as their first language, for example, is entirely dependent on their specific cultural context and exposure.

An important aspect of neuroplasticity relates to the way that early childhood experiences do, in a sense, determine how the brain is "wired." Repetitive experiences, both healthy and traumatic ones, strengthen neural pathways in specific ways that become literally structured into the neural pathways of the brain. In other words, parts of the brain either become active or inactive based on environmental experiences and inputs (Perry & Pollard, 1997; Perry, Pollard, Blakley, Baker, & Vigilante, 1995). Neurobiologists have estimated that the number of neural connections can go up or down by 25% or more, depending on the richness of the environment. Importantly, one's early neurology "likely impacts the healthy growth and development in ways that could potentially lead to later negative sequelae, including a lack of capacity for healthy, secure interpersonal relationships" (Altman & Altman, 2014, p. xx). In other words, brain structuring that takes place early in the life can, in many cases, set the neurological stage for the remainder of the lifespan. While this does not lessen the power of neuroplasticity or the capacity of individuals to change throughout life, it provides a sobering reminder about the nature of early experiences. Neurological structures and networks are being laid that may prove stubbornly resistant to subsequent change.

Remarkably, God has formed our brains for lifelong growth. Our brains are especially responsive to growth during the periods when we need it the most—early in our lives or after we have experienced injury. A review of some of our fundamental biological structures displays the way that growth is an innate part of our being.

The means of our physical growth provides important lessons about development. At our core level, our behaviors are formed by neurological pathways. Patterns of behavior literally become entrenched in our brains over time, many of which are therefore stubbornly resistant to change. Neuroplasticity suggests that change can and does occur throughout the lifespan, but that pathways must be accounted for. Behaviors and psychological processes learned over time become habitual ways of being in the world. Trauma in one's past, for example, can encode defensive ways of thinking and behaving in one's life. Because patterns can be deeply structured in one's brain and behaviors, the road to change can be a long one. At times, change only comes with qualitatively different inputs. Often, those inputs must be repeated over long periods of time, especially when the maladaptive "learning" has been deep. Children whose earliest years have been spent in institutions, for example, may have highly structured neurological pathways that formed in response to their environments. Those pathways, while facilitating their ability to survive in that context, may be maladaptive in their lives going forward, however. Repeated inputs of an entirely different nature will be required to reform aspects of the child's behaviors and psychological processes.

Our basic neurology suggests that we are able to grow and change, but also that we form patterns that drive our functioning in the world. The possibility of change and the formation of life-giving, positive patterns is enormously hopeful. In our work with persons, however, it can also be sobering to account for the roles of maladaptive patterns. We can be formed in ways that facilitate both healthy and unhealthy learning about ourselves, God, and the world.

We marvel at the ways God has explicitly designed our physical bodies for growth and learning. He has additionally created a system in which human growth is partly universal and partly dependent on environmental inputs, especially relational ones. This combination of the innate and the intentional mirrors, in some respects, the way God consistently upholds human relationality. While all development could be experience-expectant, there are aspects of who we are that will always be dependent upon the actions of others. In this respect, our development, even our survival, is dependent upon the actions of others. Not only must we be cared for by others when we are infants, for example, but aspects of very brain structure depend on the inputs of other people. At our deepest levels, from conception to death, we are made both for growth and for dependence on others.

Principle 2: Change is Always Possible

Many applications from neuroplasticity—the lifelong ability of the brain to reorganize neural pathways in response to new experiences—are relevant to social work practice. One area relates to the power to change or "retrain" our brains. Who of us would not like a new and improved brain, one that thinks before it speaks, is naturally full of wisdom, and is consistently characterized by compassion? If neuroplasticity says that our brains change in response to repetitive inputs, are there inputs that can *positively* change us? Are there ways to help our clients lessen the negative patterns they have learned over time?

Neuroplasticity explains why helping people to change their behavior often feels like an uphill battle. Children who experience chronic stress, for example, have brains that modify themselves to survive their stress through reactivity, inattention, and poor emotional regulation. Their brains adapt to their unstable environments by being on constant alert, learning to respond quickly to the chaotic and rapidly changing nature of their lives. These learned characteristics are useful under stress, but translate poorly to academic settings where focus, attention, and emotional regulation are required (Franke, 2014). Social workers often assist young people in the slow and tedious work of learning new and productive coping mechanisms. Learned behaviors can be resistant to change, though, especially when they are part of a person's way of surviving in the world.

Emerging research with chronically-stressed children emphasizes activities that account for the child's neurological patterns. For example, exposure to chronic stress has been connected with neural losses in the hippocampus (negatively impacting memory and learning) and overactivation in the amygdala (increasing emotional reactivity). These processes can additionally result in impairment in the prefrontal cortex where executive functioning skills such as logical reasoning and decision-making occurs (Blair & Raver, 2016; Hair, Hanson, Wolfe, & Pollak, 2015). To be effective, therefore, interventions must slow the activation of an over-sensitive system in which the child feels easily threatened. Interventions must focus on interrupting learned responses, such as defensive aggression, and retraining the child's brain to detect actual threats to their safety. Effective interventions also strengthen the prefrontal cortex by teaching all-important executive functioning skills (Fisher, Beauchamp, Roos, Noll, Flannery, & Delker, 2016).

Research in empathy provides another example of the application of neuroplasticity to social work. It is widely known that a lack of empathy leads to problems with interpersonal relationships (Segal, 2011). Empathy is comprised of two different realms—affective and cognitive. Affective empathy allows us to feel what others are feeling. It is more of an instinctual response triggered by visual or auditory stimuli than cognitive empathy, which involves a conscious effort to understand what another person is feeling and intending (Zaki, Weber, Bolger, & Ochsner, 2009; Gerdes, Segal, & Harmon, 2014). These two processes, located in different regions of the brain, work together to form a rich quality of empathy that combines emotion and reasoning. Under normal circumstances, our brains are hardwired for empathy, but development of the two aspects of empathy requires environmental inputs.

When individuals lack the necessary inputs, however, empathy can still be cultivated through targeted interventions which have been shown to stimulate the brain's capacity for affective and cognitive empathy. Mindfulness is a promising example of an intervention that can heighten awareness of one's own emotions and increase the ability to attend to the emotions of others (Creswell, Way, Eisenberger, & Liberman, 2007; Hölzel et al., 2010). Other creative means of increasing empathy include asking clients to read fiction and nonfiction as a means of "hearing" the inner dialogue of those facing difficult situations (Kidd & Castano, 2013). Repeatedly asking individuals to mimic the facial expressions illustrated in movie clips or photos stimulates underdeveloped brain regions and increases empathy (Stoddard, 2007). Stimulating awareness of one's own emotions through journaling has also been linked in increasing empathy for others (Hofmann, Sawyer, Witt, & Oh, 2010; Ramasubramanian, 2017).

We need to be realistic in our expectations of these types of interventions. We continue to experience the limits of biology as well as the effects of sin. However, the malleability of our brains is deeply encouraging. Among many things, it means that our brains can learn characteristics of Christ-likeness. Patterns of faithfulness can be cultivated in our very beings. Through the consistency of specific shaping inputs such as Bible reading, meditation, prayer, and individual and corporate worship, we are slowly, but surely, being changed. In small, but steady increments, we can learn the way of the cross. With submission and obedience, our entire being can be transformed by the knowledge that we belong to God.

Principle 3: Every Body Matters

Every body (and everybody!) matters. But a brief review of historical views about the body demonstrates longstanding disagreement about the importance of the body. During the period of the early church, and later through Greek philosophers of the first and second centuries, a belief system known as **gnosticism** emerged. The system taught that the material world (including our bodies) was evil because it was created by an evil being. In order to overcome the evil of the material world, individuals needed to have an experience with a transcendent, good God (King, 2005). Gnosticism divided the world into good and evil. But it also effectively denounced the "goodness" of the physical parts of creation. It encouraged distancing from the material world (and the findings of science) and focusing on the *nonmaterial*. This view eventually became known as the **dualistic** perspective because it separates persons into material and immaterial parts. In terms more familiar to us, it implies separating a person into a body and a soul (Shobris, 1994).

The Apostle Paul denounced gnosticism, but its influence has been experienced throughout history and remains in our contemporary context. For example, in their focus on the soul and not the body, some 20th century American evangelicals supported evangelism and deemphasized other forms of social action (Noll, 2001). Some contemporary faith groups prioritize the work of evangelism over activities, such as digging wells, microenterprise, and creation care. Some Christians have dismissed the contributions of medicine or science in lieu of biblical teachings. At times, it is the devaluing of the material world that underscores positions like these.

Important points are raised by such groups, but it is also critical to place any activity within a holistic belief system that appropriately values both the material and immaterial dimensions of persons. The meeting of basic material needs is critical to human flourishing. Caring for creation is a part of fulfilling God's call. The material world is not to be de-emphasized, but embraced for its inherent goodness. An understanding of our bodies and the resources of the natural world as sacred parts of creation appropriately guides the range of our activities in the world.

The importance of the body is perhaps best understood by the incarnation and resurrection of Christ. Jesus entered the world in a human body, one which was ultimately resurrected. A theology of the atonement states that Christ had to be both fully human and fully divine in order for his death to be a true substitution. The physical body of Christ is central to our faith and simultaneously elevates the importance of our physical selves.

Our bodies are important because they are part of the good creation and because Christ took on a physical body. But what if we were just invisible, shapeless spirits? Wouldn't it have been easier to be created without physical bodies which require a great deal of time and energy to sustain? Perhaps, but having a physical body also enhances our relationships with other people (Balswick, King, & Reimer, 2016). Our physical bodies allow us to hold hands with our spouse, comfort a distressed toddler, and embrace a lonely person. They facilitate and convey love, attachment, comfort, compassion, and intimacy. The importance of compassionate human touch has been demonstrated in persons of all ages. Our bodies are important because they are part of a good creation, but also because they play a role in drawing us closer to others and, indirectly, to God. In this way, our bodies ultimately contribute to our highest goals and purposes as persons.

We turn now to three perspectives related to the biological realm and the study of HBSE—determinism, the medical model, and biological risk factors and protective factors.

Determining Determinism (my genes made me do it)

All of us have heard the line, "the devil made me do it"—a clever way of excusing actions and shifting the blame for wrongful behavior. An overemphasis on biological explanations—"my genes made me do it"— can lead to a similar, unproductive blame game. The interaction of the biological causes of behaviors and the ability to make choices about our actions raises important, yet difficult, questions. At the core of this dilemma lie questions about how "free" we are if explanatory genes can be located for many, perhaps even most, of our behaviors.

Our understanding of various phenomena has been altered as new genetic markers have been identified. Genetic locations for numerous realities including risk-taking (Zuckerman & Kuhlman, 2000), personality, introversion and extroversion (Power & Pluess, 2015), mental health disorders (Gratten, Wray, Keller, & Visscher, 2014), criminal behaviors (Appelbaum & Scurich, 2014; Sabatello & Appelbaum, 2017), and even aging are being identified (Rodríguez-Rodero, Fernández-Morera, Menéndez-Torre, Calvanese, Fernández, & Fraga, 2011). Consider, for example, a study that pinpointed the dopamine receptor genes that predict psychopathic personality traits (Wu & Barnes, 2013) or one that found neural correlates for sensory processing sensitivity—the trait that makes some people more emotionally sensitive than others (Acevedo, Aron, Aron, Sangster, Collins, & Brown, 2014). Findings like these are remarkable and exciting. Yet they can also be worrisome as they raise questions about how free we really are as persons.

If every behavior can be explained by a source—a view known as **determinism**—then our sense of agency is illusory. This point relates not only to our genes, but to our environment as well. Some people believe there are specific causes for every behavior and every aspect of environment which can be identified if only one looks hard enough. This raises important questions for social workers, as our work often entails efforts to change human behavior and/or environments, questionable activities if the claims of determinism are true.

There are problems with determinism, however. Our created nature as agents and our responsibility for our wrongful behavior come to mind. The Bible speaks at length about our ability to make choices related to our behavior. The belief that all behavior is determined by genes or our environment seems to contradict the sense of responsibility and the related consequences of the biblical record.

A concept related to determinism is *self-determination,* or the ability to make choices regarding one's own life. Self-determination suggests that making choices about one's life is actually empowering and fosters healthy self-confidence and self-efficacy. For this reason, social workers strongly advocate for self-determination for their clients. We teach people that they are not victims of their circumstances, but they can make choices amidst the worst scenarios. A rigid view of determinism, stating that all choices and behaviors are predetermined, can diminish such empowerment and self-efficacy. Decision-making opportunities can provide a healthy sense of control when experiences feel entirely out of control. So, while a great deal of the world and our lives may be determined by forces outside of our control, levels of personal choice remain. And while determinism explains many things, it does not fully account for this aspect of the human experience.

Determinism also fails to explain our *experience* of ourselves as free agents. Despite the variables beyond our control at any given moment, we still experience ourselves as choice makers. This experience, at least at the present time, is not entirely explainable by biology or environment.

A related point applies to subjective emotional experiences, such as feeling love, empathy, or compassion. None of us wants our richest affective experiences to be predetermined, solely the products of brain chemistry. On the other hand, we do not experience deep feelings as disconnected from our bodies, but as real and authentic. It does not seem that our bodies and subjective emotions are incompatible, but that they co-exist in a unified manner. Indeed, we live in a mysterious reality in which we are fully embodied, yet we are free to experience deep emotions.

Directly related to determinism, persons of faith hold different philosophical views regarding the nature of our bodies. Some hold to the ancient view of **dualism**, which separates the body and soul. Others hold the view of **monism**, or the belief that a person is one, completely unified entity. From this view, the soul is not an additional component of a person (Cooper, 2000). In general, dualists view choices as the products of our immaterial selves (emphasizing free will or agency) and monists view choices as the products of our material selves (emphasizing determinism). Still others hold to nuanced views, believing, for example, that the body and soul are separate, but interactive in the sense that our brains interpret and control the ways we respond to our souls.

Many scholars of faith agree, however, that determinism goes too far and that the evidence supporting biological and environmental determinism is inconclusive. They indicate that, while scientific evidence proves that genes and environment strongly *influence* human behavior, current evidence fails to prove that these factors actually *cause* behavior (Bauermeister, 2008). Others decry a strict dichotomy between determination and free will and suggest, instead, that we are both determined *and* free. David G. Myers (2008) writes about the biblical emphasis on both constructs:

> When the holy texts address us directly, they emphasize our responsibility for failings and our decisions. When talking to us about others, especially the poor and outcast, it [the Bible] frequently advocates the complementary perspective. Act with compassion. "Judge not." … The book of Proverbs admonishes self-control of one's passions, receptiveness to instruction, and hard work. But when it turns to our outlook on others, it admonishes concern "for the cause of the helpless." …Thus, science and religion concur in affirming both a determined order and the benefits of perceived freedom. We are the product of our biological and social histories, and we are the architects of our future (p. 42).

Also emphasizing a holistic, interactive approach, Moes and Tellinghuisen (2014) write,

> We fear that the discovery of a genetic aspect to traits such as personality means we lose our sense of freedom, but genes implicated in behavior give us predispositions, not a predicted life course. Even the combination of genes and environment, predictive as they are, still do not completely determine the outcome of our choices (p. 58).

In the end, whatever our precise physical make-up, we are people of choices. We experience ourselves as created agents, decision-makers who make choices throughout our lives. God has formed us to be agents and, as agents, we also have responsibility. We experience a range of subjective emotions, including love, compassion, anger, and empathy. Accordingly, we are wise to view ourselves as "greater than the sum of our neurobiological parts" (Moes & Tellinghuisen, 2014, p. 45).

The Medical Model

It is important to review the tenets of the medical model as it is the philosophy and paradigm that underlies most of the mental health services of the Western world. It is also important because social workers routinely work in settings that are formed by the medical model. The medical model holds that mental health disorders result from underlying physiological factors. Mental health disorders are treated as biological problems, often with medications broadly known as psychotropics. In essence, the medical model approaches mental health disorders in the same manner as diabetes or a broken ankle. The range of symptoms are assessed and form the basis for the diagnosis and treatment protocol.

The medical model has dominated the field of psychiatry for many years. Its emphasis on the biology underlying mental health problems provided an important corrective to earlier views about mental health difficulties. From the ancient world until the modern period, punitive beliefs that connected mental illness to morality were common (Farre & Rapley, 2017). For example, "madness" was seen as the result of one's behaviors for many years. For many years, the medical model was dominant within social work until its exclusive emphasis on biology began to be challenged in the 1960s. After this point, social workers advocated for a systems theory approach, an approach which is still used to understand mental health problems today (Casstevens, 2010; Zastrow, 2010).

Many social work practitioners believe that the medical model remains a highly useful approach because it removes the stigmatization that has long surrounded mental health problems. By emphasizing the physical etiology of mental health disorders, the tendency to hold people responsible for alleviating their own problems has decreased. Many social workers, however, feel the medical model falls short of the holistic understanding of humans that is emphasized by the overall discipline.

Despite philosophical differences, there can be synergy between those working within a medical model and those practicing more holistic approaches. In psychiatric facilities, for example, multidisciplinary teams with people representing varied approaches can contribute to strong client outcomes. A multi-faceted approach is important because mental health disorders often have holistic causes and accompanying psychological, spiritual, and social factors limit a person's functioning when unaddressed.

The medical model encapsulates well the biblical theme of embodiment. It appropriately highlights the importance of the biological dimension to a person's overall functioning. But in its one-dimensional approach to mental health problems, many Christians in social work find it limiting. It fails to fully account for the robust view of human nature described in our biblical themes, including our core relationality and, as mentioned previously, the importance of our agency. Social workers will want to consider every problem, including mental health and substance disorders, from multiple angles. Always we will want to hold biology, relationality, and agency in tension. In other words, we want to highlight our clients' abilities to make choices, even in situations where there are clear physiological bases for their problem. And we see their social and psychological well-being, in addition to their physical well-being, as core to their flourishing.

Biological Risk and Protective Factors

We continue our discussion of the physical dimension by looking at the area of biological risk and protection. We are well aware of specific risky health behaviors such as smoking or poor eating habits and protective behaviors such as vaccinations and preventive medical care. Instead of identifying specific risk or protective factors (important as they are), we will broadly consider biological risk and protection from the perspective of our biblical themes and model for development. Aligning ourselves with God's intentions means that we seek to rightly order our physical selves along with other aspects of our humanness. In other words, a rightly ordered view of the body provides protection in a way that exceeds simply the avoidance of risky behaviors. It appreciates the body and its critical role in the types of relationships for which we formed.

An important way to consider biological risk and protection is in terms of the importance the physical dimension assumes in one's life. There are risks associated with imbalance in this area, either when the body becomes overly important or when the body is minimally valued. Conversely, a rightly ordered view of the body serves as an important means of "protection."

Placing too much emphasis on the body can lead to problems such as anxiety about one's health, preoccupation with a youthful appearance, and eating disorders. A focus on exercise can become obsessive and facilitate additional problematic behaviors, such as anxiety, irritability, and judgmental attitudes toward others. On the other hand, minimizing the importance of the body can contribute to abusing the body through activities such as overeating, smoking, use of illegal drugs, incompliance with prescribed medications, denial of physical symptoms, and lack of physical activity.

How does one achieve the difficult balance of honoring physical needs without becoming obsessed with the body, particularly in a culture that grossly inflates the importance of one's outward appearance? This is a challenging question and one that will require individual reflection as our specific challenges differ. But as sinful people, we are prone to disorder in this area. Like our culture, we are prone to extremes that distort God's creational purposes. Anxiety and fear often underlie disorders related to our bodies. We fear having a physical appearance that will make us rejected by others. We obsess about potential illnesses and live in fear of the wrong diagnosis. We fear looking old in a culture that prioritizes appearing youthful.

Addressing fears related to our bodies is not easy. It requires consistently affirming our identity in Christ as wholly and completely beloved. It requires affirming the sacredness of the bodies of those with whom we work, especially those suffering the effects of disease. Finally, it means upholding the physical body as good, but simultaneously refusing to let "outward appearances" overshadow the internal beauty of the persons with whom we work.

Guiding Theological Principles

Finally, it is useful to summarize some theological principles that guide us in this important area. Ultimately, these principles can serve to protect us. They include:

1—The body as "good." As part of God's good creation, our bodies were formed in goodness. Shame, introduced in the fall, easily impacts our views in this area. Yet we need not be ashamed of what God and has made and believes to be good. We were physically formed according to God's design, and therefore we are called to embrace what is good in ourselves and one another.

2—The body as sacred. The sacredness of the body was demonstrated in the incarnated and resurrected Christ. As sacred objects, our bodies are to be treated with dignity and honor throughout our lives. Bodies are not simply physical "shells" to be disregarded, neglected, mocked, or abused. Our bodies provide means by which we nurture relationships with one another. Upholding the sacred nature of the body means that actions such as physical and sexual abuse are egregious because they devalue something of inestimable worth.

3—The physical body as subject to the consequences of sin. Bodies are vulnerable to the harmful or neglectful behaviors of others. Bodies are harmed through acts such as domestic violence or physical neglect. Individually, we can dishonor our own bodies through neglect or the use of harmful substances. We can overindulge our physical appetites. Bodies decline over time, gradually decreasing in their functionality. As Christians in social work, we are called to deal compassionately and graciously with those who struggle with their bodies, whether that be through eating disorders, chronic medical conditions, or the everyday habits of eating well and exercising. To varying degrees, we are all impacted by the effects of sin on our physical bodies and must uphold each other in aspects of this collective journey.

4—Our bodies, as part of our whole selves, should be engaged in the worship of God. In multiple ways such as work, dance, and play, our bodies enable worship. As "temples of the Holy Spirit" and those "who are not our own" (I Cor. 6:19), the care of ours and others' bodies can be acts of worship. That said, God Himself, and not bodies themselves, should be the object of our worship. Our sinfulness makes us prone to worship the wrong things. While our consumeristic culture cultivates worship of the body, largely to promote goods and services, pursuing this end only breeds discontentment.

5—Finally, it is important to note that we all experience physical dependence in our lives. We are all dependent as children, but physical dependence due to injury, illness, or aging can be experienced at many junctures. Like other aspects of our humanness, dependence is not to be feared by those requiring help or resented by those providing help. While it is difficult to depend on others for one's physical needs, it demonstrates our deep need for God and one another. While it is equally difficult to care for another person, it also demonstrates the tangible ways in which we emulate the hands and feet of Christ.

Chapter Summary

We are hardwired for growth, down to the cells throughout our body and the neurons throughout our brains. Much of our growth requires inputs from our environment. Aspects of our brain architecture form pathways in response to both our positive and negative experiences. Yet we struggle in relationship to our biology. Some struggle to understand agency in light of our physical selves. Some look to biology to explain everything. Bodies are susceptible to harm and neglect. Bodies can become objects of worship. Remembering our bodies as good and sacred guides an appropriate posture toward our physical selves.

Discussion Questions

1. What problems routinely encountered by social workers might be improved by a rightly ordered understanding of the body?

2. How do you work to rightly order your physical body?

3. How does the medical model contribute to and detract from an understanding of mental health problems?

4. How does the concept of neurogenesis impact the everyday activity of social workers?

References

Acevedo, B., Aron, E., Aron A., Sangster, G. M., Collins, N., & Brown, J. (2014). The highly sensitive brain: An fMRI study of sensory processing sensitivity. *Brain and Behavior, 4,* 580-594.

Altman, J. C., & Altman, R.A., (2014). Foreword, In H. Matto, J. Strolin-Goltzman, & M. Ballan, (Eds.), *Neuroscience for social work: Current research and practice* (p. xiv). New York: Springer.

Annunziato, A. (2008). DNA packaging: Nucleosomes and chromatin. *Nature Education, 1,* 26.

Appelbaum, P. S., & Scurich, N. (2014). Impact of behavioral genetic evidence on the adjudication of criminal behavior. *The Journal of the American Academy of Psychiatry and the Law, 42,* 91–100.

Ashford, J. B., LeCroy, C. W., & Lortie, K. L (2006). *Human Behavior in the Social Environment: A Multidimensional Perspective.* Belmont, CA: Wadsworth Publishing.

Balswick, J.O., King, P.E., & Reimer, K. S. (2016). *The reciprocating self.* Downers Grove, IL: InterVarsity Press.

Baumeister, R. (2008). Free will, consciousness, and cultural animals. In J. Baer, J.C. Kaufman, & R.F. Baumeister (Eds.), *Are we free: Psychology and free will* (pp. 65-85). New York: Oxford University Press.

Blair, C., & Raver, C. C. (2016). Poverty, stress, and brain development: New directions for prevention and intervention. *Academic Pediatrics, 16,* S30–S36.

Casstevens, W.J. (2010) Social work education on mental health: Postmodern discourse and the medical model, *Journal of Teaching in Social Work, 30,* 385-398.

Creswell, J. D., Way, B. M., Eisenberger, N. I., & Lieberman, M. D. (2007). Neural correlates of dispositional mindfulness during affect labeling. *Psychosomatic Medicine, 69,* 560 –565.

Cooper, J. W. (2000). *Body, soul and life everlasting: Biblical anthropology and the monism-dualism debate.* Leicester: Apollos.

Dennis, M., Spiegler, B. J., Juranek, J. J., Bigler, E. D., Snead, O. C., & Fletcher, J. M. (2013). Age, plasticity, and homeostasis in childhood brain disorders. *Neuroscience and Biobehavioral Reviews, 37*(10), 2760-2773.

Dick, D. M. (2011). Gene-environment interaction in psychological traits and disorders. *Annual Review of Clinical Psychology, 7,* 383–409.

ENCODE: Encyclopedia of DNA Elements (2019). Retrieved from https://www.encodeproject.org/.

Farre, A., & Rapley, T. (2017). The new old (and old new) medical model: Four decades navigating the biomedical and psychosocial understandings of health and illness. *Healthcare, 5,* 1-9.

Fisher, P.A., Beauchamp, K.G., Roos, L.E., Noll, L.K., Flannery, J., Delker, B.C. (2016). The neurobiology of intervention and prevention in early adversity. *Annual Review of Clinical Psychology, 12,* 331-57.

Franke, H. A. (2014). Toxic stress: Effects, prevention and treatment. *Children, 1,* 390–402.

Fuchs, E., & Flugge, G. (2014). Adult neuroplasticity: More than 40 years of research. *Neural Plasticity, 5,* 1-10.

Garland, E., & Howard, M. O. (2009). Neuroplasticity, psychosocial genomics, and the biopsychosocial paradigm in the 21st century. *Health & Social Work, 34,* 191–199.

Gerdes, K. E., Segal, E. S., & Harmon, J. K. (2014). Your Brain on Empathy: Implications for Social Work Practice. In *Neuroscience for Social Work Current Research and Practice* (pp. 9-37). New York: Springer Publishing Company.

Gratten, J., Wray, N.R., Keller, M.C. & Visscher, P.M. (2014). *Large-scale genomics unveils the genetic architecture of psychiatric disorders. Nature Neuroscience, 17,* 782–790.

Haight, W. L., & Taylor, E. H. (2013). *Human Behavior for Social Work Practice, Second Edition: A Developmental-Ecological Framework* (2nd ed.). U.K: Oxford University Press.

Hair, N.L., Hanson, J.L., Wolfe, B.L., Pollak, S.D. (2015). Association of child poverty, brain development, and academic achievement. *JAMA Pediatrics,169*, 822–829.

Hofmann, S. G., Sawyer, A. T., Witt, A. A., & Oh, D. (2010). The effect of mindfulness-based therapy on anxiety and depression: A meta-analytic review. *Journal of Consulting and Clinical Psychology, 78*, 169–183.

Hölzel, B.K., Carmody, J., Evans, K.C., Hoge, E.A., Dusek, J.A., Morgan, L., ... Lazar, S.W. (2010). Stress reduction correlates with structural changes in the amygdala, *Social Cognitive and Affective Neuroscience, 5*, 11–17.

Institute of Medicine and National Research Council. (2015). *Transforming the workforce for children birth through age 8: A unifying foundation.* Washington, DC: The National Academies Press.

Kidd, D.C., & Castano, E. (2013). Reading literary fiction improves theory of mind. *Science, 342*, 377-380.

King, K.L. (2005). *What is gnosticism?* Cambridge, MA: Belknap.

Kolb, B., Gibb, R., & Robinson, T. E. (2003). Brain plasticity and behavior. *Current Directions in Psychological Science, 12*, 1-5.

Lourenco, F., & Casey, B. (2013). Adjusting behavior to changing environmental demands with development. *Neuroscience and Biobehavioral Reviews, 37(9)*, 2233-2242.

Noll, M. A. (2001). *American evangelical Christianity: An introduction.* Oxford: Blackwell Publishers.

Matto, H. C., Strolin-Goltzman, J., & Ballan, M. S. (2014). *Neuroscience for social work current research and practice.* New York: Springer Publishing Company.

Moes, P., & Tellinghuisen, D. J. (2014). *Exploring psychology and Christian faith: An introductory guide.* Grand Rapids, MI: Baker Academic.

Myers, D.G. (2008). Determined and free. In J. Baer, J.C. Kaufman, & R.F. Baumeister (Eds.), *Are we free: Psychology and Free will* (pp. 32-43). New York: Oxford University Press.

Perry, B.D., Pollard, R.A., Blakley, T.L., Baker, W.L., Vigilante, D. (1995). Childhood trauma, the neurobiology of adaptation and use-dependent development of the brain: How states become traits. *Infant Mental Health Journal 16*, 271-291.

Perry, B.D. & Pollard, R.A. (1997). Altered brain development following global neglect in early childhood. *Society for Neuroscience: Proceedings from Annual Meeting*, New Orleans.

Power, R.A., & Pluess, M. (2015). Heritability estimates of the big five personality traits based on common genetic variants, *Translational Psychiatry, 5*, 1-4.

Ramasubramanian, S. (2017) Mindfulness, stress coping and everyday resilience among emerging youth in a university setting: a mixed methods approach, *International Journal of Adolescence and Youth, 22*, 308-321.

Rodríguez-Rodero, S., Fernández-Morera, J. L., Menéndez-Torre, E., Calvanese, V., Fernández, A. F., & Fraga, M. F. (2011). Aging Genetics and Aging. *Aging and Disease, 2*, 186–195.

Sabatello, M., Appelbaum, P.S. (2017). *Behavioral genetics in criminal and civil courts. Harvard Review of Psychiatry, 25, 289-301.*

Segal, E.A. (2011). Social empathy: A model built on empathy, contextual understanding, and social responsibility that promotes social justice, *Journal of Social Service Research, 37*, 266-277.

Shobris, J.G. (1994). The dualism of psychology. *Genetic, Social, and General Psychology Monographs, 120*, 375-92.

Stoddard, J. D. (2007). Attempting to understand the lives of others: Film as a tool for developing historical empathy. In A. S. Marcus (Ed.), *Celluloid blackboard: Teaching history with film* (pp. 187-214). Charlotte, NC: Information Age Publishing.

Wu T., & Barnes J. C. (2013). Two dopamine receptor genes (DRD2 and DRD4) predict psychopathic personality traits in a sample of American adults, *Journal of Criminal Justice 41*, 188-195.

Zaki, J., Weber, J., Bolger, N., & Ochsner, K. (2009). The neural bases of empathic accuracy. *Proceedings of the National Academy of Sciences, 106*(27), 11382-11387.

Zastrow, C. (2010). *Introduction to social work and social welfare* (10th ed.). Belmont, CA: Brooks Cole.

Zuckerman, M. & Kuhlman, D.M. (2000). Personality and risk-taking: Common biosocial factors. *Journal of Personality, 68*, 999-1029.

Glossary

Amygdala – almond-shaped groups of nuclei located deep within the brain. Plays a primary role in the processing of memory and emotional regulation

Ceiling effects – upper limits to the brain's capacity for development

Critical periods — limited times during development when the nervous system has heightened sensitivity to environmental stimuli

Executive functioning — the ability to differentiate among conflicting thoughts, determine good and bad, predict consequences, and control impulsivity

Myelination — the process of developing a myelin sheath around a nerve fiber which is vitally important to healthy central nervous sytem functioning

Neurogenesis — the process of new neurons being generated from neural stem cells. Most active during the prenatal period, neurogenesis is responsible for populating the growing brain with neurons throughout the life cycle

Neuroplasticity — the lifelong ability of the brain to reorganize neural pathways based on new experiences

Ontogeny — the development of an organism

Plasticity — the capacity for continuous alteration of the neural pathways and synapses of the living brain and nervous system in response to experience or injury

Prefrontal cortex — Part of the frontal lobes responsible for planning, reasoning, and self-control

Synapse — the meeting point between two neurons

Synaptic gap – Space between the axon of one neuron and the dendrite of another by which impulses pass through the diffusion of a chemical neurotransmitter

Synaptic pruning – Process of the brain reducing the overall number of neurons and synapses, leaving room for more efficient synaptic configurations. Occurs through age 12 and approximately 50% of neurons do not survive until adulthood

Chapter Five

The Psychological Dimension

his chapter will explore the psychological dimensions of HBSE. We will identify key themes raised by dominant psychological theories that explain various aspects of human behavior including object relations theory, psychosocial theory, learning theories, psychoanalytic theory, psychodynamic theory, attachment theory, life structure and transitional theory, faith development theory, and moral development theory. The theories will also be considered in light of the biblical themes discussed in Chapter 1 and the model for development of Chapter 2.

Slips from Freud

We begin with perhaps the most well-known psychological theory, psychoanalytic theory. Psychoanalytic theory originated with the writings of Sigmund Freud (1913/2010), an Austrian physician whose work during the late 19th and early 20th centuries has been influential in many disciplines, including social work. Psychoanalytic theory is best known for its emphasis on the role of the unconscious mind in affecting, even determining, human behavior. Freud believed the unconscious mind—its feelings, intentions, and passions—were key to understanding the core motivations underlying human behavior. He also believed the unconscious to be problematic as it is highly influential, yet largely unknown to us. Therefore, psychoanalytic techniques, such as free association, are used to expose the unconscious for the purpose of understanding its role in driving one's thoughts, feelings, and behaviors.

An important contribution of the theory was Freud's identification of defense mechanisms—actions one uses to decrease anxiety by distorting reality, thereby making reality more acceptable and less potent. Examples of defense mechanisms include repression, denial, displacement, projection, rationalization, and reaction formation. Psychoanalytic techniques illuminate defense mechanisms by bringing them to a person's conscious attention. The techniques strive to decrease reliance on defenses and to facilitate the facing of fears directly and authentically.

Psychoanalytic theory shares points of connection and disconnection with our biblical themes.

First, it is important to note that psychanalytic theory has deterministic characteristics, meaning that it points to sources of our actions outside of free will and agency. The theory teaches that our personality and behaviors emerge from the conflict between our internal drives and our internal controls, a conflict between three different parts—the id, ego, and superego (Jones, Watson, & Butman, 2011). Parts of our personality and behaviors also result from the influence of our unconscious minds which are largely shaped by our early experiences. If the unconscious mind significantly determines one's personality and actions, the role and importance of human agency naturally recedes. This high level of determinism seems inconsistent with the biblical theme of human agency.

Second, our core relationality and the importance of social connections are minimized in this theory. Psychoanalysis views the person as a self-contained psychological system (Jones, Watson, & Butman, 2011). One's behavior and personality are said to be products of internal, individualized sources and are not seen as by-products of one's relationships with others or with God. This individualistic view fails to grasp the richness and power of relationships in our lives and formation.

Third, the theory entails no concept of sin. Psychoanalytic theory highlights the fact that humans are fundamentally driven by the need to seek pleasure for themselves, a notion that resembles original sin. This concept, however, is tied more to a biological urge necessary for survival than a core understanding of a self-centered, sinful posture. Freud wrote about selfishness as a repressed emotion, but the Christian view of sin as pervasive, affecting all aspects of a person, is absent from the theory (Moes and Tellinghuisen, 2014).

Fourth, while Christians concur with Freud that persons are driven by a self-centered desire for pleasure, particularly within cultures where pleasure is idealized, many authors argue that the need to discover meaning and purpose in life is actually a more fundamental drive (Pytell, 2000). The search for meaning and purpose often *includes* pleasure-seeking behaviors, but ultimately, these pleasure-seeking behaviors are secondary to the primary search for meaning and purpose. Persons of faith likely agree with Freud that while we frequently act out of deep selfishness, our selfishness and sinfulness do not fully incorporate or explain who we are. That is better explained by our image-bearing nature. And as image-bearers of God, we carry innate positive drives, including creativity and love (Jones, Watson, and Butman, 2011).

Finally, the end goal, or *telos,* of psychanalysis does not match the goal of right connections with God, self, and others. Instead, the goal is self-knowledge because it is seen as the means to maturation. This includes freedom from the power of one's unconscious drives and defense mechanisms. While Christians greatly value self-knowledge, its primary value relates to its ability to improve our relationships with God, ourselves, and others. For people of faith, self-knowledge often (paradoxically) produces humility and dependence and not greater self-actualization or pride. In other words, knowledge of ourselves leads to an increased awareness of our dependence on God more than a release from the power of our innate drives.

Many Christians in social work have thoughtfully adapted psychoanalytic theory to their purposes. Many have broadened the approach to include relationships and softened the theory's deterministic aspects. The theory's emphasis on identifying our hidden motivations is one that many Christians find very helpful. From this perspective, Hoffman (2007) writes,

> My supreme desire…is to chronicle…the redemption of psychoanalysis from the shroud of godlessness that has hung over its rich contributions, familiarizing a new generation of Christian professionals with the metamorphosis of psychoanalytic work. Through God's sovereign influence via the writings of theorists steeped in the Judeo-Christian narrative, relational psychoanalysis practiced within a Christian worldview has become, for me, the place where Spirit and truth, transcendence and immanence, law and grace meet in the context of life-changing relationship (p. 75).

The contributions of psychanalytic theory extend across many disciplines, including social work. The frequent use of terms like "denial" and "repression" underscore the theory's widespread influence. It continues to influence our approaches to understanding human behavior.

To Freud and Beyond

Post-Freudian theories emerged as Freud's followers became dissatisfied with the deterministic bent of psychoanalysis. Yet they appreciated aspects of the original theory including its emphasis on the lasting influence of childhood, the role of the unconscious, and the difficulty of psychological struggle. Many psychodynamic theories were developed, including self-psychology and ego psychology. Here we will focus on psychodynamic theories as a category, focusing on the themes they hold in common.

Psychodynamic theorists softened the deterministic aspects of psychoanalysis by focusing more on the influence of relationships and less on sexual drives. A central tenet of psychodynamic theories is that persons have internal memories and images from the past that influence, often unknowingly, the present. These memories form templates that unconsciously shape their thinking and behavior in the here-and-now (Mangis, Jones, & Butman, 2011). Internalized memories affect behaviors in the present because we often "recreate" dysfunctional relational patterns from the past. We may also view our present selves in ways that actually represent dysfunctional self-perceptions from the past. The focus in psychodynamic work is identifying and correcting dysfunctional historical patterns that harm present relationships within ourselves and with others.

Psychodynamic theories contribute to our understanding of sin. They do not account for original sin, use the language of sin, nor allude to its pervasive nature. However, the theories helpfully identify wrongful behavior as a reaction to unmet psychological needs. Identifying the psychological function underlying wrongful behavior does not remove accountability. But identifying the psychological function can be helpful in altering the behavior. For example, if someone lies because they feel inferior and lying inflates their sense of self-importance, addressing their psychological need for significance will often be critical to changing the behavior. At times, sinful behaviors are manifestations of unmet psychological needs. Psychodynamic theory helps us to see this link and to consider the underlying issue along with the problematic behavior.

Psychodynamic theories are less deterministic by accommodating human agency. While we are strongly influenced by patterns from our past, we are not entirely subject to them. Certainly we are influenced, but not slavishly so. Our past creates probabilities, but does not determine the choices we will make. We retain a sense of freedom and accountability for our actions.

The primary goal of psychodynamic theories is to be free from unhealthy historical patterns. Through such freedom, individuals are able to realistically see themselves and to form healthy relationships with others. As one article states, "Immaturity is marked by seeking out unhealthy individuals with whom to engage in pathological relational patterns that repeat old, unresolved interactions (Mangis, Jones, & Butman, 2011, p. 144)." We again affirm this goal and purpose, but want to understand it in light of our ultimate telos. We pursue freedom from unhealthy historical patterns in order to rightly relate to God, ourselves, and other people.

While Christians in social work may find points of departure from psychodynamic theories, these theories can provide a helpful theoretical base. Faith-based practitioners using psychodynamic approaches will need to incorporate discussions of relationships with God and others. They will also need to carefully integrate a theology of sin and its consequences along with interpretations about the psychological functions underlying behaviors.

What's the Objective?

Object relations theory originated in the 1940s through the work of British psychologists, W.R.D. Fairbairn, D.W. Winnicott, Harry Guntrip, and Melanie Klein. They believed that an individual's self was developed in direct relationship with another person, typically their primary caregiver. Drawing on aspects of psychoanalytic theory, theorists believed that children unconsciously internalized an "object" into their psyche. The object was a representation of their early primary caregiver. If the caregiver was loving and responsive, the object was internalized as positive. The opposite was internalized when caregivers were unloving. According to the theory, the nature of the object predicts behaviors as the person responds to present relationships based on the unconscious object. The way an object is internalized predicts health or dysfunction in current and future relationships (Hamilton, 1990).

Christian researchers have studied object relations theory for its extensions to understanding individualized responses to God and faith. Linkages have been found between the nature of internalized objects and views toward God and faith. For example, one study confirmed a positive relationship between the nature of a person's internalized object and the level of their spiritual maturity (Hall, Brokaw, Edwards, & Pike, 1998). Of this particular finding, Benner wrote that "psychological and spiritual functioning are inextricably linked because people relate to God through the same psychological mechanisms that mediate relationships with other people" (1988, p. 304). The study authors described a reciprocal relationship where,

> ...individuals who tend to experience others as critical and to emotionally withdraw to protect themselves are more likely to experience God as critical and to emotionally withdraw from God when this experience occurs. Likewise, when positive and negative relationship experiences occur with God, these may influence one's internal object relations and relationships with other people (p. 310).

Hall and Edwards (2002) developed an instrument, *The Spiritual Assessment Inventory*, which measures spiritual development based on object relations theory and theological anthropology. About the measure, Brokaw and Edwards (1994) wrote that it, "draws on the theoretical insights of object relations theory...and a sizable literature on God image/ representation, indicating that one's relational/emotional development is mirrored in one's relationship with the Divine, however that is perceived by the individual" (p. 341). Jones (1991) wrote, "Religion...is understood as a relationship with God that reflects and reenacts an individual's deep structure of internalized relationships. Individuals' relationships with God may be healthy or pathological, to varying degrees, and parallel their object relations maturity..." (p. 16).

Object relations theory reflects well the biblical theme of relationality. Not only does it shed light on the nature of one's relationship with God and others, it underscores the ways that relationships are a core to our being and central to our actions. It is important, however, to understand that while there are correlations between the past and present, these are not entirely predictive and may be influenced by mediating factors. An internalized object may be negative, but be mediated by the presence of other loving persons in a person's life. Additionally, the nature of one's formative relationships do not entirely predict their future. Healthy relationships with God and other people have the power to change the way one sees and experiences relationships. Realizing the love of God and others in the present can modify longstanding views of others as untrustworthy, manipulative, or unloving.

The link between one's early experiences and future relationships, including those with God, holds great value for Christians in social work. This linkage underscores the need to improve upon early childhood relationships whenever possible. We ought to facilitate healthy and secure early childhood relationships in order to lessen future relational obstacles. However, nurturing secure primary relationships at *any* point in the lifespan is valuable as it contributes to holistic relational growth.

Loved into Loving

Attachment theory built upon object relations theory (Ainsworth, 1969). The theory originated in England in the 1950s through the work of psychoanalyst, John Bowlby (Bowlby, 1958, 1968). Observing the anxiety of children who were separated from their primary caregivers, Bowlby theorized that children inherited a relational model based on the quality of this relationship. In practical terms, if the parent-child relationship was secure, he believed that children would react negatively when separated. He saw anxious reactions as indications that the child had properly attached to their caregivers. Anxious children who were ambivalent toward their caregivers demonstrated poor quality attachments where they did not trust the caregiver to be attentive. Like object relations theory, the quality of this attachment was believed to create a template, an "internal working model" (IWM) that predicted the quality of future relationships.

A series of well-known experiments conducted by Mary Ainsworth (1969) called the *Strange Situation Protocols* studied attachment theory, quantifying the responses of young children after their caregivers left the room, a stranger was introduced, and the child was reunited with their caregiver. Their attachments were categorized as secure, anxious-resistant, avoidant, and disorganized.

Like object-relations theory, attachment theory has been of interest to Christian researchers. It has been extended to study attachment to God. Maltby and Hall (2012) write,

> ...it did not take long for attachment theory to make its way into the psychology of religion. Parallel to...prior work applying object relations theory to understand people's experiences of God, researchers quickly realized that people experience God as an attachment figure, and subsequently began applying attachment-based categories to describe attachment to God (p. 303).

Indeed, many scholars have indicated that human and divine attachments do not have different points of origin. Hall and colleagues (2009) write:

> A number of theorists have addressed the issue of the relationship between psychological and spiritual development. These authors all point to...the meaning that the internal dimension of persons is not separable into "spiritual" and "psychological" components. In other words, the processes that govern one's experience of relationship with God, a typical understanding of "spirituality," are the very same "psychological" processes...that govern one's relationships with self and others (Hall, Fujikawa, Halcrow, Hill, & Delaney, p. 233).

Change, according to attachment theory, occurs through corrective present-day relationships which are characterized by trustworthiness, consistency, and unconditional love. While a corrective relationship could be represented by one's relationship with God, most researchers conclude that these occur more frequently through human relationships which are then transferred to one's relationship with God (Maltby & Hall, 2012).

Attachment theory resonates well with many biblical themes, particularly our relational nature. Hall and Maltby (2014) summarize this point well:

> We believe that numerous areas of attachment theory...resonate with a Christian worldview...including our relational nature and the image of God, internal working models, and growth and healing as a relational process... the relational paradigm of attachment theory resonates deeply with a rich Trinitarian theme in Christian theology suggesting that relationality is at the core of what it means to be created in the image of God...it is equally clear that a person who lacks attachment relationships and other forms of meaningful human connection does not manifest the fullness of what God intended personhood to be (pp. 200, 202).

This rich extension of attachment theory—that is, as highlighting the relationality that resonates with our image-bearing nature—adds important depth. The theory itself suggests only that humans are hardwired to attach for purposes of survival, not as the result of our core relational nature as modeled by the Trinity.

Attachment theory highlights no conception of sin. It only draws attention to the core problem of insecure attachments. Interestingly, an integrated understanding of original sin suggests that among all early attachments, even secure ones, infants develop imperfect IWM because of their *own* sinful tendencies and responses (Hall & Maltby, 2014). In other words, infants themselves, in addition to caregivers, may play a role in the nature of the attachment because of their inherent sinfulness.

Attachment theory is highly useful to Christians in social work because of its strong relational paradigm. It also accurately portrays human growth and development as primarily relational processes. As the theory implies, while people can be deeply harmed by relationships, they can also be deeply restored to God, themselves, and others *through* them.

Setting the Stage

Erik Erikson's (1963) psychosocial theory identifies eight linear stages that individuals move through sequentially throughout their lives. Erikson based his work on Freud's psychosexual theory, but focused uniquely on the way that relationships impact development of the ego—the conscious sense of one's self. He concluded that all persons face a series of crises of a psychosocial nature as the psychological needs of the individual conflict with the social needs of others. Erikson believed that internal strength grew as the person successfully resolved each subsequent developmental crisis, resulting in an ability to maintain one's core identity in the face of external conflict. Erikson's stages reflect his interest in personal and social identity—the part of one's identity that comes from group memberships. He believed that the identity crisis culminated in adolescence when experimentation with various identities eventually results in a singular, integrated identity.

Erikson believed that individuals need to master each predictable developmental crisis in order to proceed to the next crisis. Each stage is typified by two conflicting forces. When an individual successfully resolves these conflicting forces, they emerge from the stage with the corresponding virtue. Persons could proceed to the next stage without resolution of the crisis, but Erikson believed they would experience negative consequences.

Erikson's psychosocial theory—highly influential in conceptualizing human development—has both points of congruence and incongruence with biblical themes. First, the theory resonates well with the biblical emphasis on relationality. Unlike psychoanalytic theories which look solely to a person's internal world, Erikson understood that relationships play a critical role in the formation of one's identity. Similarly to attachment and object relations theories, Erikson's emphasis on the quality of early social interactions as the foundation for future relationships is important. This foundation has also been extended to understanding the nature of adult faith. Conn (1977) writes:

> It seems particularly illuminating…that the first psychosocial crisis of Erikson's life cycle - the infant's struggle to work out a balance favoring basic trust over against mistrust - brings forth, if successfully resolved, the fundamental strength or virtue of hope. For more than anything else, it is the rudimentary trust or hope resulting from this first critical stage that forms the bedrock for adult faith (pp. 256-257).

Secondly, Erikson's theory importantly prioritizes the development of virtues, virtues that mirror those developed as a result of increased spiritual maturity. Each stage, successfully resolved, results in the formation of a virtue such as hope, purpose, competence, fidelity, love, care, and wisdom. The theory additionally encourages movement over the span of a lifetime from selfish preoccupation to loving concern for others. Erikson's emphasis on developing virtues that move beyond one's self is congruent with the Bible's emphasis on growth as a gradual process of moving away from selfishness and toward others. Conn writes further:

> The critical point to be grasped here is that within Erikson's epigenetic model every crisis that marks a further developmental stage has a built-in criterion of self-transcendence. In other words, one develops in a fully human way only insofar as at each critical juncture one achieves a measure of self -transcendence in moving beyond one's self to the good of others (p. 261).

Learning Theories

We turn next to another important category of the psychological dimension, theories about how we learn. These theories are critical, of course, to social workers who spend a great deal of time assisting people in learning. Because they share a philosophical base, we will first review behavior and social learning theory and then consider both theories in light of our biblical themes.

Ringing Pavlov's Bell

The brainchild of John B. Watson during the early 20th century, behavior theory was originally based on observable behavior. Watson believed that everything, even fear, is learned and not innate. Children are born as blank slates who need to be taught everything and, unfortunately, are taught unhealthy things along the way (Watson, 1913, 1930). Behaviorism originated during a historical period that emphasized logical positivism. This philosophy stated that in order to be true, things needed to be observable and empirically verifiable. In contrast to psychoanalytic theory, behavior theory was seen as logical, verifiable, and rational. All humans are believed to learn through classical conditioning—when a neutral event becomes reflexively associated with new eliciting stimuli.

Behavior therapy was built upon in the 1950s by B.F. Skinner, who described operant conditioning—changes that occur when learned responses are modified by their consequences. Related to this, reinforcement represents things that increase the likelihood of the behavior and punishments decrease the likelihood of the behavior (Skinner, 1953; Ferster & Skinner, 1957). Negative reinforcement is the increase of a behavior due to withdrawal of an unpleasant consequence. In essence, behavior theory indicates that learning across the lifespan is the product of negative and positive consequences. Human problems are the by-product of three mechanisms: the learning of inappropriate responses, the lack of learning of appropriate responses in the past, and wrong consequences provided for maladaptive behavior (Ashford, LeCroy, Lortie, 2006; Jones, Flanagan, & Butman, 2011). A child's poor behavior may be the result of all three, for example, if she has learned from her parents' example to yell when she is angry, not been taught to effectively manage her anger, and received the attention she is craving for angry behavior.

Learning through Modeling

Many people felt that behavior theory was incomplete as it did not include cognition as a factor in human behavior. Subsequent learning theories sought to include the contributions of cognition. An important example with relevance to social work is social learning theory.

Originating with Albert Bandura, social learning theory suggests that learning is not passive, as behavior theory suggests, but incorporates individual thinking and processing (Bandura, 1977). Social learning theory emphasizes learning from modeling, not simply from consequences. We learn not solely from direct experiences, but also from observed experiences. We are shaped by role models, choosing behaviors to imitate or reject. In this regard, we are active participants in our own learning, not passive recipients. Social learning theory also indicates that the things we focus on in our environments influence our thinking and behavior.

Learning theories are deterministic, meaning they point to the causes of actions as lying outside of an individual's will. Behavior theory, for example, states that external consequences cause human behaviors as individuals make changes to either avoid negative consequences or to gain positive ones. While this practical line of thinking is helpful in understanding individual motivation and actions, Christians in social work will likely find it overly simplistic and incomplete. Behavior theory, by not highlighting the human ability to make choices that transcend instinctual urges, fall short of incorporating the biblical theme of human agency. As Jones, Flanagan, & Butman (2011) write:

> Christians must claim that human beings are capable of acting out higher motives, such as the desire to serve God, and that these higher motives cannot always be reduced to the drive for tangible reinforcement (p. 186).

Social learning theory comes closer to a biblical view of human agency by incorporating reciprocal determinism, meaning that behavior is not solely the product of our environment on us, but also a product of our interaction with the environment (Ashford, LeCroy, & Lortie, 2006). It notably includes one's cognition and, in doing so, comes closer to a biblical view of human agency and responsibility.

Learning theories also provide no sense of human sinfulness. They speak instead of survival in the here-and-now as the ultimate goal and behaviors as predictable if one understands the consequences operating behind the scenes. In this sense, behavior theories oversimplify behavior, missing something critical to a holistic understanding of persons. As Jones and colleagues (2011) write, "The fundamental and irrevocable weakness of behavior modification is that in the process of reducing complexity to fundamental processes, all that is recognizably and distinctly human disappears" (p. 189).

Christians in social work ought not dismiss the tenets of learning theories, however. Indeed, the Bible speaks of rewards, punishments, and consequences. Understanding the basic ways behavior is motivated by rewards and consequences is helpful. A Christian view of behavior, however, encompasses more than what is externally observable. The Bible connects behaviors to the condition of the heart. So while right behaviors matter, they are not always connected to pure internal motivations. Behaviors can look outwardly admirable, for example, but be driven the prideful need to receive praise from others. Conversely, wrong behaviors may have complex inner causes that require careful and compassionate exploration.

An important contribution from learning theories is their emphasis on the ways we are shaped by habitual, repetitive responses. This is a helpful consideration in the pursuit of faith development. Habitual practices such as prayer, Scripture reading, and meditation have the ability, over time, to change the hearts and actions. Related to this, the importance of modeling has significant application as it underscores activities such as faith-based or secular mentoring programs for children, adolescents, parents, and families.

Social workers frequently utilize learning theories, particularly in work with children or developmentally disabled persons, where scenarios with clearly delineated expectations, rewards, and consequences are strongly indicated. Structured environments can provide anxiety-reducing predictability. Modeling behaviors or lifestyles is also helpful across populations. This may be especially true when people feel isolated in their struggle. We should be aware, however, that changing behaviors or gaining behavioral compliance does not always indicate deep motivational change or "heart-level' change. Christians in social work will want to be mindful of this, looking for ways, whenever possible, to encourage change that incorporates the whole person.

Developing the Mind

Jean Piaget, a 20th century Swiss psychologist, developed a stage theory related to human intelligence which has been influential in cognitive psychology—the study of sensation, perception, and cognition (Piaget, 1932, 1936, 1957). Sensation is the process by which a person detects internal and external stimulation at its various receptor sites. Perception is the interpretation of sensory input, and cognition is the process of obtaining, organizing, and utilizing sensory and perceptual information from the environment and past experiences (Ashford, LeCroy, & Lortie, 2006).

Piaget's theory identifies the ways by which persons acquire and build upon already-existing learning. He believed cognitive development resulted from an ongoing process of adapting what one already knows to environmental discrepancies that occur as one develops. He referred to this as adaptation. Related concepts are *assimilation*—adapting new information to existing thought structures—and *accommodation*—changing thought structures to incorporate new environmental inputs. Piaget also highlighted the importance of organization, the idea that we make sense of what we perceive by placing thoughts into categories.

According to the theory, children typically move through four stages of organizing their thoughts—sensorimotor, preoperational, concrete operational, and formal operational. The sensorimotor stage is characterized by the movement from reflexive actions to the initiation of symbolic thought. The preoperational stage demonstrates an increase in symbolic play and egocentrism. The concrete operational stage is illustrated by the development of logical thinking and conversation and a decrease in egocentrism. Finally, the formational operational stage is characterized by the forming of high-level cognitive tasks including abstract thinking, counterfactual thinking, deductive reasoning, and metacognition.

While the theory has been criticized for its unilateral, one-size-fits-all approach, Piaget's stages have been widely influential. They continue to assist educators and practitioners in accurately tailoring educational approaches to the cognitive capabilities of the child. Social workers regularly use them to align interventions with the intellectual proficiencies of individual children or groups of children.

Piaget's theory correlates well with the biblical theme of embodiment. The theory entails brain-centered cognitive developmental process. Through the mechanisms of sensation, perception, accommodation, and assimilation, children typically move from basic thought processes to complex abstract thinking. The role of biology is critical to the model and rightly reflects the biblical emphasis on persons as embodied.

The theory of cognitive development devotes little attention to relationality. The theory is deterministic in the sense that cognitive growth is the result of unfolding biological maturation and learning experiences. However, the theory does not highlight the ways that relationships facilitate or inhibit cognitive growth. Relationships can both bolster or harm the speed and quality of a child's cognitive developmental process. Piaget's theory also draws little attention to the child's agency or reciprocal participation in the learning process.

Piaget's theory has limitations for Christians in social work as it does not incorporate a broad, holistic view of the person. The theory, however, has appropriately drawn attention to the need to create developmentally appropriate interventions. This has enormous implications for social workers working with children. Various forms of therapy with children are indirectly built on the principles of Piaget when they emphasize cognitively appropriate methods of relating to children.

Learning Right from Wrong

Moral development theory was developed by American psychologist, Lawrence Kohlberg (1973, 1981, 1984). Kohlberg's theory of moral development has influenced many secular and faith-based practitioners. The theory was based on his research into how individuals responded to the now-famous Heinz dilemma (a man must decide whether or not to steal a drug needed to save his dying wife's life after a greedy pharmacist inflates its price). Based on people's responses to the moral dilemma, Kohlberg identified six stages of ascending moral development: punishment/obedience, rewards, good intentions, obedience to authority, difference between moral and legal right, and individual principles of conscience.

The six stages are divided into three categories: pre-conventional, conventional, and post-conventional morality. Kohlberg believed that an individual increased in moral development as they moved from decisions to avoid punishment into decisions involving abstract reasoning. Kohlberg felt that children were in the first two stages, adolescents and adults were in stages three and four, and that some adults (but not all) reached stages five and six. Kohlberg believed that people did not skip stages and rarely regressed to lower stages.

Interestingly, Carol Gilligan, who worked as Kohlberg's research assistant, criticized his approach as not accounting for the ways that gender differences relate to morality. She argued in her well-known work, *In a Different Voice* (1982), that women approach morality more from an "ethics of care" approach that considers their responsibilities within relationships than the sense of fairness and justice identified in Kohlberg's theory.

Among persons of faith, Kohlberg's theory has both critics and supporters. Some scholars, for example, point out that Kohlberg's theory is based on a hypothetical dilemma which is too far removed from daily life, where moral decisions are actually made (Moroney, 2006; Clouse, 1985). Others are concerned with the theory's lack of a concept of sin. In fact, some question whether morality can actually be grasped without an understanding of humans as inherently sinful and, therefore, wired to make wrong moral choices (Clouse, 1990). Gibson (2004) additionally points out the failure of the theory to measure moral *behavior*, the way in which moral reasoning is manifested. The concern is that one can endorse mature moral reasoning in the abstract, but live out something entirely different. In this respect, Gilligan's emphasis on assessing morality within relationships better encompasses the practical versus abstract nature of moral decision-making.

Balswick, King, and Reimer (2016) raise an important concern related to the theory's inability to account for *theological* motivations when making moral decisions. They make the important point that Christians may choose right actions as a product of their love for God and a desire to obey his moral laws. For Christians, morality needs to be linked to God's moral laws and our relationship to Him in order to be fully understood. Gibson (2004) summarizes this well,

> ...for persons who acknowledge God as the source of absolute Truth and the divine lawgiver and who wish to benefit from Kohlberg's insights, it is necessary to offer an alternative model. In maintaining that moral law extends from a higher being...the Christian worldview integrally ties morality with one's relationship to God. In essence, then, the Christian understands morality as extending from one's holistic spiritual development (p. 297).

Some scholars have pointed out that Kohlberg's theory contains bias against religious belief because individuals who believe that God's moral truths must be obeyed are by definition not seen as post-conventional (Johnson, 1996). Therefore, acting morally out of a desire to please God is not seen as a mature sign of development although it is desirable by biblical standards. It has also been pointed out that the Bible appeals to various grounds for obedience, including avoidance of punishment and the achievement of rewards. Yet the theory correlates these motivations with immature moral development. Indeed, there may be cases in which acting morally in light of a future reward is mature. Choosing to forgive someone, for example, may be motivated by the future "reward" of freedom from resentment and anger.

At the same time, many Christian scholars and practitioners have embraced and applied Kohlberg's theory. Many highlight congruence between the theory and a biblical emphasis on individual moral differences as well as the connection of internal reasons for external behavior (Moroney, 2006). The biblical emphasis is on not simply "doing the right thing," but doing it from a place of pure motivation, a concept mirrored in Kohlberg's theory.

Gibson (2004) has integrated Kohlberg's theory with stages of moral development in a helpful model that can be summarized as follows:

Level 1	Level 2	Level 3	Level 4
Accommodation to God's law out of fear of punishment or hope of a reward	Imitation of godly exemplars with growing respect for and obedience to the Ten Commandments	Personal, principle-centered commitment to Christian worldview	Movement beyond a focus on individual piety to corporate piety and the redemption of creation's broken structures
Source of Authority	Source of Authority	Source of Authority	Source of Authority
Self	Others	One's principles	The Kingdom of God

Kohlberg's theory is highly useful for Christians in social work as it characterizes moral growth as moving from punishment-avoidance to the consideration of a larger context. That said, we ought to consider moral development in a broad sense that encapsulates God's moral laws and obedience to him. For Christians, the hope is that moral growth comes from a deepening trust in God. In other words, there is strong correlation between moral and spiritual development. At times, we appropriately fear punishments and crave rewards, but mature moral behavior is motivated more from love than fear. A deepening of love for God facilitates trust and a desire to submit to his laws, both for our good and the good of others.

Moral development theory has strong implications for many social service programs. Most programs should be governed by firm, yet loving, consequences. Children will benefit from structured and consistent consequences as illustrated by the pre-conventional stage of moral development. The broader principle of moving from fear-based compliance to intrinsically-based self-control should guide interventions, however. Across the lifespan, high-quality relationships are key to the development of strong morality. Such relationships set the stage for the loving relationship with God we hope to model and foster.

Growing a Faith

James Fowler, a 20th century American theologian and Methodist minister, took Piaget's theory of cognitive development, Kohlberg's theory of moral development, and Erikson's psychosocial theory and adapted them into a theory of faith development. Fowler was also strongly influenced in the development of the theory by theologians Paul Tillich and H. Richard Niebuhr. He aimed to provide a theory for understanding the phenomenology of how people develop ways of relating to the world and themselves in light of their understanding of transcendent reality. Faith development theory (1981) includes seven stages, but was later expanded to eight (Moseley, Jarvis, Fowler, & DeNicola, 1993). According to the theory, persons move from an undifferentiated stage of faith at birth to a universalizing faith where there is concern for the justice of all people.

It is important to understand that Fowler broadly defines faith as the primary motivation of one's life. His theory accordingly characterizes "faith" as a construct that is present among *all* persons, even in cases when someone does not identify or engage with a specific religion or religious practices (Green & Hoffman, 1989). Faith is understood as "a generic human phenomenon – a way of leaning into or meeting life, whether traditionally religious, or Christian, or not (Fowler, 1986, p. 16)." By universalizing faith development, the theory was influential in moving faith from something seen as subjective to something that could be quantified, studied, and understood. It also elevated the role of faith as a critical part of the human experience, one deserving of attention and exploration.

However, the theory's attempt to be universal may present its greatest weakness. Many Christians believe that the theory lacks enough specificity to be valuable. As McDargh (2001) writes,

> ...what some have found Fowler's greatest usefulness, namely that he understands faith as a human universal, not always or even necessarily religious in its content or context is, for these critics, his greatest limitation (p. 192).

Some have argued that by equating faith with openness or a generic human phenomenon, faith loses its core essence as a loving and covenantal relationship between persons and the divine. Indeed, openness to spirituality is an early component of faith development, but further growth entails specifically confessing the redemptive work of Christ and growth in love and obedience toward God and others. Jones (2004) elaborates on this point:

> The core content of Fowlerian stage-development appears to me to be openness to that which is "other"—both to the relative otherness of fellow humans and to the ultimate otherness of the transcendent realm. It is the development of this openness that Fowler's stages so admirably describe. Christian faith emerges from this openness to that which is "other;" however, because Christian faith requires not only an openness to Ultimate Reality but also a confession that Ultimate Reality is encountered uniquely and consummately in Jesus Christ, Christian faith has its own developmental structure, formed by its distinctive content (p. 354).

Many scholars believe that the theory's concept of maturation is overly reliant on human efforts and therefore underemphasizes the role of the Holy Spirit. In this respect, the role of human agency is believed to be exaggerated. Theological criticism has centered on the fact that, from a Christian viewpoint, "faith" is a human response to God's grace and a gift from God, as opposed to something humanly manufactured (McDargh, 2001).

Similar to the Piagetian movement from literal to abstract understanding, faith understanding begins through the teaching of parents and institutions, such as churches and schools. A more mature faith embraces mystery and life's paradoxes. In this respect, the theory provides a useful means of understanding Christian growth. Growth as a Christian certainly does not imply denying one's intellect or logical reasoning, but there is a sense that faith growth makes one more aware of mysteries that lie outside of our understanding. Paradoxically, greater acceptance of mystery does not equate with greater anxiety, but instead a deeper trust in God as all-knowing. As the theory suggests, an ability to trust God despite the presence of mystery is indeed a mark of Christian growth.

While studies have both supported and refuted aspects of faith development theory (Genia, 1990; Parker, 2010), it has been helpful in faith-based settings. Awareness of the theory helps to match interventions to the stage of the person. Also, Fowler notably highlighted education about faith through institutions such as family and church. In this respect, he provided a framework by which to broadly understand the trajectory of faith development, although teaching and understanding the Christian faith entails considerably more specificity.

Psychological Risk and Protection

We conclude this chapter with a brief discussion of risk and protection in the psychological realm. Risk factors in the psychological realm have been defined as "anything that compromises mental functioning" and "disharmony in the psychological system or a lack of opportunity to develop the mental and motor processes needed to cope with life's demands" (Ashford, LeCroy, Lortle, 2006, p. 112)." On the other hand, psychological protective factors facilitate coping during crisis and enhance mental functioning. Some observations related to building psychological protection—based on the theories from this chapter—are offered here.

First, there is overwhelming support that loving and stable early attachments provide psychological protection. While a lack of healthy attachments can be overcome, doing so can be a lengthy, even lifelong, process. With this in mind, Christians in social work ought to labor proactively, facilitating healthy familial attachments whenever possible. Critical time periods make this work urgent for practitioners assisting young families. Facilitating healthy attachments is often complicated by psychosocial crises within the life of the family. Despite the presence of multiple stressors, priority must be given to parent-child relationships. The correlation of primary caregiver attachment and future attachment to God only strengthens the importance of this focus.

Related to this point, an emphasis, as highlighted by psychoanalytic and psychodynamic theories, on healthy childhood experiences is critical. While all parents are sinful, patterns of consistency, love, and stability bear significant fruit in the lives of children. In cases where parents undervalue their importance, they can benefit from education about their formative role. In other cases, parents need feedback about how they are modeling dysfunction from their own past. They need help forming new and productive patterns with their children. Some parents lack self-confidence, overwhelmed by feelings of hopelessness and frustration toward themselves and their children. Both insight-oriented and behavioral approaches are needed in the critical, but challenging, process of strengthening struggling parents.

Second, psychological protection involves the ability to successfully manage crises. Social workers frequently engage with persons during periods of crisis. Crisis creates disequilibrium, even in stable systems, and regaining equilibrium is often difficult. Acknowledgement of crisis and the depth of its impact is a critical and necessary part of coping. Unfortunately, some faith-based groups nurture a culture of perfection which discourages the disclosure of struggle. The church has many resources to help people in crisis, but in such cases, people do not feel free to be honest. Christians in social work serve well by normalizing struggle within the body of Christ, treating it as an inherent part of the human experience versus a display of inferiority or weakness.

Third, several theories focus on the ways we learn. Learning is a complex process involving many different components, but it is important to consider the ways that we are continually learning, consciously and unconsciously. Psychologically, we are both harmed and protected by the things we learn from our environments. Our clients, for example, learn things from media and culture that place them at risk. They learn that they need to appear a certain way to be considered physically attractive. They learn to fit into social groups by being violent. They learn that people of their racial background are viewed with suspicion. Daily, they are being consciously and unconsciously learning about themselves and the world through themes such as materialism, individualism, and racism.

To counter learning that places people at risk, numerous interventions from numerous places are needed. These may include teaching clients to challenge risky messages from the culture, encouraging client participation in countercultural institutions such as schools and churches. They may include nurturing psychological dispositions such as self-efficacy and self-confidence which serve as counterpoints to the narratives of their environments. Indeed, the Christian faith provides extraordinary psychological protection as it affirms individuals as unique, worthy, and beloved.

Finally, moral and faith development provide a strong foundation for coping with crisis and gaining resilience as persons. There are many connections between strong faith, strong morality, and human flourishing. Therefore, encouraging moral growth by helping someone to consider the impact of their decisions on others, is encouragement toward flourishing. Nurturing someone's openness to faith encourages their flourishing. Christians in social work see natural connections between moral choices and a person's well-being. We encourage activities that psychologically protect our clients, not simply because such activities are good things to do, but because they align them more closely with God's purposes.

Chapter Summary

Various psychological theories contribute to our understanding of human behavior, although each also has shortcomings when viewed from a faith-based perspective. Because Christians in social work spend a great deal of their time working directly or indirectly on psychological issues with their clients, it is important to critically consider the nature of such theories. Insights from our faith and theoretical insights provide a rich context for assisting others in forming and maintaining healthy emotions, thoughts, and behaviors.

Discussion Questions

1. How do moral and faith reasoning interconnect? On the other hand, how is it that highly moral people may have no faith?

2. Write a one-sentence slogan for each of the theories covered in the chapter.

3. What do you think is taking place when individuals have healthy early attachments, but have considerable relational problems throughout the remainder of their lives?

4. In what specific ways does behavior theory play a role in your daily life?

5. Fowler and Kohlberg said that few people reach the ultimate stages of their theories. Do you agree with this? Why or why not?

References

Ainsworth, M. D. S. (1969). Object relations, dependency, and attachment: a theoretical review of the infant-mother relationship. *Child Development, 40,* 969-1025.

Ashford, J. B., LeCroy, C. W., & Lortie, K. L. (2006). *Human behavior in the social environment: A multidimensional perspective.* Belmont, CA: Wadsworth Publishing.

Balswick, J. O., King, P. E., & Reimer, K. S. (2016). *The reciprocating self: Human development in theological perspective.* Downers Grove, IL: Intervarsity Press.

Bandura, A. (1977). *Social learning theory.* Englewood Cliffs, N.J.: Prentice-Hall.

Benner, D. (1988). *Care of souls: Revisioning Christian nurture and counsel.* Grand Rapids, MI: Baker Book House.

Bowlby, J. (1958). The nature of the child's tie to his mother. *International Journal of Psychoanalysis, 39,* 1-23.

Bowlby, J. (1968). *Attachment and Loss, Vol. 1: Attachment.* New York: Basic Books.

Brokaw, B. F., & Edwards, K. J. (1994). The relationship of God image to level of object relations development. *Journal of Psychology and Theology, 22,* 352-371.

Clouse, B. (1990). Jesus' law of love and Kohlberg's stages of moral reasoning. *Journal of Psychology and Christianity, 9,* 5-15.

Clouse, B. (1985). *Moral development: Perspectives in psychology and Christian belief*. Grand Rapids, MI: Baker Book House.

Conn, W.E. (1977). Erikson: The ethical orientation, conscience and the golden rule, *The Journal of Religious Ethics*, 5, 249-266.

Erikson, E. (1963). *Children and society*. New York City, NY: W. W. Norton & Company.

Ferster, C.B. & Skinner, B.F. (1957). *Schedules of reinforcement*. New York: Appleton-Century-Crofts.

Fowler, J. W. (1981). *Stages of faith: the psychology of human development and the quest for meaning*. New York: HarperCollins.

Fowler, J. W. (1986). Faith and the structuring of meaning. In C. Dykstra & S. Parks (Eds.), *Faith development and Fowler* (pp. 15-42). Birmingham, AL: Religious Education Press.

Freud, S. (2010). *The Interpretation of Dreams*. (A. A. Brill, Trans.). New York, NY: The Macmillan Company. (Original work published 1913).

Genia, V. (1990). Religious development: a synthesis and reformulation. *Journal of Religion and Health*, 29, 85-99.

Gibson, T.S. (2004). Proposed levels of Christian maturity, *Journal of Theology and Psychology*, 32, 295-304.

Gilligan, C. (1982). *In a different voice: Psychological theory and women's development*. Cambridge, MA: Harvard University Press.

Green, C. W., & Hoffman, C. L. (1989). Stages of faith and perceptions of similar and dissimilar others. *Review of Religious Research*, 30, 246–254.

Hall, T.W., Brokaw, B.F., Edwards, K.J., & Pike, P.L. (1998). An empirical exploration of psychoanalysis and religion: spiritual maturity and object relations development, *Journal for the Scientific Study of Religion*, 37, 303-313.

Hall, T.W. & Edwards, K.U. (2002). The spiritual assessment inventory: a theistic model and measure for assessing spiritual development. *Journal for the Scientific Study of Religion*, 41, 341-357.

Hall, T.W., Fujikawa, A., Halcrow, S.R., Hill, P.C. & Delaney, H. (2009). Attachment to god and implicit spirituality: clarifying correspondence and compensation models, *Journal of Psychology & Theology*, 37, 227-244.

Hall, T. H., & Maltby, L. E. (2014). Attachment-based psychoanalytic therapy and Christianity: Being-in-Relation. In E. Bland (Author), *Christianity & psychoanalysis: A new conversation*. Downers Grove, IL: Intervarsity Press.

Hamilton, N.G. (1990). *Self and others: Object relations theory in practice*. Lanham, MD: Rowman and Littlefield Publishers.

Hoffman, M. (2007). From libido to love: relational psychoanalysis and the redemption of sexuality, *Journal of Psychology & Theology*, 35, 74-82.

Johnson, E.L. (1996). The call of wisdom: Adult development within Christian community, Part I: The crisis of modern theories of post-formal development. *Journal of Psychology and Theology*, 24, 83-92.

Jones, J. W. (1991). *Contemporary psychoanalysis and religion*. New Haven: Yale University Press.

Jones, T.P. (2004). The basis of James W. Fowler's understanding of faith in the research of Wilfred Cantwell Smith: an examination from an evangelical perspective, *Religious Education*, 99, 345-357.

Jones, S. L., Flanagan, K., & Butman, R. E. (2011). Behavior therapy, In S. L. Jones & R. E. Butman (Eds.), *Modern Psychotherapies: A Comprehensive Christian Appraisal* (2nd ed., pp. 166-200). Downers Grove, IL: Intervarsity Press.

Jones, S.L., Watson, and Butman, R.E. (2011). Classic psychoanalysis, In S.L. Jones & R. E. Butman (Eds.), *Modern Psychotherapies: A Comprehensive Christian Appraisal* (2nd ed., pp.94-134). Downers Grove, IL: Intervarsity Press.

Kohlberg, L. (1973). Stages and aging in moral development: Some speculations. *Gerontologist, 13*, 497-502.

Kohlberg, L. (1981). *The philosophy of moral development: Moral stages and the idea of justice*. San Francisco: Harper & Row.

Kohlberg, L. (1984). *The psychology of moral development: The nature and validity of moral stages*. San Francisco: Harper & Row.

Maltby, L.E. & Hall, T.W. (2012). Trauma, attachment, and spirituality: a case study, *Journal of Psychology & Theology*, 40, 302-312.

Mangis, M. W., Jones, S. L., & Butman, R. J. (2011). Contemporary Psychodynamic Psychotherapies. In S. L. Jones & R. E. Butman (Eds.), In *Modern Psychotherapies: A Comprehensive Christian Appraisal* (2nd ed., pp. 135-166). Downers Grove, IL: Intervarsity Press.

McDargh, J. (2001). Faith development theory and the postmodern problem of foundations, *The International Journal for the Psychology of Religion*, 11, 185-199.

Moroney, S. (2006). Higher stages? Some cautions for Christian integration with Kohlberg's theory. *Journal of Psychology and Theology*, 34, 361-371.

Moes, P., & Tellinghuisen, D. J. (2014). *Exploring psychology and Christian faith: An introductory guide*. Grand Rapids, MI: Baker Academic.

Moseley, R. M., Jarvis, D., Fowler, J. W., & DeNicola, K. B. (1993). *Manual for faith development research*. Atlanta, GA: Center for Research in Faith and Moral Development, Candler School of Theology, Emory University.

Parker, Stephen (2010). Research in fowler's faith development theory. *Review of Religious Research*, 51, 233-252.

Piaget, J. (1932). *The moral judgment of the child*. London: Routledge & Kegan Paul.

Piaget, J. (1936). *Origins of intelligence in the child*. London: Routledge & Kegan Paul.

Piaget, J. (1957). *Construction of reality in the child*. London: Routledge & Kegan Paul.

Pytell, T. (2000). The missing pieces of the puzzle: a reflection on the odd career of Viktor Frankl, *Journal of Contemporary History*, 35, 281-306.

Skinner, B.F. (1953). *Science and human behavior.* New York: Macmillan.

Watson, J. B. (1913). Psychology as the behaviorist views it. *Psychological Review,* 20, 158-178.

Watson, J. B. (1930). *Behaviorism* (revised edition). Chicago, IL: University of Chicago Press.

Chapter Six

The Social Dimension

This chapter will explore the social dimensions of HBSE. We will ask ourselves what role a person's social environment—their family, peer groups, institutions, and cultural and societal context—plays in their behavior. While research is continually adding to our understanding of the ways social realities—moving targets in a rapidly changing culture— influence behavior, there is much current insight upon which we may draw.

In looking at the social dimension, we will identify the key emphases of theories including social development theory, ecological systems theory, the person-in-environment perspective, developmental systems theory, and family development theory. The chapter concludes with a discussion of aspects of social risk and protection. Along the way, each theory will be considered in light of the biblical themes discussed in Chapter 1 and the model for development from Chapter 2.

Social Fitness

We begin with social development theory. Social development theory originated through the work of Leo Vygotsky, a Russian psychologist who lived during the Russian Revolution. His life was unfortunately cut short by tuberculosis, years before his work gained recognition in developmental psychology. Vygotsky's theory (1962, 1978) became widely influential after his research was published in the West in the 1960s.

Social development theory takes a different perspective than biological or psychological theories, arguing that one's *social* interactions represent the starting point of development. It suggests that higher mental processes, such as cognition and learning, are actually by-products of socialization. Understanding development, therefore, requires understanding the social and cultural contexts in which persons are embedded. Unlike many other theories, social development theory does not identify linear stages, but instead highlights important concepts.

Vygotsky believed that language particularly demonstrated the manner in which social relationships directed the development of children. He differed from Piaget in this regard. Piaget believed that infants developed speech internally (an inside-out approach), preparing themselves for eventual verbal interaction with others. Vygotsky believed the opposite, that language developed from social interactions (an outside-in approach). He believed that cognitive development resulted from the internalization of language as children were stimulated by their social contexts to develop language skills which allowed them to interact with others. Language was seen as important to understanding both children's cognitions (Vygotsky, 1987; Balswick, King, & Reimer, 2016).

Vygotsky extended the importance of social inputs to the process of learning. While Piaget felt that children learn best through independent exploration, Vygotsky believed they learn best from guided social interactions within a "zone of proximal development." A zone of proximal development describes the space in which a person receives the optimal amount of assistance and encouragement to master new skills. That is to say, learning occurs most optimally through instruction from someone who skillfully challenges and supports. He identified the importance of "scaffolding"—strategies that support, but also extend—the learner's cognitive abilities. These also worked to increase their sense of self-efficacy.

The theory additionally indicates that a child's internal mental representation of his or her self is dependent on their social and cultural context. Mental representations are important because they are the building blocks that comprise our thoughts. They are the "symbols, images, feelings, or commitments that constitute our thinking" (Balswick, King, & Reimer, 2016, p. 91). Therefore, social relationships are critical not only to learning; they directly influence the formation of one's self-perceptions.

Social development theory has significant relevance to the understanding of HBSE. In many respects, the theory laid the groundwork for social work's commitment to improving the environment as a means of improving individual lives. Importantly, it underscores the fact that development is highly impacted and, in many ways, initiated, by social relationships. Relationships influence many critical areas, including one's level of cognitive development and their perceptions of themselves.

The theory has many implications for social work practice. Many of our clients have inadequate early relationships and thus have formed extremely negative self-representations. Negative self-perceptions can contribute to numerous poor outcomes. For example, children can internalize a sense of inadequacy as learners, limiting their potential and creating a sense of futility about their future. They can respond to a negative self-perception by looking to risky peer groups for validation. They can develop a grandiose sense of self as a paradoxical means of coping with the invalidation they have internalized from others. A deep appreciation for the innumerable ways that social development contributes to individual self-representations is important for social workers. Indeed, many of the core problems of those with whom we work are related to the impact of their social environment upon their view of themselves.

The theory also indicates that development is particularly transmitted through language and therefore varies by culture. This thesis underscores social work's core commitment to understanding cultural context as a means of understanding differences among persons. Cultural contexts are not seen as minor sources of formation, but substantive contributors to learning and self-perceptions.

Social development theory encapsulates extraordinarily well the biblical theme of relationality. By highlighting the way that social interactions impact the development of language, trigger cognitive development, and influence our concepts of ourselves and the world, the theory certainly upholds the importance of relationships. These concepts correlate well with a biblical concept of humanness where one's sense of self develops in the context of formative relationships with God and other people.

The theory specifically draws our attention to the role of culture, suggesting that culture impacts the ways persons see themselves and the world. In this respect, the theory supports a biblical emphasis on cultural differences as an important and valuable way that people differ. Cultural differences are not to be ignored nor minimized as they represent the different ways that individuals reflect the image of God. At the same time, the theory suggests a universal process wherein people essentially grow and learn through relationships, whatever their cultural context.

Social development theory identifies no concept of sinfulness beyond indirectly implying that relationships have the potential to create significant developmental harm. Indeed, relationships are significant mechanisms for the manifestation of sin and brokenness. The theory also does not identify a concept of inherent sinfulness playing a role in the way that, for example, perceptions from the outside world are internalized. Nor does it identify the ways that culture can powerfully transmit sinful postures, such as nationalistic arrogance or ethnic superiority.

Related to other biblical themes, the theory does not diminish human agency, but it does not emphasize it either. It focuses considerably more on the way we are shaped "from the outside in." While it is accurate to say that we are highly influenced by our social environments, we also make choices about how to respond to internalized messages about ourselves and the world. At some level, the role of individual agency extends even to social situations dominated by negativity, minimal support, and sinful misperceptions.

An understanding of the formative power of the social dimension implies thoughtful decision-making about one's social context. To varying degrees, we exert agency by making conscious choices about our relationships, institutions, and the cultural contexts in which we place ourselves. We can place ourselves within relationships and contexts that affirm the truth of our status as beloved image-bearers. Conveying the importance of relationships to development is important for our clients, particularly for young people who are still forming their identities.

Parts of the Whole

Next, we turn to ecological system theory. *Ecology* refers to the study of the relationships of organisms with each other and with their physical surroundings. Ecological systems theory refers to the study of persons within their various systems. It indicates that persons cannot be understood without an examination of their relationships with one other and with their social environments. These relationships are interactive and reciprocal in the sense that we are both influenced by and directly influence other people and our social environments.

Urie Bronfenbrenner was a Russian-born psychologist who first identified ecological systems theory. He delineated four levels of systems that influence persons: the microsystem (home), mesosystem (daycare, school, peer groups), exosystem (parental work places and local governments), and macrosystem (historical events, national and international culture) (Bronfenbrenner, 1977).

Central to ecological systems theory is an emphasis on understanding the whole versus simply the parts, a concept referred to as *holism* (Ashford, LeCory, & Lortie, 2006). The theory focuses on the interrelationships between humans and their environments and emphasizes the ways in which even the smallest parts form a component of something far larger. It looks to the largest systems for understanding of the smaller systems. Ecological system theory is the opposite of reductionism, which studies individual parts in order to understand the whole.

Ecological systems theory has been important in social work. The theory implies that social work practice at any level can positively impact other levels. In other words, interventions that facilitate individual healing and growth for a struggling adolescent can indirectly contribute to the good of the teen's family, friends, school, and community. Conversely, macro-level interventions, such as fair housing practices, can facilitate health among schools, families, and children.

Ecological systems theory implicitly endorses the goodness of creation by drawing attention to the full range of social influences. The theory rightly identifies national and local governments, communities, schools, and churches. Such institutions and social contexts are critical components of a good creation. At levels close to the individual, families serve as laboratories for rich instruction in relating to others, learning to communicate, and finding one's way through conflict. The components within every system play integral roles in forming and developing humans well.

Bronfenbrenner's theory does not identify a notion of sin within or between the levels of the systems. This is indirectly implied, as the theory is often used to identify problematic relationships within or between levels, but the theory specifies no means of understanding sin. It is helpful to consider the fact that while positive changes in one system may impact another system, sin can work similarly. Sinful behaviors by an individual can impact whole communities, for example, when crimes are committed. In the opposite manner, ethnic discrimination within a nation can trigger individual-level hatred and revenge-seeking.

Human agency is not directly addressed by this theory, although we can imply that while one is free to act independently, they are never entirely free from the influences of their immediate and larger environmental systems. In this regard, the theory resonates with the limited sense of freedom that is highlighted in the Bible, although the theory's limitations relate to environmental influences and not biological or theological restrictions. The theory minimizes the importance of embodiment, drawing attention instead to the way that relationships trigger biological processes, such as cognitive development.

Ecological systems theory upholds well the biblical theme of relationality. Its core emphasis of understanding the nature of "within-level" and "between-level" relationships as a means of understanding human development is extremely useful. The theory identifies well a truth related to our relationality—that our actions are not in a vacuum, but impact someone or something larger than ourselves.

This principle is important to Christians in social work in two aspects. First, it is encouraging to know that interventions in any system have potential for impacting the greater good. Individuals who develop well have the potential to impact others and to create an ever-widening circle of positive influence. Growth as a Christian also involves an increasing ability to see the ways in which one's actions impact other people. We often grow in self-control or compassion, for example, when we can honestly hear how our actions have been received by another. This is also an important aspect of Christian accountability in which we lovingly speak truth in order to support one another and strengthen our relationship.

Second, social institutions play a critical role in human flourishing and therefore deserve our sustained attention. This is certainly true on the highest levels of government where social workers advocate for just policies, but also on the middle levels where churches, schools, and neighborhoods represent highly formative mechanisms of human development. Indeed, the familial level is arguably the most important social influence in the formation of the individual.

Context is Everything

The person-in-environment approach represents a perspective for practice rather than a theory explaining behavior. However, its strong relevance to social work makes it important in our discussion of social influences on human development. First developed by Karls and Wandrei (1994), the person-in-environment approach is structured similarly to the Diagnostic and Statistical Manual—a classification of mental disorders used by practitioners. The person-in-environment approach identifies four factors to use when describing client problems: Factor I: Social-role problems, Factor II: Environmental problems, Factor III: Mental disorders, and Factor IV: Physical disorders.

The person-in-environment approach draws attention to the multiple influences on a client's situation by emphasizing factors both inside and outside of persons. The perspective rightly understands persons in light of a complex range of internal and external factors. The person-in-environment approach has been said to differentiate the profession of social work from sister disciplines, such as psychology, which tends to be more person-centered, and sociology, which tends to be more environment-oriented (Kondrat, 2015).

Examining the person-in-environment approach in light of biblical themes and the model for development is important as the perspective is widely embraced by social work. Similar to ecological systems theory, the perspective's emphasis on the interactive relationship between persons and environments highlights well the biblical theme of relationality and the reciprocal nature of our relationships with one another and the world around us. The approach is more descriptive than prescriptive. Our telos directs us more specifically toward *right* relationships with God, others, and the world, but the person-in-environment approach is a helpful tool in viewing the web of relationships and contexts around a person.

The person-in-environment perspective grasps well our interconnected nature. However, it does not extend far enough to include the responsibilities *implied by our interconnectivity*. The Bible is clear that our connections with others are to be characterized by love. We ought not simply consider the ways we are shaped by the environment and vice versa, but the ways we can better *love* within our particular contexts. In other words, for Christians in social work, the encouragement is to move beyond the description of the person-in-environment relationship to a consideration of how specific interconnections can become mechanisms for loving one another and powerfully influencing the world.

Like ecological systems theory, in the person-in-environment perspective, discussion of the ways that all relationships are impacted by sin is absent. Incorporating the concept of brokenness and the need for restoration within every level of interaction potentially adds significant depth to the perspective. Specifically, it helps to conceptualize the way that individuals are impacted from the outside world by systemic sin and also how individual brokenness negatively impacts the outside world.

Systems of Development

Developmental systems theory emerged in the 1990s as a metatheory—an overarching approach that integrates a range of theories. Influenced by research in genetics, American psychologists Richard Martin Lerner and Donald Herbert Ford sought to develop a relational metatheory that moved beyond reductionistic views that tried to delineate either nature or nurture. Instead, they sought an approach that integrated variables from the biological and environmental realms, emphasizing the study of different levels of organization as a means of understanding life-span human development (Ford & Lerner, 1992; Lerner, 2006, 2012).

Lerner and Ford organized developmental systems theory around two core concepts—*epigenesis* and developmental dynamics. They describe epigenesis as the development caused by relationships between the individual and the complete environmental context (Balswick, King, & Reimer, 2016) and developmental dynamics as the overarching idea that development is constantly changing. This concept is referred to as *relative plasticity*, an idea which moves us past the mechanistic versus organismic debates to an understanding that change constantly occurs, but is also relative, or limited by the relationship between genes and environment. According to the approach, development at each stage builds upon the results of the development from earlier stages.

Developmental systems theory is a metatheory, but is best understood through its themes. Overall themes of the theory include: development as a product of multiple interacting sources, organisms inheriting resources from the environment in addition to genes, organisms shaping their own environment, individuals as unique combinations of the relationship between genetic endowment and environmental variables, humans as active agents in their own development, humans as created for community, and lack of a singular source of influence in an organism's development (Lerner & Schmid, 2013).

Developmental systems theory is unique in its refusal to focus on one variable related to development—genes, culture, society, history—but instead strives to emphasize the *relationship* between each of the variables and the whole person. This is referred to as *relationalism* as it emphasizes the interaction between the person and context throughout their lifespan (Balswick, King, & Reimer, 2016). According to the theory, it is neither nature nor nurture that lead to development, but the relationship between the two that is important. Understanding that often-complex relationship, proponents argue, is where our focus should center.

According to developmental systems theory, persons are active participants in their own development, not simply organisms acted upon by genetics and the environment. Balswick and colleagues write, "Developmental systems theory moves us beyond an additive model (heredity plus environment equals human behavior) to an interactive model in which the relationship between systems is the primary influence of behavior" (2016, p. 109). In developmental systems theory, there is an inherent optimism about the potential for change, identified by what are termed *adaptive developmental regulations* (Lerner, 2002). Adaptive developmental regulations are positive changes in both the person and their surrounding context.

Analyzing developmental systems theory in light of biblical themes is important as this approach has become highly influential. Developmental systems theory beautifully affirms the reciprocal relationship between persons and their contexts, seeking to understand relationships on every level and in every stage. The theory emphasizes the relationships between persons and their contexts, but also suggests that one's context does not necessarily predict their future behavior. In and of itself, one's context does not hold that power. It is the interaction of the person with that context that influences behavior. This is a genuinely hopeful viewpoint as it appropriately limits the influence of context, implying that persons can make right choices despite difficult contexts.

This point relates to human agency as well. Developmental systems theory rightly endorses the concept of limited agency, which mirrors the biblical idea that humans are not passive, but active participants in their own development. It also, however, affirms the important reality that persons are limited by contexts which include their genes, social lives, cultural realities, and historical time periods. As indicated by the concept of "relative plasticity," we have the power to change, but within our God-given biological, social, and cultural limits.

Developmental systems theory highlights a telos or goal that is ultimately related to evolutionary theory. That is, the ongoing adaptations between a person and their environment are seen as critical to survival. While we can affirm the theory's strong emphasis on embodiment and certainly the importance of this purpose, a Christian worldview points to a telos that exceeds that of mere survival, involving right connections with God, with others, and with the world. We long to see humans develop toward a particular purpose, meaning that the interactions between persons and their contexts facilitate their flourishing.

Development in the Family

Family development theory (also known as family life cycle theory) emerged through research published by Reuben Hill (1949) and Evelyn Duvall (1957). Family development theory was the first approach that sought to systematize the way that families, not just individuals, move through stages as they develop (Hill & Rodgers, 1964). The theory suggests that families typically progress through a series of stages that are also characterized by transitional events. The stages are triggered internally by the demands of the family—their biological, psychological, and social needs—and externally through social expectations and environmental constraints (Mattessich & Hill, 1987).

While the number of stages varies depending on the researcher, Duvall's (1957) eight stages have been widely used in social work. He identifies the following stages: married couples without children, the childbearing years, the preschool years, the school-age years, the adolescence years, the launching of children, middle-age, and aging. Gladding (2009) and Carter & McGoldrick (1988) suggest six stages: persons leaving home, the joining of families through partnership, families with young children, families with adolescents, launching of children, and later life.

The stages of families can be studied on three different levels: the psychology of the individuals in the family, the interactions between members of the family, and the influences of society and various institutions upon the family (Rodgers & White, 1993). The theory seeks to inform the ways families change over time, the nature of the family unit, and the ways families are impacted by their societal contexts. The theory implies that families develop in predictable ways and that families in one stage share similarities with other families in the same stage.

Because family development theory emphasizes change over time, families must then be viewed over time in order to be accurately understood. The theory also highlights the reciprocal nature of families wherein individuals in the family influence other members of the family (Mattessich & Hill, 1987). This implies that the maturity of the family is tied to the maturity of individual members. In other words, family units do not mature properly if individual members are immature and unable to manage the tasks and transitions of their developmental stages.

Family development theory is important in social work as it creates a framework for understanding, and often normalizing, the challenges faced by families. Families with young children, for example, experience physical and emotional demands that reduce the time available for individual or marital needs. Couples in old age often face the demands of declining functioning or increased caretaking responsibilities that require significant physical and psychological adaptation. Identifying individuals and families according to stages assists with normalizing their struggles and targeting appropriate interventions.

From the perspective of our biblical themes, family development theory captures well an emphasis on relationality. Highlighting relationships within families is especially important as families arguably represent the most influential God-ordained institution. Understanding the progression of families through stages is also helpful as this progression reflects the creational design for families. This does not imply that there is a singular path individuals or families must take; some married couples, for example, choose not to have children. Some adults never marry. Families suffer the loss of members to divorce or death. But all persons and families, regardless of their particular circumstances, are subject to changes over time. Therefore, a perspective that seeks to understand their unique progression through stages can be extremely useful.

The telos, or ultimate goal, of family development theory is the successful achievement of the tasks connected to each stage, not specifically the *maturation* of the family. Young families, for example, have to navigate the demands of child caretaking while also attending to their marital relationship. They have to agree on methods of discipline and a host of everyday decisions related to their children. In this sense, the theory provides a practical approach.

However, Christians in social work desire not only family mastery, but also family maturation. These goals are related, but not the same. Families actually mature over time when they grow in love and grace for one another. In some cases, families master the tasks of their particular stage by, for example, successfully launching young adult children, but are not simultaneously growing in love. This can produce new crises as the couple may remain committed, but the commitment is not undergirded by love. Over time, such scenarios can produce resentment. In other words, families develop optimally when they successfully achieve the tasks of their stages, but are simultaneously growing in love and grace. Progressing through the stages alone is not sufficient for the type of growth described in this text.

Individual human agency is not specifically addressed by the theory, as the focus is on the functioning of the family unit. Like other family theories, its view of individual agency is likely too weak. Family development theory also does not conceptualize the difficulties experienced by families as relating to sin, but as reflections of their particular stages or their difficulties in transitioning to a new stage. It describes common struggles of each phase, but these are attributed to the challenges of the stage rather than the sinful proclivities of the individuals within the family or the larger influences which are impacting the family.

Family Systems Theories: Take One and Take Two

Family systems theory actually refers to two separate, but related, approaches. One originated from the work of Murray Bowen and the other emerged later through general systems theory. The concept of *holism*— that the system must be understood as a whole and not the parts in isolation—is central to both manifestations of family systems theory. The whole is seen as greater than the sum of its parts. We will review both approaches, starting with Bowen's work, as both are influential in social work.

Murray Bowen, an American psychiatrist, developed family systems theory (Bowen, 1966, 1974, 1978). The theory holds that families function as emotional units, and therefore, changes in the emotional functioning of one family member are "compensated for" by changes in the emotional functioning of other family members. The family, not the individual, is the basic unit of emotional functioning. Families are then the most effective place for intervention.

Bowen's theory highlights further the connection between the functioning of the family unit and its members. The nature of the emotional connection in a family is so important that it contributes to high or low functioning among its individuals (Bowen, 1974). This point has significant implications because it ties the problems within an individual, at least in part, to problems in the family. Dysfunction in the family unit, for example, can very well be the primary contributor to the mental health problem manifested by an individual member. From this viewpoint, assistance should be directed at the family, the source of the problem, and not solely at the person displaying problematic symptoms.

The emotional interconnection of the family implies that everyone is impacted when even one individual member changes. This reality is helpful when a family is unwilling to get help, but an individual is willing. While the family is the preferred "client," the theory implies that individual growth benefits the family unit. Individual crises, on the other hand, can negatively impact the whole family as well.

Bowen (1974) identified mechanisms for identifying the nature of a family's emotional state. These include differentiation of the self, triangles, the family's emotional process, the family's projection process, multi-generational transmission processes, sibling positions, and emotional cutoffs. To visually illustrate these dynamics, especially intergenerational patterns, genograms were developed which continue to symbolize the core principles of family systems theory (McGoldrick Gerson, & Petry, 2008).

The second approach, also termed *family systems theory*, evolved from general systems theory—a scientific perspective indicating that a system is characterized by the interactions of its parts. A system is defined as a bounded set of interrelated elements that exhibits coherent behavior (Constantine, 1986). Therefore, knowing one part of a system allows us to know something about other parts.

Researchers saw application from systems theory to work with families (Broderick, 1993). Indeed, families function like systems. A family system is the sum total of all of the interrelationships within the family and the boundaries between the family and its environment. Family systems theory identifies the predictable patterns of interaction within a family that maintain their emotional equilibrium and guide the behavior of the members. This occurs through the use of unconscious rules which inform the roles and responsibilities of members. Importantly, family rules may be functional or dysfunctional in nature.

The concept of boundaries is critical to this version of family systems theory. Family boundaries may be open or closed. Open boundaries permit the influence of external elements upon the family. Closed boundaries isolate family members from the environment. Family systems also have subsystems such as sibling groups which are also defined by boundaries, rules, and expectations. Dynamics assessed in family systems theory include the family's functioning, communication, distribution of power, management of conflict, level of cohesion, and adaptation to change or crisis (Broderick, 1993).

Both forms of family systems theory uphold human relationality, highlighting the uniquely formative power of family relationships. Viewing families as systems illuminates the ways that family members knowingly and unknowingly influence one another. The theories rightly point beyond individuality to our corporate identities in families. The theories' high view of families affirms the sacred role God has given them in forming individuals, particularly children.

On the other hand, both approaches minimize individual agency, pointing to the family unit as shaping decision-making and behavior. While highlighting the importance of the family is the strength of these approaches, they simultaneously underestimate the power of individual agency and other social influences. There are exceptions to family roles and expectations when individuals intentionally step away from entrenched patterns. For example, this occurs when a person chooses abstinence despite growing up in an alcoholic family. Beyond the family, the theory fails to acknowledge other important social influences on an individual's choices, such as schools, churches, and neighborhoods.

Neither theory directly conceptualizes sin, although the direct and indirect effects of sin are well-illustrated in dysfunctional family dynamics. Examples of this include the authoritarian use of power by a parent toward a child or emotionally abusive communication between spouses. Additionally, the emphasis on sinful behaviors and patterns potentially extending across generations is an apt biblical theme. While cross-generational patterns can be pernicious, they never lie beyond healing. Indeed, authentic forgiveness, which involves confession and trusting God to parcel out justice, can break down the most entrenched cross-generational patterns.

In her important work, *Family Ministry: A Comprehensive Guide* (2012), Diana Garland casts an inspiring vision for the ways that Christian family systems, through the covenantal commitments to each other, can be powerful living demonstrations of God's love and faithfulness. She describes the ways in which families, like all relationships, evolve from contracts—where meeting one another's expectations is not the essential condition for the furthering of the relationship—to covenants—where the members choose the relationship whether or not expectations are met. Garland rightly suggests that covenantal commitments within a family create the stable structure by which the family can endure both expected and unexpected changes.

Many have found the descriptions of families offered by both of these perspectives to be insightful. Others have gained freedom from destructive psychological and behavioral patterns by better understanding their family system. They have identified patterns within their present behavior that are the tacit by-products of past family dynamics. Such insight is often tantamount to moving people toward lives marked by healthy, life-giving choices and patterns.

Social Risks and Protective Factors

We conclude this chapter with a discussion of risk and proctective factors within the social realm. Social risks have been described as "the impoverishing of the child's world so that the child lacks the basic social and psychological necessities of life" (Garbarino & Abramowitz, 1992, p. 35). While this definition specifies children, persons of all ages are affected when key components of their social lives—families, schools, churches, communities—fall short of what they need to develop and flourish. That said, there are many protective factors in the social realm that bolster growth and minimize developmental risk. Some overarching principles related to social risk and protection will be identified. We will refer back to biblical themes related to the nature of humanity as healthy social institutions carefully account for these characteristics—relationality, sinfulness, and agency.

First, in the area of relationality, we certainly need relationships, but they need to be of a particular nature. Unsurprisingly, persons thrive within relationships characterized by unconditional love. There is likely no form of greater developmental protection than unconditional loving relationships. Here lies, however, the place where developmental needs are also most often at risk. A remarkable number of the individuals with whom we work have experienced patterns of conditional love. Conditional love places acceptance of the recipient within parameters. This has the effect of diverting the recipient's focus from healthy developmental tasks to perpetual, sometimes lifelong, attempts to gain acceptance and approval. Unconditional love works entirely differently by removing the possibility of rejection and allowing true maturation to occur. Qualifications are eliminated, always superseded by love.

Indeed, unconditionally loving relationships are critical because they mirror the type of love God has for us. Because they are initiated and sustained by humans, such relationships will never match the perfect love of God. We easily veer into unloving and judgmental postures toward one another. But offerings of unconditional love touch the relational needs which lie at our core. Authentic and loving relationships affirm something deep within our souls because they confirm what is true—that we are deeply and unequivocally loved by our creator.

The benefits of unconditionally loving relationships are innumerable. When persons are freed from the fear and anxiety of rejection, they are able to more fully embrace themselves and others. A preoccupation with pleasing others in order to be loved is eliminated. Unconditionally loving families provide a safe place for children to manage the wide range of developmental tasks that come their way. It is important to add that unconditionally loving families are not necessarily free of crisis. Problems including poverty, death, or conflict can and do occur. However, the constancy of unconditional love in a family provides an inestimable resource for coping with the typical and atypical tasks that arise.

The nature of the relationships in other areas of one's social life—their school, job, neighborhood, community—are also critical to well-being. Like families, ideal social environments have, within natural limits, the characteristics of authentic love. Schools, neighborhoods, churches, and communities play surprisingly significant roles in developmental protection. Caring and supportive peers, teachers, coworkers, neighbors, and community members create a wall of protection around vulnerable persons. Religious institutions serve as enormous protective factors when they exhibit non-judgmental, compassionate care to those within their membership and communities.

Persons are enormously protected developmentally when the social worlds they regularly inhabit are emotionally and physically safe and supportive. Those who routinely fear their physical or emotional safety will unfortunately be thwarted in the tasks of normal development. At its core, fear is a healthy survival instinct, but persistent or chronic fear overwhelms us biologically and psychologically, circumventing growth. Sadly, the nature of social environments is often one of risk. For example, some neighborhoods are highly transient, facilitating few interpersonal connections. For many, schools are places of fear, where individuals must continually defend and protect themselves. Some workplaces breed more competition and antagonism than support and collaboration.

Schools, colleges, and universities can represent places of either great protection or great risk. Protective schools demonstrate academic challenge and individualized support for all persons within their care, especially those struggling emotionally and academically. But schools increase developmental risk for their students when they fail to provide proper academic support, are physically or emotionally unsafe, or reflect an impersonal, uncaring atmosphere.

The importance of social institutions to human development cannot be overstated. As part of the creational design, they are threads of the social fabric intended to support persons within their spheres. When social structures are strong and stable, persons benefit in numerous ways. For example, individuals and families benefit emotionally as they internalize the affirmation that comes from belonging to a genuinely supportive and caring group. They benefit when others become aware of their psychological or physical needs and are able to meet them.

That said, many persons lack adequate or caring social supports and are physically, emotionally, and spiritually diminished as their relational needs go unmet. Sometimes persons lack trust in social institutions and intentionally distance themselves from them. Other times, persons long for social support, but lack viable options. As Christians in social work, one of our roles is to strengthen social institutions, such as families, schools, non-profit organizations, and churches, and to better connect individuals to them. These connections are important as stable and supportive social structures answer unspoken, yet universal, questions about one's worth and value. In doing so, they affirm their God-given roles by strengthening the social fabric around individuals, particularly those who desperately need love and affirmation.

Second, the ways that social institutions interact with human agency can either increase developmental protection or risk. For example, the growth of children is protected when they are regularly allowed to make independent, age-appropriate decisions. Couples flourish when their individual and corporate identities are each given space and nurture. Employees grow when they are given appropriate levels of autonomy and support. Communities flourish when the opinions of members are carefully considered in decisions that relate to them. Prioritization of individual and group agency is vitally important across the range of social institutions. In general, restricting agency places people at risk as it potentially stifles their creativity, self-confidence, and sense of mastery. Open and safe communication is important to sustaining agency because it allows opportunities for the discussion and negotiation of varying viewpoints.

Third, in a different but equally important way, social institutions must appropriately respond to sinfulness and wrongdoing. The ways that social institutions respond to wrongdoing contributes to either developmental risk or protection. As a general principle, sin and wrongdoing must be addressed within each context, but needs to be paired with redemption and restoration. In families, this certainly entails healthy limitations and the age-appropriate discipline of children. More broadly, it entails fostering a confessional atmosphere where members of the family are accountable for hurtful behaviors, whether intentional or unintentional. But confession must be followed by grace and forgiveness where persons and relationships are restored.

The ways that families respond to wrongdoing is developmentally important. When, for example, the behaviors of children are held against them or continually brought to their attention, children can internalize shame, the sense that they are inherently flawed persons. True forgiveness is critical because it separates wrongful behavior and unhealthy shame. Shame represents a particular developmental risk and it contributes to several problematic characteristics, including self-loathing and poor self-confidence. Shame blurs self-perception as individuals see themselves as persistently flawed.

Social institutions such as schools, churches, and communities generally have formal policies for addressing wrongdoing. This is necessary as wrongful behaviors can and do occur. But, like families, constituents benefit most when such policies combine appropriate boundaries with grace and forgiveness. Opportunities for redemption and restoration can be built into school, work, and program policies. Granted, some people will not make better choices even given the opportunity, but policies oriented toward forgiveness, reconciliation, and redemption still bend in the right direction.

How are these risk and protective factors relevant for Christians in social work? Practically speaking, we may not have the ability to directly reduce risk or increase developmental protection in a client's life. Certain areas of intervention, although important and greatly needed, may fall outside of the scope of our practice or our access. Other times we have opportunities to encourage change but persons, for their own reasons, either choose to move in life-giving directions, or they are unable to move in those same directions.

Risk and protective factors, however, provide Christians in social work with insight into the ways things "ought to be." Risk factors often mirror sin within social institutions. For example, violence, neglect, and authoritarianism in families are significant developmental risk factors. Protective factors, on the other hand, often reflect God's intentions. Firm but caring schools, neighborhoods that cherish children, and churches where every participant is seen as valuable serve as enormous means of developmental protection.

Though our faith provides a vision of ideal contexts for development, we ought not be surprised by the limitations of social institutions. At times, they hurt and disappoint, falling far short of their potential. We should not lose hope in the developmental potential of families, schools, churches, and communities, however. They remain the building blocks of human development despite their imperfections. Like all parts of the world, their broken states necessitate continual growth, healing, and restoration. But they remain critical mechanisms for how God reaches, develops, and forms his beloved image-bearers.

Chapter Summary

As Christians in social work, theological truths inform a great deal of what we know about social development. It is not surprising that our clients need loving families, schools, neighborhoods, and communities as we have been created for loving relationships. The formative role of social institutions is not surprising as they reflect God's creational design. Though broken, these structures are critical components in helping persons to connect meaningfully with others and with God. Therefore, it is also not surprising that much of social work practice and intervention rightly revolves around the restoration of these institutions from micro-level work with families to macro-level work with organizations and policies.

Discussion Questions

1. You are the principal of a new school for children with behavioral issues who have been suspended from other schools. What approach will you take in setting policies in your setting?

2. What dynamics contribute to shame? Think about this in relation to families, work places, and churches. Recall a time when you felt shame and ponder the dynamics of the scenario.

3. What are the advantages and disadvantages of family development theory which breaks down family progression into stages?

4. Do you agree or disagree with connecting principles of risk and protection with the dynamics of sin and God's intentions? Why or why not?

5. Write a one-sentence "slogan" that summarizes the ideal social environment for human development.

References

Ashford, J. B., LeCroy, C. W., & Lortie, K. L (2006). *Human behavior in the social environment: A multidimensional perspective*. Belmont, CA: Wadsworth Publishing.

Balswick, J. O., King, P. E., & Reimer, K. S. (2016). *The reciprocating self: Human development in theological perspective*. Downers Grove, IL: Intervarsity Press.

Bowen, M. (1966). The use of family theory in clinical practice. *Comprehensive Psychiatry, 7*, 345-374.

Bowen, M. (1974). Toward the differentiation of self in one's family of origin. In F.O. Andres & J.P. Lorio (Eds.). *Georgetown Family Symposia, Vol. 1,* Washington, DC: Georgetown University Medical Center, Department of Psychiatry, Family Section.

Bowen, M. (1978). *Family therapy in clinical practice,* Northvale, NJ: Jason Aronson, Inc.

Broderick, C.B. (1993). *Understanding family process.* Thousand Oaks, CA: Sage Publications.

Bronfenbrenner, U. (1977). Toward an experimental ecology of human development. *American Psychologist, 32* (7), 513-531.

Carter, B., & McGoldrick, M. (1988). *The changing family life cycle: A framework for family therapy* (2nd ed.). New York: Gardner Press.

Constantine, L. L. (1986). *Family paradigms: The practice of theory in family therapy.* New York: Guilford Press.

Duvall, E. R. (1957). *Family development.* Philadelphia: J.B. Lippincott.

Ford, D.L., & Lerner, R.M. (1992). *Developmental systems theory: An integrative approach.* Newbury Park, CA: Sage Publications.

Garland, D. R. (2012). *Family Ministry: A Comprehensive Guide* (2nd ed.). Downers Grove, IL: InterVarsity Press.

Gladding, S. T. (2009). *Counseling: A comprehensive profession* (6th ed.). New York, NY: Pearson Education.

Garbarino, J., & Abramowitz, R. H. (1992). Sociocultural risk and opportunity. In J. Garbarino, *Children and families in the social environment,* (2nd ed.), (pp. 35-70). New York: Aldine de Gruyter.

Hill, R. (1949). *Families under stress.* New York: Harper & Row.

Hill, R., & Rodgers, R. H. (1964). The Developmental Approach. In H. T. Christensen (Ed.), *Handbook of Marriage and the Family.* Skokie, IL: Rand McNally & Company

Karls, J. M., & Wandrei, K.E. (1994). *Person-in-environment system: The PIE classification system for social functioning problems.* Washington, DC: National Association of Social Workers

Kondrat, M.E. (2015). "Person-in-Environment." *Social Work - Oxford Bibliographies*, Oxford University Press, Retrieved from www.oxfordbibliographies. com/view/document/obo-9780195389678/obo-9780195389678-0092.xml.n.

Lerner, R. M. (2002).*Concepts and theories of human development* (3rd ed.). Mahwah, NJ: Erlbaum.

Lerner, R.M. (2006). Developmental science, developmental systems, and contemporary theories of human development. In R. M. Lerner & W. Damon (Eds.), *Handbook of child psychology: Theoretical models of human development* (pp. 1-17). Hoboken, NJ: John Wiley & Sons.

Lerner, R.M. (2012). Essay review: Developmental science: Past, present, and future. *International Journal of Developmental Science, 6,* 29-36.

Lerner, R. M., & Schmid, C. K. (2013). Relational developmental systems: Theories and the ecological validity of experimental designs. *Human Development, 56*, 372-380.

Mattessich, P., & Hill, R. (1987). Life Cycle and Family Development. In M. B. Sussman & S. K. Steinmetz (Eds.), *Handbook of Marriage and Family* (pp. 437-469). New York, NY: Plenum Press.

McGoldrick, M., Gerson, R., & Petry, S. S. (2008). *Genograms: Assessment and intervention* (3rd ed.). New York, NY: W.W. Norton.

Rodgers, R. H., & White, J. M. (1993). Family development theory. In P.G. Boss, W.J. Doherty, R. LaRossa, W.R. Schumm, & S.K. Steinmetz (Eds.). *Sourcebook of family theories and methods: A contextual approach* (pp. 225-254). New York, NY: Plenum Press.

Vygotsky, L.S. (1962). *Thought and language.* Cambridge, MA: MIT Press.

Vygotsky, L.S. (1978). *Mind in society: The development of higher psychological processes.* Cambridge, MA: Harvard University Press.

Vygotsky, L.S. (1987). Thinking and speech. In R.W. Rieber & A.S. Carton (Eds.), *The collected works of L.S. Vygotsky, Volume 1: Problems of general psychology (pp. 39–285).* New York: Plenum Press. (Original work published 1934).

Part Two

Now that we have a big picture of human development, we will consider ways to apply a biblical view of human development to the stages of life. Starting with infancy and concluding with old age, we focus on a few noteworthy aspects of each stage. In doing so, we will refer back to the biological, psychological, and sociological themes in earlier chapters. As in Part 1, our goal is to assist our clients in developing closer relationships with God, themselves, and the created world. Part II takes us farther down that road by asking, "But how do we best do that?" And also, "What types of environments help individuals in this stage to develop in the right direction?"

Chapter Seven

Infancy:
Early Growth toward
God and Others
(ages 0–2)

*Most potential mental health problems will not become mental
health problems if we respond to them early.*

Center on the Developing Child (2013)

W
e begin our study of the life span by exploring infancy, a
stage of unique and foundational human growth and development. The case of an infant will be described first,
followed by a discussion of key characteristics of infancy,
and concluded by a review of the case from the perspective of the key
characteristics and the biblical themes outlined in an earlier chapter.

As we consider infancy (ages 0-2), it is important to recognize that persons at every stage are developing toward something. As Christians in social
work, our goal is for infants to develop in the direction of healthy connections with God, themselves, and other people. In this chapter, we will ponder how development of this nature may be fostered within infants. This
may sound like a grandiose goal when we consider the limited speech and
cognition of infants, particularly newborns. However, as discussed in Part
1, numerous theories indicate that one's relational foundation is laid during
this stage. This makes infant development vitally important.

Beyond the important tasks of their stage, infants themselves are full
image-bearers who beautifully reflect and respond to their Maker. This
point is well-illustrated by Jesus' response in Matthew 21:15-16 (NIV)
where he quotes from Psalm 8:

> But when the chief priests and the teachers of the law saw
> the wonderful things he did and the children shouting in the
> temple courts, "Hosanna to the Son of David," they were in-
> dignant. "Do you hear what these children are saying?" they
> asked. "Yes," Jesus answered, "Have you never read, 'From the
> mouths of children and infants you have ordained praise?'"

Remarkably, infants are identified as worshippers. As we will see, we can learn a great deal about our formation as image-bearers by observing the nature of infants.

We begin by examining the life of one infant, Anastasia, and her family.

The Case of Anastasia

Anastasia is a six-month old infant who is being raised in a "ring" suburb of Chicago—one that falls just outside the perimeter of the inner city. She was born to a 20-year old mother, Luisa, who is in an on-again, off-again romantic relationship with the father of Anastasia, a 23-year old man named Carlos. Luisa also has a two-year old daughter, Carmela, from a different father—Juan—with whom she has no current relationship. Juan pays child support when he is employed, but he is frequently unemployed. He has no current relationship with Carmela and has not seen her in over a year.

Luisa essentially functions as a single parent as neither Juan nor Carlos take an active role in parenting their daughters. When Luisa and Carlos are together, Carlos attempts to help with Anastasia's care, but this takes the form of activities such as shopping for groceries or doing laundry. He has minimal emotional attachment to Anastasia and rarely interacts with her during the times he is present in the home. It is clear that Anastasia does not actually recognize her father as she cries when he picks her up and looks in the direction of her mother.

Anastasia was born four weeks early and weighed 4 pounds at birth. She was healthy overall, but remained in the hospital for two weeks in order to gain weight. Luisa did not consume alcohol or drugs during the pregnancy, but smoked cigarettes daily. Luisa was relatively healthy during the pregnancy, but she has an extensive mental health history that dates back to her childhood.

Currently, Anastasia is up to date on all of her vaccinations, but is slightly behind in some developmental markers. She is not sitting up unassisted or crawling. She is, however, "cooing" and responding verbally when prompted. Anastasia is small for her age, at the fifth percentile for the national average of height and weight, although she was slightly premature at birth. She has been formula-fed since birth as Luisa chose not to breastfeed. Anastasia is currently being introduced to cereal. Her sleeping patterns are erratic and unusual for her age. She rarely sleeps for more than two hours at night before waking.

Luisa was born in the same suburb where she currently resides. The community is primarily populated by first and second generation Hispanic immigrants. Luisa's parents immigrated from Mexico a year before she was born. They recently became naturalized United States citizens. Luisa was born in the U.S. and is fluent in Spanish and English. Spanish was spoken in her family of origin and is the primary language of her current home. Luisa had planned to attend a community college to study nursing, but became pregnant with Carmela at age 17 and dropped out of high school in the second semester of her junior year.

Luisa and her daughters qualify for public assistance as their income is considerably below the federal poverty line. Their income comes from two sources—child support (although this is inconsistent) and Temporary Assistance for Needy Families (TANF) government assistance. They additionally receive Supplemental Nutrition Assistance Program (SNAP) benefits which assist with food, Women, Infants, and Children (WIC) which helps to pay for formula and diapers, and basic medical insurance through Medicaid. Luisa has no current employment. To receive TANF cash assistance, she is required to demonstrate attempts to find work, but the jobs she qualifies for pay minimum wage. If employed, daycare expenses for two children would represent a large percentage of her income.

Luisa and her daughters live in a one-bedroom apartment on the third floor of an aging building. The neighborhood is comprised of sturdy, but aging, apartment buildings and modest single-family homes. She has lived in the apartment for the past two years and has remained current with her rent and utility payments, but her housing costs consume most of her monthly income, leaving little money for additional expenses. She has no debt, but also has no money in savings.

The neighborhood around the apartment building has a significant amount of crime. Luisa rarely ventures out at night, fearing for her and the children's safety. Two gangs reside in her neighborhood and there are frequent uprisings, occasionally involving the use of guns. Luisa and her children have thankfully not been directly affected by gang violence, but this is a constant fear. Not owning a car, Luisa uses public transportation for appointments, grocery shopping, and outings, but she remains at home much of the time because of the challenge of transporting two young children. There are convenience stores within walking distance, but no public parks or playgrounds where she can take her young children.

Luisa is the second of four children born to her parents. The siblings are all two years apart in age. Her parents divorced when she was eight years old and she and her siblings spent weekdays with her mother and alternate weekends with her father after the divorce. Both of her parents remarried shortly after their divorce. Luisa has a good overall relationship with her mother who lives in the same suburb. Luisa's mother works full-time as a restaurant cook and is unable to help much with childcare, but she does try to come over on Saturdays to see her granddaughters. Luisa is not close to her stepfather, although he is not unkind, just distant. Luisa's father also resides nearby and works long hours as a car mechanic. Luisa has historically had a distant relationship with her father. She has minimal emotional attachment to her father as she has experienced him as harsh, critical, and unsupportive throughout her life. She currently sees her father very infrequently. Her stepmother is a nice person, but she rarely sees her either due to the disconnection with her father.

Luisa was an average student throughout school. She attended a large public school where she was a quiet, reserved student with few close friends. She complied with most academic expectations, but was minimally motivated at school. Her teachers viewed her as an immature and unassertive student.

This perception mirrors Luisa's general perception of herself as insignificant and unimportant. She has struggled with depression since she was a young girl, even before her parent's divorce, although it has never been professionally diagnosed or treated. As a result of her depression, or perhaps more accurately as its root cause, she views herself very negatively. She describes herself as physically unattractive and not particularly smart or talented.

Luisa's negative self-perception led to several relationships with young men who took advantage of her emotional vulnerability. She became sexually active at age 11 and had a series of short-term, sexual relationships with males. In her sophomore year of high school, Juan, a popular but immature male, pursued her and the two began dating. Luisa felt proud that Juan was dating her. Their relationship was unfortunately a chaotic one with repeated conflicts and breakups due to Juan's possessiveness and jealousy. Despite the instability of the relationship, Luisa was excited to learn that she was pregnant. Juan distanced from her which was initially hurtful, but Luisa focused instead on the pregnancy and her hopes of having a baby to love and be loved by unconditionally.

Luisa's first pregnancy was uneventful and Carmela was born full-term. Luisa's style of parenting is an emotionally-stunted, mechanical one. She cares for the physical needs of her children relatively well—feeding and bathing them regularly—but is highly limited when it comes to emotionally connecting with her children. She rarely plays with them and is almost exclusively focused on their physical needs. She disciplines Carmela harshly with yelling and swats to her bottom.

Her parenting behavior may largely be explained by the current state of her mental health. Since Anastasia was born, Luisa has struggled with postpartum depression, including symptoms of severe fatigue, irritability, feelings of hopelessness, poor sleep, and intermittent thoughts of suicide. This is not a new development in light of her long-term depression but her symptoms have been markedly worse in the last six months since Anastasia's birth. She has not shared the extent of her depression with anyone as she is embarrassed by her inability to cope. Luisa sees her current struggle as confirmation of her overall ineptitude as a person. Thankfully, Luisa does not think about harming her children, but she often wishes they were never born.

Luisa lost her high school friends when she dropped out of school and has very little current social contact or support. Beside her mother and Carlos when he is present, she has no other social support. She stays away from her neighbors as she does not trust them. She does not attend church, although she was raised Catholic and attended church on major holidays while growing up. Luisa believes in God and sometimes asks him to give her a better life, but that is the extent of her faith involvement.

At this time, Luisa's main hope lies with Carlos. She believes that if they married, her life would improve significantly. Unfortunately though, he resembles her father in the sense that he is emotionally cold and minimally communicates with her. Carlos also secretly maintains relationships with other women. He has struck Luisa twice during arguments, but apologized and each time indicated it would not happen again. Luisa does everything she can to appease him and keep the relationship going because she sees it as her only hope for a better life.

We will return to a discussion of Anastasia and her family later in the chapter, but first we need to explore **two key characteristics of infancy**.

Infants are Hardwired to Survive

Ashford, LeCroy, and Lortie (2006) write, "Before modern times, the major developmental task of infancy was simply to survive it" (p. 214). Sadly, this is not just an historical phenomenon; it is a contemporary reality as infant mortality rates remain high in many parts of the world. Importantly, this quote draws our attention to a critical characteristic of infancy. That is, regardless of their context, infants are hardwired to survive, to live. Indeed, a remarkable array of life-affirming biological, psychological, and social mechanisms are embedded in infants.

But how can infants be hardwired to survive when they are so ill-equipped to meet their own needs? They lack the ability to run from danger or even to identify situations that are life-threatening. Beyond this, they cannot meet their basic physical needs for food, water, and shelter.

They are entirely dependent on others. Remarkably, infants are hardwired to survive through the mechanism of attachment. That is, they are physically and emotionally drawn toward the persons upon whom their survival depends. Indeed, it is incredible to note how relational attachment—an infant's core means of survival—is supported by a host of emerging biological, psychological, and social processes.

For example, there are many biological processes that support attachment. There is no life stage with more biological growth than infancy. By the end of the first year of life, infants typically triple their birth weight, crawl or walk, and speak their first word. They gain gross and fine motor strength and control. The cerebral cortex, the center of language and emotional regulation, increases in sophistication through extensive nerve myelination, laying the foundation for the transition from involuntary to voluntary responses (Gross, 2019).

Eyesight changes rapidly. A newborn's vision is limited to objects that are 8-10 inches away. Cells are not separated by function and type as myelination is incomplete, meaning newborns cannot discriminate between objects. But within just three months, infants can visually follow moving objects and reach for objects within their sight line. By five months, depth perception permits coordinated movement toward objects. Vision improves from 20/400 at birth to approximately 20/25 by six months of age (Slater, Field, & Hernandez-Reif, 2007).

Each of these biological processes supports and nurtures attachment, the infant's hardwiring for survival. For example, developing infants can see, recognize, and move toward their parents. Increased motor development allows them to crawl toward and physically embrace their caregivers. Early language creates the ability to communicate recognition and interpersonal connection—interestingly, the first words of English-speaking babies are often "Da-da" or "Ma-ma." These behaviors work to strengthen the parent-child relationship.

Psychological processes also facilitate attachment for survival. Relating to others requires the ability to recognize one's self as distinct and separate from those with whom you are interacting. One study indicated that infants produced a more robust sucking response when touched on the cheek by another person as opposed to touching their own cheeks, implying knowledge of the difference between their own bodies and external stimuli (Rochat & Hespos, 1997). Researchers have also pinpointed self-consciousness or embarrassment—indicators of the ability to imagine the perception of others—during the second year of life (Rochat, 2003). In other words, infants are developing the psychological tools for attaching to caregivers now and forming more complex relationships in the future.

Though they are dependent on caregivers, infants are simultaneously developing as unique persons. Individuation is triggered as their temperaments emerge. Their likes and dislikes become increasingly evident as they gravitate toward certain foods, toys, and persons. Developing individualized characteristics increases the child's awareness of how they are separate from those around them. Indeed, individuation and self-awareness are core psychological components of relationships with others (Rochat, 2001, 2003).

Social processes also facilitate attachment. The hardwiring for survival through attachment can also be seen in the way that infants respond socially. By two months, infants demonstrate socially-elicited smiling. By smiling at a parent, for example, positive feelings are elicited within the parent which stimulate further interaction. By three months, infants learn to cry in ways that garner the attention of others. Between two and six months of age, they expect certain responses during social exchanges and display negative affect when, for example, someone is playing with them and abruptly stops (Rochat, Querido, & Striano, 1999). Such responses demonstrate hardwiring for survival as they solidify and deepen relationships with those on whom the infant depends.

Ultimately, biological, psychological, and social growth contribute to the formation of agency—the child's ability to act on their world. Agency forms the basis for future relationships and represents an extension of the infant's survival hardwiring. While initial attachment is necessary for one's basic needs, over time, children typically shift toward relationships increasingly driven by choice (Margoni & Surian, 2018). As a child matures and is more able to meet their own needs, relationships become motivated by goals beyond mere survival. Although independence will not come fully until years into the future, agency represents a critical part of the child's future.

In sum, early in life, children attach to their caregivers to survive. Over time, they grow in the agency which will be needed for their future thriving. The biological, psychological, and social processes embedded within infants contribute the ingredients necessary for rich relationships, both in the present and future. Indeed, from birth, infants display clear characteristics of the biblical themes of relationality and agency. The stage is being set for their flourishing in the world.

Infants are Vulnerable

The shadow side of dependency is vulnerability. Unfortunately, persons with high levels of dependency are also at high risk for harm. Granted, dependency is not entirely negative as it often facilitates qualities such as humility, but it can place someone at the mercy of persons with impure motives or harmful behaviors. It is important to appreciate the vulnerability of infants if, as social workers, our role is to promote their flourishing. To illustrate vulnerability, we will discuss two different examples of risk— the lack of necessary developmental inputs and child abuse and neglect.

Vulnerable to Missing Inputs

The brain operates on a pre- and post-developmental trajectory, meaning that while core mechanisms are in place at birth, they mature in response to specific environmental inputs. Brain formation involves the interaction between genetic programming, cell functioning, and inputs from the environment. Therefore, early experiences have the potential to actually shape the brain.

The quality of early emotional interactions directly influences core psychological and social development. Neural pathways develop in response to relational inputs, a process described as "experience-dependent" development (Twardosz, 2012). Without the experiences, particular desirable developmental outcomes may not occur. Maladaptive brain development may also result from poor-quality environmental inputs, negatively impacting the child's future psychological or social functioning. Perry (1999) writes:

> Despite the genetic potential for bonding and attachment, it is the nature, quantity, pattern and intensity of early life experiences that express genetic potential. Without predictable, responsive, nurturing and sensory-enriched caregiving, the infant's potential for normal bonding and attachments will be unrealized. The brain systems responsible for healthy emotional relationships will not develop in an optimal way without the right kinds of experiences at the *right times* in life (pg. 3).

This means that while infants are hardwired to survive, they are entirely dependent on others to supply the inputs they need to mature and thrive. The importance of high-quality inputs cannot be overstated. Such inputs impact neurological formations that underlie nearly every human behavior imaginable. Environmental inputs take many forms, but to illustrate their importance, we will briefly focus on one example, the child's home environment.

A large body of research highlights the connection of a high-quality home environment and positive child outcomes. For example, the degree to which a home environment is stimulating is linked to higher child cognitive performance (Bradley et al., 1994). Specific parental behaviors, such as speaking frequently to the infant, asking questions while reading, and spending time gazing at the infant, are all correlated with executive functioning and cognitive development (Obradovi, Yousafzai, Finch, Rasheed, 2016). Emotionally warm parent–child interactions during daily routines are positively linked to child communication skills (Camp, Cunningham, & Berman, 2010). High-quality home environments additionally predict the level of child fine and gross motor performance (Saccani, Valentini, Pereira, Muller, and Gabbard, 2013).

A high-quality home environment also relates positively to academic performance. For example, enriching experiences, such as regularly reading to young children, are linked to increased competence in math (Bradley and Corwyn, 2016; Melhuish et al., 2008). Reading to infants and toddlers also related to improved attitudes towards reading and language ability (Hartas, 2012; LeFevre, Polyzoi, Skwarchuk, Fast, & Sowinski, 2010; Westerlund & Lagerberg, 2008).

Notably, the importance of a high-quality home environment has been demonstrated across cultures. In a study from Italy, the home environment demonstrated considerably more influence on infant neurological development than socioeconomic status (Ronfani et al., 2015). A study in Portugal reported a strong association between the quality of the home environment and infant motor and cognitive development (Pereira, Valentini, & Saccani, 2016). An Australian study reported that a stimulating home learning environment correlated with language development and school readiness (Yu & Daraganova, 2014). In a large Taiwanese study exploring numerous physical, psychological, and social factors, home environment explained nearly two-thirds of the variance in infant developmental outcomes (Hwang, et al., 2014).

In home environments that lack stimulation, such as those where a parent is depressed, infants display more negative outcomes. Maternal depression poses risks for children's cognitive, language, and socioemotional development (Downey & Coyne, 1990; Goodman & Gotlib, 2002). Maternal depression contributes to poor child outcomes through either intrusive or withdrawn parenting. Such responses disrupt the attachment process as infants typically respond to such parental behaviors by reducing their own engagement (Dix, Cheng, & Day, 2009; Dix, Stewart, Gershoff, & Day, 2007).

Importantly, a high-quality home environment has the ability to offset other risk factors, such as a low socioeconomic status. While socioeconomic status has been shown to account for approximately 20% of the variance in childhood IQ (Brooks-Gunn & Duncan, 1997), explanations related to the qualitative nature of the home environment often explain the disparity. That is to say, socioeconomically disadvantaged children are more likely to experience homes with less linguistic, social, and cognitive stimulation than children from higher socioeconomic backgrounds (Bradley & Corwyn, 2016; Hart & Risley, 1995; Rowe & Goldin-Meadow, 2009).

It is important to note that while children from economically disadvantaged households demonstrate poorer outcomes across several domains, this does not have to be the case. A high-quality home environment can serve to offset many of the negative effects of poverty. One study, for example, demonstrated that the quality of the home environment mediated the effect of poverty on the cognitive abilities of toddlers (Benson, 2014). Indeed, while income impacts parents' ability to afford expensive enrichment activities, many aspects of a high-quality home environment are not directly related to economic status (Tandon et al., 2012).

Indeed, infants are vulnerable to the effects of poor-quality home environments. They have no ability to control their circumstances and many aspects of their healthy development are entirely dependent on the provision of stimulation and love. For this reason, the nature of the inputs in an infant's life must be carefully evaluated.

Vulnerable to Abuse and Neglect

Unfortunately, the high dependency level of infants also are makes them vulnerable to abuse and neglect. Abusive and neglectful behaviors fail to provide basic human needs for safety and protection. An understanding of the attachment process highlights the difficulties connected with abuse and neglect. Young children are hardwired to survive physically and psychologically. But in abusive situations, such hardwiring means that infants will not attach to the unsafe person. Similarly, neglectful behavior communicates threat and marks the caregiver as an unsafe attachment object. Psychologically distancing from the unsafe person is a critical self-protective response (Perry, 1999, 2002).

Abuse and neglect toward infants not only exploits their dependency, it also is extraordinarily poorly timed. The infant brain grows at an astonishing speed. Infancy is a highly neurologically sensitive period. But the high sensitivity of the infant brain also means that damaging experiences are highly potent. In this sense, a neurological window of opportunity is simultaneously a window of vulnerability to harm. Perry (2002) writes, "While experience may alter the behavior of an adult, experience literally provides the organizing framework for an infant and child" (p. 88). Indeed, the earlier and more severe abuse and neglect are, the greater the impact on the developing child.

These realities mean the abuse and neglect of infants can lead to a number of negative outcomes. Importantly, many of the damaging outcomes come through the pathway of trauma—extreme and sustained stress—which, in essence, hijacks the survival hardwiring. In the presence of sustained trauma, the brain's core mechanism for survival, its fight-or-flight response, is continually triggered. This differs from healthy development where threats and the ensuing stress response are occasionally triggered. In some cases, the stress response functions adaptively. When over activation of the stress response occurs during the sensitive infant period, the brain is formed maladaptively. The hippocampus, amygdala, prefrontal cortex, and endocrine system are implicated in the complex physiological response to trauma (Shonkoff and Garner, 2012).

In a general sense, the brains of children who have been abused and neglected have been formed to view the world as threatening. Unsurprisingly, with brains that are hypersensitive, they demonstrate high levels of emotion, including aggression, in response to everyday stressors. Their perceptions of stress have been skewed by early trauma, a factor with wide-ranging implications. The negative impact of trauma on brain formation can contribute to a wide range of potential outcomes. These include numerous long-term physical (Lee, Chioun, Coe, & Ryff, 2017), behavioral, and psychological problems (Freeman, 2014). For example, adults with histories of early trauma may demonstrate high anxiety (Sperry & Widom, 2013), poor emotional regulation (John, Cisler, & Sigel, 2017), criminal behavior (Herrenkohl, Jung, Lee, Klika, & Skinner, 2015), substance abuse (Banducci, Hoffman, Lejuez, & Koenen, 2014), depression (Jung, Hyunzee, Herrenkohl, Lee, Klika, & Skinner, 2015), self-injurious behaviors (Auerbach et al., 2014) and a higher risk for suicide (Harford, Yi, & Grant, 2014).

This daunting list of outcomes clearly illustrates the vulnerable nature of the infant. Vulnerability will extend into later stages of development, but it will never again be as profound as during the infancy stage, when dependency is highest and neural pathways are primed for growth. These realities have implications for social work practitioners.

Understanding the fragile nature of this stage is important for Christians in social work who long for infants to develop in the right direction. Those working in the field of child welfare particularly encounter situations where the vulnerability of infants is exploited. The nature of infancy and our view of children as sacred image-bearers requires the highest view of their protection and safety. It also requires the strongest reproach of those who intentionally harm them.

An understanding of the nature of the infant stage also highlights its developmental opportunity. Intervening with children and families at this stage has potentially lasting impact. Educating, nurturing, and supporting families during this time period can profoundly influence the future. Indeed, it is vital to influencing the earliest human development in the right direction.

Now that we have explored some big ideas regarding infant development, we will return to the case of Anastasia and her family.

Anastasia Revisited

At six months of age, Anastasia is in an exciting stage of life. Her developing brain is fully primed for growth and her abilities are quickly expanding. She is a compact bundle of opportunity. Though only six months old, Anastasia is a relational being whose current relationships are laying a foundation for her future connections to God, others, and the world as a whole.

Biologically, Anastasia's rapid neurological growth is resulting in improved fine and gross motor control. She can eagerly extend her arms towards others. Her eyesight, memory, and language are expanding. She can see, remember, and verbally respond to familiar persons in her world. Appropriately, Anastasia displays self-protection when she exhibits anxiety toward persons and objects that are frightening to her. Anastasia is a small, but growing agent, displaying affinity for the things she likes and withdrawal from those she dislikes.

Psychologically, Anastasia is developing self-awareness, growing in the realization that she is a unique and separate being. Her self-perception is steadily being formed as others engage with her. She is growing in cognitive skills that allow her to actively connect to others in the present and future.

Yet Anastasia is vulnerable, and several areas of risk must be addressed in order for her to develop in the right direction. Anastasia's relationship with her mother presents developmental concerns. Luisa is parenting alone, and while this does not preclude secure and attached parenting, it does introduce risk. The challenge of parenting two young children alone places significant physical and emotional responsibility on Luisa. Time for emotional bonding and play is necessarily limited by the demands of caring for two young children. Time for Luisa to attend to her own needs is also limited by the demands of single parenting. Her energy is strained by the daily realities of poverty.

Luisa's own developmental stage is an area of concern. As an adolescent mother, her own developmental needs were undoubtedly shortchanged. Luisa's early sexual activity and general immaturity suggest a young woman with unmet psychological needs, including the need for unconditional love and affirmation. Luisa needs and desires close relationships, but these will undoubtedly be difficult in light of her emotional wounds and current emotional state. Luisa admirably demonstrates resourcefulness by responsibly maintaining her apartment and financial responsibilities.

An immediate concern is Luisa's postpartum depression which is impacting her functioning to the dangerous point of contemplating suicide. Luisa needs an immediate psychiatric assessment and psychotherapy. The initial goals of these referrals will be stabilizing her depression, decreasing her problematic symptoms, and improving her daily functioning. Once her mood is stable and her symptoms are under better control, insight-oriented psychotherapy to address underlying issues related to her depression and hopelessness is strongly indicated. Areas of focus in psychotherapy include her relationships with Carlos and her family of origin, vocational future, experience as a parent, and social isolation.

Another significant concern is the absence of a strong emotional attachment between Luisa and Anastasia. While she is capably caring for her physical needs, Luisa's depression and compromised emotional capacity impact her growing daughter. Anastasia is at risk for adopting withdrawal and distrust as her primary ways of being in the world. Instead of healthy dependence and trust, she may be internalizing an anxious posture that will cause her relational difficulty in the future. Instead of feeling cherished and loved unconditionally in the present—the root of her self-esteem and ability to experience the nature of God's love someday—she is at risk for experiencing and internalizing herself as a burden in her mother's life. Additionally, it is unlikely that Anastasia is receiving the stimulation she needs to fully develop cognitively, physically, and psychologically.

In addition to postpartum depression, there are areas of unresolved need and concern in Luisa's life that also impact Anastasia. Luisa appears to be relatively connected to her mother, which is a protective factor. The positive relationship with her mother may represent a model or template for Luisa's current and future parenting style. There is no indication that Luisa was abused or neglected by either parent, another positive factor. Luisa's distant relationship with her father raises concern, however. At this point, the impact of this relationship on Luisa is unknown. However, the nature of the relationship should be explored, especially as Luisa demonstrates a pattern of poor choices in romantic relationships, which could be rooted in her family of origin.

The relationship between Luisa and Carlos introduces particular risk as domestic violence is present. Violence in the home creates a high level of risk for both daughters who will, directly or indirectly, witness its effects and likely internalize anxiety. Both children are at higher risk for physical abuse when partner violence is present (Bragg, 2003). The situation is further complicated by the fact that Luisa has pinned her hopes for the future on a lasting relationship with Carlos. Her determination for the relationship to work may produce undesirable effects. Luisa's desperation could cause her to make decisions based on her need to preserve the relationship versus using good judgement. A break in this relationship could also destabilize Luisa's fragile mood and increase her hopelessness about the future. This is risky for an individual with suicidal ideation who is parenting two children alone.

After her depression has stabilized, Luisa will need to identify short- and long-term goals that are independent of her relationship with Carlos. Affirmation of her strengths and abilities, including caring for two young children alone, is critical. A strengthening of her sense of agency—her ability to make informed and independent decisions—is important. Further, she will need assistance in exploring the impact of her history on her current relational patterns. Like many young women, she is looking to a romantic relationship to fulfill her unmet emotional and social needs.

Beyond her interpersonal and psychological challenges, Luisa is ill-prepared to financially support her family as a high school dropout and single mother. The poverty of the family and the sustained stress related to chronic economic instability place each member of this family at developmental risk. A further concern relates to the safety of the neighborhood. Viable future possibilities, including GED completion, eventual community college for nursing, and subsidized, quality daycare should be explored. Luisa has a long path to adequately caring for her family financially, but her original vocational plan could likely be achieved with sustained assistance.

Another risk to Anastasia's development is her family's social isolation. This is particularly concerning for Anastasia as Luisa is not functioning well and the home environment therefore lacks appropriate stimulation. Because Anastasia's exposure to others and her world within the apartment is highly restricted, there are few alternative sources of social stimulation in her life. Beyond her mother, Luisa also has little social support, a situation that is undoubtedly exacerbating her depression and hopelessness about the future. She also has no faith community as the family lacks a church connection. This is particularly significant in the life of a family lacking the psychosocial support that a church could offer.

There is additional concern related to the role of Carlos as Anastasia's father. He is intermittently in Anastasia's life, a reality that likely prevents emotional bonding. Anastasia's memory is minimally developed, so she requires the consistent presence of her father in order to retain familiarity. Carlos is not facilitating an emotional connection with Anastasia through time spent together and play. This prevents Anastasia from forming a positive internal perception of her father. It is unsurprising that Anastasia interacts with her father as a stranger. This relationship could be nurtured and developed, however. If Carlos regularly spends time with Anastasia, she will retain a positive memory. If he interacts calmly with Luisa, Anastasia's anxiety toward her father will eventually decrease.

Finally, there are risks related to Anastasia's physical development. As a premature infant who is small for her age, she remains at mild risk for developmental delays. It is possible, however, that her delays are the product of a lack of adequate stimulation. With conscious attention to enrichment activities, Anastasia's gross and fine motor control may markedly improve. Luisa should also consult with her pediatrician regarding Anastasia's sleep patterns. The lack of consistent sleep for both Anastasia and Luisa undoubtedly place additional strain on the entire family.

In sum, there is no question that Anastasia has been born into a fallen world. There are numerous challenges in her immediate environment, including poverty, domestic violence, and a depressed mother. This is concerning because Anastasia is in a stage of highly sensitive neurological development. The trauma of her current environment could create entrenched neural patterns that prove problematic in her future. Her life is just beginning, but changes are needed to help Anastasia to develop in the right direction. Without intervention, we fear that her future ability to see herself accurately, as one who is deeply and unconditionally loved by God, may be affected.

Immediate changes are needed in order for Anastasia to develop in the right direction. Her key means of developing well—the relationships around her—currently lack the stability she will need to experience the world as reliable, stable, and emotionally safe. Anastasia is wired for survival, so she will find ways to adapt to her environment, but her adaptation will likely be maladaptive. However, with the interventions suggested, the direction of Anastasia's development could be refocused toward the purposes for which she was created.

Chapter Summary

Infants are tiny image-bearers latent with potential and primed for growth. Their entire being is oriented toward stable connections with others. Infants illustrate our human need for one another and for God. Remarkably, they have the capacity for worship, an innate desire to praise their maker. Their level of dependency beautifully reflects the dependency that is core to our nature. Yet in their dependency they are also vulnerable to the effects of a broken world. Infancy represents a stage of tremendous opportunity and an important time for intervention all around the growing child. Indeed, many infants can benefit from interventions that refocus their development in the right direction.

Discussion Questions

1. How are dependency and vulnerability both positive and negative realities in our lives?

2. What implications do the principles from this chapter have for work in child welfare?

3. In terms of Anastasia's future, what are your greatest concerns? What are your greatest hopes for her?

4. Now answer the same questions for her mother, Luisa. What are your greatest concerns and your greatest hopes for her?

5. Think about the model for development—connections with God, ourselves, and others. Now summarize a telos for Anastasia's development in two or three sentences.

References

Ashford, J. B., LeCroy, C. W., & Lortie, K. L (2006). *Human behavior in the social environment: A multidimensional perspective*. Belmont, CA: Wadsworth Publishing.

Auerbach, R. P., Kim, J. C., Chango, J. M., Spiro, W. J., Cha, C., Gold, J., . . . Nock, M. K. (2014). Adolescent nonsuicidal self-injury: Examining the role of child abuse, comorbidity, and disinhibition. *Psychiatry Research, 220,* 579-584.

Banducci, A. N., Hoffman, E., Lejuez, C., & Koenen, K. C. (2014). The relationship between child abuse and negative outcomes among substance users: Psychopathology, health, and comorbidities. *Addictive Behaviors, 39,* 1522-1527.

Benson, J.G. (2014). Socioeconomic status and cognitive outcomes: Mediating role of the home environment. Retrieved from http://digitalrepository.unm.edu/psy_etds/9.

Bradley R.H., Whiteside-Mansell, L., Mundfrom, D.J., Casey, P.H., Kelleher, K.J., Pope, S.K. (1994). Early indications of resilience and their relation to experiences in the home environments of low birthweight, premature children living in poverty. *Child Development, 65,* 346–60.

Bradley, R. H., & Corwyn, R. F. (2016). Home life and the development of competence in mathematics: Implications of research with the HOME inventory. In B. Blevins-Knebbe & A.M. Berghout Austin (Eds.). *Early childhood mathematics skill development in the home environment,* (pp. 29-49). Switzerland: Springer International.

Bragg, H.L. (2003). *Child protection in families experiencing domestic violence.* Child Abuse and Neglect User Manual Series. Washington, DC: U.S. Department of Health and Human Services, Children's Bureau Office on Child Abuse and Neglect.

Brooks-Gunn, J., & Duncan, G. (1997). The effects of poverty on children. *Future Child, 2,* 55-71.

Camp, B. W., Cunningham, M., & Berman, S. (2010). Relationship between the cognitive environment and vocabulary development during the second year of life. *Archives of Pediatrics & Adolescent Medicine, 164,* 950-6.

Center on the Developing Child (2013). *Early Childhood Mental Health* (In-Brief). Retrieved from www.developingchild.harvard.edu.

Dix, T., Cheng, N., & Day, W. H. (2009). Connecting with parents: Mothers' depressive symptoms and responsive behaviors in the regulation of social contact by one- and young two-year-olds. *Social Development, 18,* 24-50.

Dix, T., Stewart, A. D., Gershoff, E. T., & Day, W. H. (2007). Autonomy and children's reactions to being controlled: Evidence that both compliance and defiance may be positive markers in early development. *Child Development,* 78 (4), 1204-1221.

Downey, G., & Coyne, J. C. (1990). Children of depressed parents: An integrative review. *Psychological Bulletin, 108,* 50-76.

Freeman, P. A. (2014). Prevalence and relationship between adverse childhood experiences and child behavior among young children. *Infant Mental Health Journal, 35,* 544-554.

Goodman, S. H., & Gotlib, I. H. (2002). *Children of depressed parents: Mechanisms of risk and implications for treatment.* Washington, D.C.: American Psychological Association.

Gross, D. (2019). *Infancy: Development from birth to age 3* (3rd ed.). Lanham, MD: The Rowan and Littlefield Publishing Group.

Harford, T. C., Yi, H., & Grant, B. F. (2014). Associations between childhood abuse and interpersonal aggression and suicide attempt among U.S. adults in a national study. *Child Abuse & Neglect, 38,* 1389-1398.

Hart, B., & Risley, T. R. (1995). *Meaningful differences in the everyday experience of young American children.* Baltimore, MD: Paul H. Brookes Publishing Company.

Hartas, D. (2012) Inequality and the home learning environment: predictions about seven-year-olds' language and literacy. British Educational Research Journal, 5, 859-879.

Herrenkohl, T. I., Jung, H., Lee, J. O., Klika, J. B., & Skinner, M. L. (2015). Effects of physical and emotional child abuse and its chronicity on crime into adulthood. *Violence and Victims, 30,* 1004-1018.

Hwang, Ai-Wen, Liao, Hua-Fang, Chen, Pau-Chung, Hsieh, Wu-Shiun, Simeonsson, Rune J., Weng, Li-Jen, & Su, Yi-Ning (2014). Applying the ICF-CY framework to examine biological and environmental factors in early childhood development. *Journal of the Formosan Medical Association, 113,* 303-312.

John, J.S., Cisler, J.M., & Sigel, B.A. (2017). Emotion regulation mediates the relationship between a history of child abuse and current PTSD/depression severity in adolescent females. *Journal of Family Violence, 32,* 565-575.

Lee, C., Coe, C. L., & Ryff, C. D. (2017). Social disadvantage, severe child abuse, and biological profiles in adulthood. *Journal of Health and Social Behavior, 58,* 371-386.

LeFevre, J., Polyzoi, E., Skwarchuk, S., Fast, L. & Sowinski, C. (2010). Do home numeracy and literacy practices of Greek and Canadian parents predict the numeracy skills of kindergarten children? *International Journal of Early Years Education, 1,* 55-70.

Margoni, F. & Surian, L. (2018). Infants' evaluation of prosocial and antisocial agents: A meta-analysis. *Developmental Psychology, 54,* 1445–1455.

Melhuish, E.C., Sylva, K., Sammons, P., Siraj-Blatchford, I., Taggart, B., Phan, M. & Malin, A.(2008). Preschool influences on mathematics achievement. *Science, 3,* 1161–1162.

Obradovi , J., Yousafzai, A., Finch, J., & Rasheed, M. (2016). Supplemental material for maternal scaffolding and home stimulation: Key mediators of early intervention effects on children's cognitive development. *Developmental Psychology, 52,* 1409-1421.

Pereira, K. R., Valentini, N. C., & Saccani, R. (2016). Brazilian infant motor and cognitive development: Longitudinal influence of risk factors. *Pediatrics International, 58,* 1297-1306.

Perry, B. D. (1999). *Bonding and attachment in maltreated children: Consequences of emotional neglect in childhood.* CTA Parent and Caregiver Education Series, Volume 1: Issue 3. Child Academy Press.

Perry, B. D. (2002). Childhood experience and the expression of genetic potential: What childhood neglect tells us about nature and nurture. *Brain and Mind, 3,* 79-100.

Rochat, P. (2001). *The infant's world.* Cambridge: Harvard University Press.

Rochat, P. (2003). Five levels of self-awareness as they unfold early in life. *Consciousness and Cognition, 12,* 717-731.

Rochat, P., & Hespos, S. J. (1997). Differential rooting response by neonates: Evidence for an early sense of self. *Early Development and Parenting, 6,* 150–150.

Rochat, P., Querido, J. G., & Striano, T. (1999). Emerging sensitivity to the timing and structure of protoconversation in early infancy. *Developmental Psychology, 35,* 950–957.

Ronfani, L., Brumatti, L. V., Mariuz, M., Tognin, V., Bin, M., Ferluga, V., Barbone, F. (2015). The complex interaction between home environment, socioeconomic status, maternal IQ and early child neurocognitive development: A multivariate analysis of data collected in a newborn cohort study. *Plos One, 10,* 1-13.

Rowe, M. L., & Goldin-Meadow, S. (2009). Differences in early gesture explain SES disparities in child vocabulary size at school entry. *Science, 323,* 951–953.

Saccani, R., Valentini, N. C., Pereira, K. R., Müller, A. B., & Gabbard, C. (2013). Associations of biological factors and affordances in the home with infant motor development. *Pediatrics International, 55,* 197-203.

Shonkoff, J. P. & Garner, A. S. (2012). The lifelong effects of early childhood adversity and toxic stress. *Pediatrics, 129,* 2011-2663.

Slater, A., Field, T., & Hernandez-Reif, M. (2007). The development of the senses. In A. Slater & M. Lewis (Eds.). *Introduction to infant development.* Oxford, UK: Oxford University Press.

Sperry, D. M., & Widom, C. S. (2013). Child abuse and neglect, social support, and psychopathology in adulthood: A prospective investigation. *Child Abuse & Neglect, 37* 415-425.

Tandon, P. S., Zhou, C., Sallis, J. F., Cain, K. L., Frank, L. D., & Saelens, B. E. (2012). Home environment relationships with children's physical activity, sedentary time, and screen time by socioeconomic status. *International Journal of Behavioral Nutrition and Physical Activity, 9,* 88.

Twardosz, S. (2012). Effects of experience on the brain: The role of neuroscience in early development and education. *Early Education and Development, 23,* 96-119.

Westerlund, M., & Lagerberg, D. (2008). Expressive vocabulary in 18-month-old children in relation to demographic factors, mother and child characteristics, communication style and shared reading. *Child: Care, Health, and Development, 34,* 257-66.

Yu, M. & Daraganova, M. (2014). Children's early home learning environment and learning outcomes in the early years of school. *The Longitudinal Study of Australian Children Annual Statistical report.* Melbourne: Australian Institute of Family Studies.

Chapter Eight

Childhood: Playing and Learning (ages 3–12)

In order to develop normally, a child requires progressively more complex joint activity with one or more adults who have an irrational emotional relationship with the child. Somebody's got to be crazy about that kid. That's number one. First, last, and always.

Bronfenbrenner (1979)

We continue our study of the lifespan by exploring childhood, a stage of remarkable human growth and development. In this chapter, childhood will be defined as the stage between ages three and 12. While this is a diverse age group developmentally, encompassing the preschool to early middle school years, we will focus on factors that apply across this stage. The case of a child will be described, followed by a discussion of key characteristics of childhood, and concluded by a review of the case from the perspective of the key characteristics and the biblical themes outlined earlier in the book.

We will maintain a focus on developing children with the telos, or ultimate goal, of healthy connections with God and other people. This is a daunting, even idealistic-sounding goal, but it reflects the unwavering belief that we develop for a purpose and that we are shaped for that purpose primarily through relationships.

Let's keep these ends in mind as we explore the life of Connor and his family.

The Case of Connor

Connor is an eight-year old Caucasian boy who lives in a small, rural town in Ohio. His hometown is located within the "Rust Belt"—an area of the country where the economy was largely buttressed by steel production until the industry vacated the region in the 1980s. This led to widespread unemployment and poverty. Connor's family has been greatly impacted by these economic realities as his grandfather was a lifelong steelworker and his father, Tom, fully expected to follow in his father's footsteps. When Tom graduated from high school, however, he entered a work force with few unskilled labor jobs. The well-paying industrial jobs that were available required technical training which he chose not to pursue. Since graduating from high school, Tom has held several jobs in retail including at a gas station and several auto supply stores. Unfortunately, his back was permanently injured in a car accident three years ago. Tom is currently receiving monthly Social Security Disability benefits related to his injury and is not formally employed.

Connor's parents met in high school and married at age 19. He is the oldest of four boys (ages 8, 6, 5, 2) and was born one year after the couple married. His mother, Sheri, is 28 years old and manages a daycare in their home, caring for several young children on a part-time basis. Tom and Sheri have been married for nine years, but were separated for a year when Connor was two years old. During this time, Connor lived with his mother and saw his father infrequently.

Tom and Sheri have a long history of instability in their relationship. They separated several years ago because the level of conflict between them was so high that they were unsure if they wanted to remain married. They eventually moved back in together with the goal of fighting less, but mainly because they needed to combine their financial resources in order to survive. The marriage is currently poor as the couple communicate ineffectively and hold significant resentment toward each other for a lengthy list of past grievances. The home is characterized by frequent loud verbal conflicts between the couple and the boys.

Because Tom and Sheri were born and raised in their current town, they have many extended family members nearby. Tom is the oldest of three children. His father lives nearby, but his mother died five years ago from cancer. His siblings also live in town, but he has a distant relationship with both of them. Tom's early home atmosphere was similar to the one he has recreated in his current family—chaotic, loud, and emotionally-charged. He had a poor relationship with both parents. He struggled academically and socially during school. These patterns have persisted and he has no current close friends or hobbies. He spends much of his days physically inactive and socially isolated and, for the past several years, has been severely obese. Tom suffers chronic pain related to his back injury and takes pain medications which cause him to sleep on and off throughout the day. In the last year, he was diagnosed with hypertension and Type 2 diabetes and takes medication to manage these conditions.

Sheri is the middle child of three children and was raised in a calmer home than her husband, but her family of origin was largely withdrawn and distant from one another. Her parents were often distracted by stressors in their lives, including finances and long work hours. As a result, they were minimally emotionally connected to each other or their children. Anger was not visibly displayed in the home, but only because family members were so disconnected from one another. A pattern of disconnection remains to this day. Sheri's extended family lives nearby and they get together on major holidays, but this group also lacks warm and connected relationships. A pattern of distance has been recreated between her parents and their grandsons as well.

Sheri has displayed symptoms of depression and anxiety, including fatigue, feelings of hopelessness, insomnia, headaches, irritability, and persistent feelings of anxiety for the past year. She has no medical insurance so has not seen a doctor about these symptoms. Sheri often feels guilty because she is short-tempered with her children and the daycare children, but she lacks patience and the ability to tolerate their behaviors, especially her boys' fighting and aggression.

Connor is currently in third grade where he is a below-average student, demonstrating delays in reading, math, and science. Academic delays have been noted by teachers and in standardized tests since he was in kindergarten. His first grade teacher recommended psychological testing as Connor exhibited symptoms of ADHD. This diagnosis was confirmed by the school psychologist. Connor is currently taking medication for ADHD. He has seen a school social worker biweekly for the past three years because of disruptive classroom behaviors, including hyperactivity, aggression, and inattention. Connor has Medicaid insurance due to a state program for children in low-income families.

Socially, Connor struggles with making and keeping friends, in large part because of his aggressive behavior. He desires friendships and often tries to interact with his peers, but other children are quickly put off by his aggressiveness. Connor is easily angered and highly reactive verbally and physically when agitated or angry, often hitting other children for minor, unintentional infractions. His teacher and the principal frequently discipline Connor by issuing after-school in-school suspensions. Connor has also received three out-of-school suspensions as the result of his many in-school suspensions. His suspensions have led to nine days out of school during this academic year. These nine days due to suspensions do not include the additional eight days he has missed because his mother could not get him out of bed and to school on time.

Connor often feels discouraged because he tries to make friends and is unsuccessful. He is aware that he is doing poorly in school, but often feels like he cannot change. Connor sometimes makes attempts to be nicer to other children and to pay attention in school, but he feels that his attempts do not make a difference. He feels that it doesn't matter if he tries or not as he gets in trouble either way. The same point applies to his schoolwork. He doesn't complete his homework because he feels that it is pointless and getting good grades is hopeless. The enjoyment Connor feels is when he is playing video games. He is skilled at several video games and feels proud of this ability, but does not feel he has any other talents.

Connor and his siblings have hostile relationships that are characterized by physical fighting, wrestling, and name-calling. The boys have moments when they get along, but they spend most of their time arguing and fighting. The atmosphere in the home is often loud as the boys are either being yelled at or are screaming at each other. Discipline consists of yelling with occasional removal of "screen time," but discipline is inconsistent. Two of the younger boys are already displaying academic delays and physical aggression in school similar to that exhibited by Connor.

The home atmosphere is highly chaotic and lacks structure and emotional warmth. Both parents feel so overwhelmed by financial strain, the demands of the home daycare, and parenting four young children that they have little energy for emotional bonding or affection. The family does not have consistent meal times and the kids often get themselves snacks throughout the evening. They also lack a consistent bed time so the children are frequently tired and difficult to wake for school in the morning. The home is disorganized and messy as laundry, cleaning, and grocery shopping are all done inconsistently.

Connor is in good overall physical health. He was a full-term infant who met all of his developmental markers on time. He is of average height and weight and enjoys physical activities, such as playing soccer. Connor's parents do not limit his "screen time" during the school year so he spends 4-5 hours a day watching TV and playing video games. During the summer, this increases to an average of 8-9 hours per day.

As mentioned before, Connor's town is small, rural, and impoverished. The tax base for his school has sharply declined in recent years and the quality of the public school district has greatly suffered from a lack of resources. Standardized scores for their school district are the lowest in their county and markedly below the expectations set by their state. Academic support services at Connor's school are minimal. The school employs one social worker, but she is woefully stretched by the many needs within the building.

Sheri and Tom did not grow up attending church and have never taken their boys to church. They think this would be a good idea, but have not had the energy to follow through on this goal. As indicated before, the family has little support from their extended family and the couple and family additionally lack close friendships. There are children in the neighborhood with whom the boys play on occasion.

We will return to the case of Connor after discussing two important aspects of child development.

Growing in Resilience

All of us, including children, experience stress. A predictable physiological response is triggered when we face something anxiety-producing such as giving a speech or meeting an important person for the first time. Stress-related hormones are released, resulting in an increased heart rate and multiple other physical responses. This activity is adaptive as our bodies prepare for the challenge before us.

At times, however, we experiences more serious incidents of stress. Tolerable stress refers to experiences involving serious stressors, such as natural disasters or the death of a family member. As the name indicates, we come through experiences of toxic stress without suffering maladaptive effects. The stress is tolerable because of the presence of critical coping mechanisms such as social supports and the ability to process the stressor (National Scientific Council on the Developing Child, 2004a, 2010, 2014). Tolerable stress is unquestionably difficult, even painful, but it is bearable because resources are in place that allow its effective management.

Conversely, toxic stress is a form of stress that is unique from normal or tolerable stress both in its severity and duration. It represents severe and, most notably, *chronic* stress. The impact of toxic stress is particularly poignant for children. To enable ongoing normal growth and development, many parts of a child's brain remain malleable and responsive to experiential inputs (Davidson, & McEwen, 2012). Like the infant period, toxic stress greatly affects the brain architecture of children because neurological sensitivity continues throughout childhood. Neurological pathways are formed in response to harmful levels of stress, interfering with many aspects of normal development, including those responsible for learning, memory and planning (Fox, Levitt, & Nelson, 2010; Shonkoff, 2010).

We cannot easily quantify what constitutes a normal, tolerable, or toxic stressor. The extent to which stressful events have lasting negative effects is not determined solely by the stressor alone, but also by the individual's response and the duration, timing, and context of the stress.

The Center on the Developing Child (n.d.) further describes the problem, writing,

> Toxic stress occurs when a child experiences strong, frequent, and/or prolonged adversity—such as physical or emotional abuse, chronic neglect, caregiver substance abuse or mental illness, exposure to violence, and/or the accumulated burdens of family economic hardship—without adequate adult support. This kind of prolonged activation of the stress response systems can disrupt the development of brain architecture and other organ systems, and increase the risk for stress-related disease and cognitive impairment well into the adult years.

Note from this description that what distinguishes tolerable from toxic stress is not only the severity of the stressor, but also the lack of resources necessary for coping. With children, who lack the cognitive ability to process stressors fully or independently, inadequate adult support is, most often, the missing resource. Though we cannot accurately predict which situations are toxic, we can support children in responding to stress in ways that minimize its negative effects on their brains and bodies.

How can children be supported in coping with stress so that their development continues normally? The obvious answer is eliminating children's exposure to toxic stressors such as abuse, neglect, violence, and poverty, among others. Indeed, eliminating or moderating sources of stress and trauma in the child's environment is necessary. We must always maintain a macro-level perspective when working at the micro level. But as important as these interventions are, there are times when the alteration of macro-level dynamics is not accessible. Helping children to respond more adaptively to the adversities around them may, however, be entirely within reach.

Facing adverse circumstances without negative effect is a characteristic referred to as resiliency. Resiliency implies tipping a child's development toward positive outcomes despite the presence of numerous factors pointing toward negative outcomes. Some researchers conceptualize a developmental teeter-totter with stress on one side and resilience on the other. Resiliency, in other words, tips the teeter-totter in a positive direction even when stressors have a weighty presence in the child's life (Blair & Raver, 2012; Cicchetti, 2010; Masten, Best, & Garmezy, 1990; Masten, 2013, 2014).

Historically, studies of children who demonstrated resilience identified the construct as a personality trait that was unique to certain individuals (Fraser, Kirby, & Smokowski, 2004). Rather than a trait that some persons inherit from their parents, resilience is now seen as a characteristic that can be developed in any child. Resilience is now referred to as an outcome, something that can be developed in response to inputs (Harper Browne, 2014; Rutter, 2012; Wright & Masten, 1997). This perspective carries great hope as we consider the opportunity to build resiliency in children living in the most difficult of situations. Not something limited to those with high IQs or agreeable personalities, it is an outcome that can be nurtured in children as a whole.

If resiliency is not an inherited personality trait, but a set of skills to be nurtured, it is important to understand its components. There are more, but we will identify three key areas underlying resilience—executive functioning, self-regulation, and agency. These characteristics are interrelated, but will be addressed separately.

Executive functioning refers to the cognitive processes that enable tasks, such as learning new subject matter, staying focused despite distraction, planning ahead, and following directions (Burgess & Simons, 2005). Executive functioning skills are expectedly critical in academic settings where following directions and staying on task correlates with school success, but how do these skills foster resilience in children? In reality, the same skills that allow children to learn English grammar rules assist them in dealing with adversity. Problem-solving abilities are useful in light of complex stressors (Diamond, 2013). While children are unable to "solve" major problems such as their family's poverty, executive functioning skills direct them toward ways of coping for themselves. This may involve behaviors such as talking to a friend or writing in a journal. The child is using executive functioning to break a complex problem into manageable tasks. Resilient children demonstrate strong executive functioning skills (Diamond, 2014; Center on the Developing Child, 2011).

A second component of resiliency is self-regulation. Self-regulation includes the ability to delay gratification, apply rationality to emotions, label one's own and others' emotions accurately, express emotions in healthy ways, and to consider the outcomes of their thoughts, feelings, and behaviors before acting on them (Baumeister & Heatherton, 1996; Choudhury, Blakemore, & Charman, 2007). The Mid-State Central Early Childhood Direction Center (2009) writes,

> A child's social-emotional development provides them with a sense of who they are in the world, how they learn, and helps them establish quality relationships with others. It is what drives an individual to communicate, connect with others and more importantly helps resolve conflicts, gain confidence and reach goals (p. 1).

Self-regulation is critical to resilience in children because it is the foundation for identity development, communication skills, and effective interpersonal relationships. Children experiencing chronic stress benefit greatly from the ability to identify their emotions. If a child can, for example, identify that he is angry when his father comes home intoxicated, he can look for ways to respond effectively to his anger. Children who cannot identify their own emotions, even in very rudimentary ways, lack insight into the ways they are being emotionally impacted by the stress. This makes them susceptible to psychological harm (Heatherton, 2011).

Identifying the emotions of others is also important because it allows children to begin to make basic sense of their environment. It allows them to differentiate their emotions from those of people around them. This skill builds resiliency because it allows children to distance from others' negative emotions in healthy ways and to avoid blaming themselves for traumatic situations. Self-regulation also enables relationship building as controlling one's emotions is necessary for nurturing friendships. Self-regulation creates pathways for supportive relationships around the child, a critical factor in thriving during adversity. Indeed, children grow in resiliency when they grow in the skills connected with self-regulation.

A third aspect of resiliency relates to agency—the ability to make choices related to our own lives. This characteristic is not just true of adults; it pertains to children as well. Agency is especially important for children experiencing toxic stress. Their lives likely contain many features that are frustrating to them, but which lie outside of their control. Children who locate some ability to make decisions about their lives, even when that ability is highly restricted, fare better in light of chronic stress (Anda, 2013; Masten, 2014). The Search Institute (2018) phrases this skill as, "I can manage life rather than letting life manage me." A child who experiences some control over their situation will experience more hope and optimism for the future than the child who lacks any sense of agency.

These areas form key aspects of resiliency. They shed light on specific areas to nurture within children in chronically stressful situations, but there is another critical component of growing resilient children.

Developmental Relationships

Children learn resiliency from adults. Children do not develop in a vacuum, but through relationships. The Search Institute (2018) has termed the interpersonal connections that best facilitate resiliency, "developmental relationships." A developmental relationship is "a close connection through which a young person develops a positive identity, agency, and a connection to community. Elements of a developmental relationship are the expression of care, challenge of growth, provision of support, sharing of power, and expanding of possibilities. This type of relationship can involve parents, mentors, non-familial adults, friends, teachers, older siblings, pastors, coaches, and program leaders. The importance of developmental relationships cannot be overstated. Researchers at The Search Institute (2018) write,

> The single most common factor for children who develop resilience is at least one stable and committed relationship with a supportive parent, caregiver, or other adult. These relationships provide the personalized responsiveness, scaffolding, and protection that buffer children from developmental disruption.

Children who do well in the face of serious and prolonged hardship have strong relationships with adults in their family and/or community (Center on the Developing Child, 2015). The quality of experiences parents and other caregivers model and facilitate for young children either strengthen or undermine the development of self-regulation, executive functions, and agency (Shonkoff & Garner, 2012). Importantly, for parents and other caregivers to help children journey through adverse experiences, they must possess and practice these skills themselves (Jones & Lesaux, 2013).

Children develop self-regulation, executive functioning, and agency—the components of resiliency—when they are in loving relationships with adults who model these abilities. Without nurturing relationships with adults who actually practice the skills of resiliency, children will not learn how to appropriately manage highly stressful situations. Children are ill-prepared to manage toxic stress, but resilient adults hold the key to nurturing these important skills in children. Indeed, the Center on the Developing Child (2015) identifies parental resilience as a key component of child resilience. They write:

> Resilience requires relationships, not rugged individualism... the capacity to adapt and thrive despite adversity develops through the interaction of supportive relationships, gene expression, and adaptive biological systems. Despite the widespread belief that individual grit, extraordinary self-reliance, or some in-born, heroic strength of character can triumph over calamity, science now tells us that it is the reliable presence of at least one supportive relationship and multiple op-

portunities for developing effective coping skills that are essential building blocks for the capacity to do well in the face of significant adversity (p. 7).

Developmental relationships help children to discover who they are, learn the skills and confidence to shape their own lives, and learn means of socially interacting with the world around them. Children who have developmental relationships experience healthy self-affirmation and settle into a core identity that stays with them in different environments. They learn to value relationships with others as they experience the rewards of giving and receiving in connections with others. In the context of safe relationships, they are free to explore themselves and to learn the critical cognitive, social, and emotional skills of being human (Champagne, 2010; National Scientific Council on the Developing Child, 2004b).

Developmental relationships have demonstrated far-reaching positive effects on children. Outcomes include academic strength, civic commitment, and numerous social-emotional characteristics. Researchers emphasize the importance of developmental relationships not only with the child's parents. Resilient children are nested within a network of developmental relationships that include their school, neighborhood, church, and community.

In summary, children experience serious neurological effects from toxic stress. They "learn" reactions based on stress and are thwarted in many aspects of normative development. However, resilient children have skills that allow them to avoid the maladaptive effects of toxic stress. Resiliency entails executive functioning skills such as problem-solving, self-regulatory skills such as emotional identification, and the determination to act as an agent in the presence of significant stress. Relationships are the key mechanisms for facilitating these skills. Children grow in these critical skills and develop resilience through nurturing relationships with resilient adults. Through such relationships, children are supported and nurtured toward skills that remarkably help them to grow in the face of adversity.

With these insights in mind, we return to Connor and his family.

Connor Revisited

Eight-year old Connor lives with his parents in a small town in Ohio. He struggles academically and socially and his family is dealing with various issues, including discipline, communication, and finances. There are several different areas that require attention in this case. Our overarching goal in working with Connor is to create developmental pathways in the present that are most likely to facilitate health and growth in his future re- relationships with God and other people. This is the *telos*—ultimate goal— of Connor's development, even at his young age. We long for Connor to have loving and supportive relationships with those in his family, school, and community. We want him to develop the resiliency that allows him to cope with, not to be harmed by, the adversity in his life in the present and future. We will keep these larger goals in mind as we explore this case.

We first consider Connor's family context. The current family envi- ronment lacks the warmth and cohesion we desire for Connor and his sib- lings. This, unfortunately, was not modeled in either Tom or Sheri's early home lives, but it can be steadily developed with some changes initiated by the parents. The modeling of new behaviors, especially new ways of resolving conflict, is an immediate need in this family. Marital counseling between Tom and Sheri, with the goal of identifying and processing the long-term, unresolved issues in their marriage, is indicated. The level of animosity between the two of them undoubtedly creates a context of neg- ativity in the household. Helping Tom and Sheri to work through a long history of disappointment and frustration in their relationship will be fun- damental to facilitating healthy relationships with the children.

It is also important to model healthy resolution of conflict for the children, but this is likely impossible considering the current state of the parents' emotional health. Each of them is significantly compromised, re- spectively, by depression and chronic pain. Sheri would benefit from a low- cost psychiatric evaluation at a community mental health facility. Until her symptoms are under better control, it will be difficult for her to make gains in parenting and household management. The same point is true of Tom, although his medical issues may be more difficult to manage due to their chronicity. It will be important, however, for him to pursue forms of pain management with less problematic side effects. His current fatigue essential- ly removes him from the family and only exacerbates the overall problems. Ideally his pain management would be accompanied by improved self-care, including a healthier diet and exercise within his physical limitations.

Improvements in both Sheri and Tom's physical and emotional health will be important to the overall functioning of this family. Related to this, the family struggles with chronic stress related to financial problems and the stress of running a daycare in their home. While this arrangement al- lows Sheri to work from home, the couple should be encouraged to look at ways to decrease stress. These may include forming and sticking to a monthly budget and also managing the daycare in a more structured and routine fashion—tasks that would be far easier if the couple's mental and physical health were improved.

The family would also benefit from the parents using consistent discipline with the children, such as time-outs or the withdrawal of privileges. Such interventions should be accompanied by "out-loud" problem-solving related to the conflicts and leading the children into some type of reconciliation with each other. This could be as simple as saying they are sorry or suggesting they play together in a joint activity. To build such skills in their children, however, Tom and Sheri must begin resolving conflicts between one another in constructive ways. This includes talking through their frustrations and letting go of previous issues that have been successfully resolved.

The chaos of the household adds stress to each member of the family. Simple, but consistent, family meals, along with regular grocery shopping days, are encouraged. The entire family should be engaged in simple household chores, and a routine should be established for parental activities, such as bill-paying and laundry. A regular daily routine, while challenging for many families to maintain, creates a sense of predictability and security that is critical for young children.

Increased family cohesion or a sense of greater emotional connection in the family are also goals. Changes such as improved communication, improved daily structure, and less unresolved conflict will all facilitate better cohesion. It will also be important for the family to have fun together and to plan inexpensive outings where they can laugh and enjoy each other outside of the family home. These should be accompanied by fun at-home activities such as watching a movie or sporting activity or playing games together.

Connor and his brothers will grow in resiliency when they see it modeled in their parents. Right now it is safe to assume that they are not steadily gaining resiliency skills as the family is not thriving, but operating in survival mode. Ideally, some basic interventions, such as learning healthy conflict resolution, would considerably help Connor with aspects of self-regulation. Learning to identify his own emotions and those of others around him would help Connor with learning ways to regulate his rapidly-changing emotions. Hearing his parents talk through emotional regulation will help Connor to form alternative pathways in his brain when faced with conflictual situations rather than relying on his instincts and acting out physically.

The same point applies to resiliency related to agency. Giving Connor healthy choices about his behaviors as appropriate will provide him with the agency he needs for healthy development. In a sense, Connor has considerable agency because he is often left to parent himself, for example, staying on a computer for many hours at a time. But agency refers to choices that are nested within an environment of healthy limitation and restriction. Agency, in other words, is not authentically present in a context of parental neglect or permissiveness.

Also critical to learning resiliency, executive functioning is an area of significant concern for Connor, with his ADHD diagnosis likely already compromising some aspects of these skills. In other words, it is critical for a child with ADHD to have more, not less, boundaries set for them by parents. The inability to easily place boundaries around their own behaviors, especially those driven by strong emotions like anger, requires more external boundary setting. Consistent and highly repetitive redirection and limits are needed to reinforce weaknesses in Connor's own internal behavioral controls. In other words, while all children require healthy boundaries as well as agency, Connor will likely require more, not less, parental interaction and direction.

A place for limitation is in Connor's screen time which is currently too high. While it is tempting for parents to allow long amounts of screen time as it effectively "silences" a noisy and chaotic household, Connor's parents will need to set time restrictions on his screen time, suggesting alternative activities. While video games can be constructive for Connor, his parents will want to consider the role of technology in the family as a whole. Much could be said about this topic, but Andy Crouch (2017) offers the following helpful point about technology in its "proper place" writing, "Technology is in its proper place when it starts great conversations. It is out of its proper place when it prevents us from talking and listening to one another"(pg. 20). Carefully thinking through the role of technology in Connor's life (as well as the entire family) will be important going forward.

In a broader sense, we are concerned about Connor's missing time from school as even relatively minimal absenteeism has negative effects on learning. Connor's disruptive behavior in school has led to out-of-school suspensions, and he has also missed school because his parents could not wake him in time. School attendance is critical for any child, but Connor is particularly at risk as he is already delayed academically and only stands to fall farther behind. If possible, the assistance of Therapeutic Support Services—someone to sit with Connor at school and provide behavioral coaching to decrease his physical aggression and emotional reactivity—seems important. Additionally, the school's policy of out-of-school suspensions seems antithetical to his learning and attendance needs. Further, Sheri and Tom are responsible for putting the children to bed on time and for a consistent morning routine. It is imperative that Connor is not given the option of "sleeping in" versus school at this young age, setting a potential pattern that will be difficult to break later on. Related to this, Sheri and Tom should be empowered to take an active role in Connor's education through communication with the teacher and school, setting up consistent times for homework, and assisting with academic problems at home as needed.

Finally, we turn to an assessment of Connor's relationships. Sadly, we can assume that he has minimal developmental relationships in his life at this time. Most importantly, he is not well connected with his parents, grandparents, or extended family members in ways that will facilitate the healthy development of his identity, self-esteem, and socio-emotional skills. In many respects, the atmosphere in the household could be characterized as emotionally and physically neglectful as both parents are withdrawn from Connor and the other children due to chronic stress and their own mental and physical health problems. The developmental outcomes of leaving Connor to make his own decisions about things like screen time, school attendance, and food choices are not only leaving Connor without resiliency-building skills, they are not communicating the presence of an unconditionally present and loving parent or parents. And as we have discussed previously, the lack of such care and support in relationships potentially leads to a poor attachment with parents and a poor relational template going forward. A pattern of reliability and trustworthiness in relationships is not internalized, but alternate patterns of survival are adopted, such as withdrawal, unhealthy self-reliance, or patterns of self-loathing.

Relationships with adults outside the family can also be excellent sources of support, but Connor is lacking in these as well. Without a church family, and caring and connected extended family, friends at school, or neighbors, Connor lacks the nested relationships critical to his development. He also lacks the potentially developmental relationships of adults through any social service or civic organizations like Boy Scouts, Big Brother Big Sister, or Boys and Girls Club. Beyond this, his connections with peers and his siblings are equally problematic and unfulfilling for him.

Connor's development is currently at risk. If present patterns continue in this family and in Connor's life, we have significant concerns about the direction of his development. Ideally, we want to see the formation of a warm and loving home characterized by emotionally connected parents and children, but also characterized by healthy limitations and boundaries. It is not too late for a healthy emotional bond to be established between Connor and his parents, one that will allow him to feel loved and cherished. Without such relationships, however, Connor's current acting-out behaviors at home and at school will likely lead to a negative internalized sense of self that can ultimately contribute to further behavioral acting-out or the depression that stems from withdrawal and self-loathing. The creation of an atmosphere where Connor feels loved unconditionally sets the stage for him to someday experience God's unconditional love for him.

Connor's ADHD necessitates the importance of a structured and consistent home and school life. At his age, he is highly reliant upon the adults around him to model such skills and to help him form more adaptive neurological pathways. Beyond this, we want to see Connor flourish and grow through fun and creative activities that stimulate his emotional and social growth and help him to identify his God-given interests and abilities. Expanding his social contexts through activities such as participation in an after-school program, extracurricular activities, or a local church would not only create possibilities for developmental relationships, it might help Connor to learn more about the remarkable person he was created to be. Patterns of negativity in the household and school and social withdrawal through heavy computer use are not leading Connor to identify the places where he excels. Instead, his shortcomings are routinely pointed out, but not counterbalanced by loving relationships that affirm him as inherently lovable and worthwhile.

There is considerable hope for Connor, but changes are needed in order for him to grow into the person he was created to be. His key means of developing well—the relationships around him—lack the ingredients he needs to experience the world as reliable, stable, and emotionally safe. Without intervention, Connor faces risks related to his future. Because, like all children, he is hardwired to survive, Connor will find ways to adapt to the realities of his environment. These adaptations, however, will likely take on maladaptive forms which do not solidly point him in the direction of the developmental *telos* for which he was created.

Chapter Summary

Childhood represents a stage of tremendous growth and opportunity. Some children are unfortunately embedded in environments dominated by stress. The exposure of children to toxic stress is highly concerning because children are still developing emotionally, physically, and socially. Resilient children use a range of executive functions, emotional skills, and the determination to act as agents in order to cope with high and sustained levels of stress. Relationships are the vehicle for developing resiliency. Through developmental relationships, children have a model for coping with crisis. They are upheld by love and nurture.

These observations highlight a role for Christians in social work—intervening in ways that facilitate positive developmental pathways for children with great potential, but also great challenges. At times, this will mean encouraging adults to practice and model resilience, and other times it will mean forming developmental relationships with our young clients. Many children face stressors with the potential to greatly derail their development. But the fact that children, with help, can grow and flourish beyond their circumstances is a message of extraordinary hope.

Discussion Questions

1. Discuss developing resiliency in light of children around the world who face considerable adversity. How might a solid understanding of resiliency impact international programs designed to support children?

2. How does an understanding of toxic stress change the way we practice and intervene with children?

3. What are obstacles to the formation of developmental relationships? How do we challenge those obstacles?

4. What are interventions that build the skills of self-regulation, agency, and executive functioning?

5. In 2-3 sentences, summarize a telos or ultimate purpose for Connor's development.

References

Anda, R. (2013). *Adverse childhood experiences: The balance of risk and opportunity.* Retrieved from jimcaseyyouth.org/adverse-childhood-experience-balancerisk-and-opportunity.

Baumeister, R.F., & Heatherton, T.F. (1996). Self-regulation failure: an overview. *Psychological Inquiry, 7,* 1-15.

Blair, C., & Raver, C.C. (2012). Child development in the context of adversity: Experiential canalization of brain and behavior. *American Psychologist, 67,* 309.

Bronfenbrenner, U. (1979). *The ecology of human development: Experiments by nature and design.* Cambridge, MA.: Harvard University Press.

Burgess, P.W., & Simons, J.S. (2005). Theories of frontal lobe executive function: Clinical applications. In P.W. Halligan & D.T. Wade (Eds.). *Effectiveness of rehabilitation for cognitive deficits* (pp. 211-231). New York: Oxford University Press.

Center on the Developing Child at Harvard University (n.d.). *Toxic stress.* Retrieved from https://developingchild.harvard.edu/science/key-concepts/toxic-stress/.

Center on the Developing Child at Harvard University (2011). *Building the brain's "air traffic control" system: How early experiences shape the development of executive function.* Retrieved from http://www.developingchild.harvard.edu.

Center on the Developing Child at Harvard University (2015). *Supportive relationships and active skill-building strengthen the foundations of resilience: Working Paper No. 13.* Retrieved from www.developingchild.harvard.edu.

Champagne, F.A. (2010). Epigenetic influences of social experiences across the lifespan. *Developmental Psychobiology, 52,* 299-311.

Choudhury, S. Blakemore, S. & Charman, T. (2007). Social cognitive development during adolescence. *Social Cognitive and Affective neuroscience, 1,* 165-74.

Cicchetti, D. (2010). Resilience under conditions of extreme stress: A multilevel perspective. *World Psychiatry, 9,* 145–154.

Crouch, A. (2017). *The tech-wise family: everyday steps for putting technology in its proper;place.* Grand Rapids, MI: Baker Publishing Group.

Davidson, R.J., & McEwen, B.S. (2012). Social influences on neuroplasticity: Stress and interventions to promote well-being. *Nature Neuroscience, 15,* 689–695.

Diamond, A. (2013). Executive functions. *Annual Review of Psychology, 64,* 135–168.

Diamond, A. (2014). Want to optimize executive functions and academic outcomes? Simple, just nourish the human spirit. *Minnesota Symposia on Child Psychology, 37,* 205–232.

Fox, S.E., Levitt, P., & Nelson, C.A. (2010). How the timing and quality of early experiences influence the development of brain architecture. *Child Development, 81,* 28-40.

Fraser, M. W., Kirby, L. D., & Smokowski, P. R. (2004). Risk and resilience in childhood. In M.W. Fraser (Ed.), *Risk and resilience in childhood: An ecological perspective* (pp. 13-66). Washington, DC: National Association of Social Workers.

Harper Browne, C. (2014). *The strengthening families approach and protective factors framework: Branching out and reaching deeper.* Washington, DC: Center for the Study of Social Policy.

Heatherton, T. F. (2011). Neuroscience of Self and Self-Regulation. *Annual Review of Psychology, 62,* 363–390.

Jones, S.M. and Lesaux, N.K. (2013). *Supporting adults to support young children.* Retrieved from https://consciousdiscipline.s3.amazonaws.com/Research/RWJF-Supporting-Adults-To-Support-Young-Children.pdf.

Lyons, D.M., Parker, K.J., Katz, M., & Schatzberg, A.F. (2009). Developmental cascades linking stress inoculation, arousal regulation, and resilience. *Frontiers in Behavioral Neuroscience, 3*, 1–6.

Masten, A.S. (2013). Risk and resilience in development. In P.D. Zelazo (Ed.), *The Oxford Handbook of Developmental Psychology*, Vol. 2. New York, NY: Oxford University Press.

Masten, A.S. (2014). Global perspectives on resilience in children and youth. *Child Development, 85*, 6–20.

Masten, A. S., Best, K., & Garmezy, N. (1990). Resilience and development: Contributions fromthe study of children who overcome adversity. *Development and Psychopathology, 2*, 425-444.

Mid-State Central Early Childhood Direction Center Bulletin (2009). *Understanding social and emotional development in young children.* Retrieved at http://ecdc.syr.edu/wp-content/uploads/BulletinSocialEmotionalDevelopment2-1.pdf.

National Scientific Council on the Developing Child. (2004a). *Children's emotional development is built into the architecture of their brains.* Retrieved from http://www.developingchild.harvard.edu.

National Scientific Council on the Developing Child. (2004b). *Young children develop in an environment of relationships.* Retrieved from http://www.developingchild.net.

National Scientific Council on the Developing Child. (2010). *Persistent fear and anxiety can affect young children's learning and development.* Retrieved from http://www.developingchild.harvard.edu.

National Scientific Council on the Developing Child. (2014). *Excessive stress disrupts the architecture of the developing brain.* Retrieved from http://www.developingchild.harvard.edu.

Rutter, M. (2012). Resilience as a dynamic concept. *Development and Psychopathology, 24*, 335–344.

Shonkoff, J.P. (2010). Building a new biodevelopmental framework to guide the future of early childhood policy. *Child Development, 81*, 357–367.

Shonkoff, J. P., & Garner, A. S. (2012). The lifelong effects of early childhood adversity and toxic stress. *Pediatrics, 126*, 232-246.

The Search Institute (2018). *Developmental relationships: The gateway to building access.* Retrieved from https://www.search-institute.org/our-research/development-assets/developmental-relationships-gateway-building-assets/

Wright, M. O., & Masten, A. S. (1997). Vulnerability and resilience in young children. In J. D. Noshpitz, J. D. Osofsky, & S. Wieder (Eds.), *Handbook of child and adolescent Psychiatry* (pp. 202-224). New York: Wiley.

Chapter Nine

Adolescence: Leaning into Identity (ages 13–18)

The young are arguably both the segment of our population whose flourishing is most subverted by our culture's obsession with maximizing experientially satisfying living and the segment of our population most open to embracing a revised account of human flourishing as they grow into their own responsibilities as citizens, parents, and leaders.

Yale Center for Faith and Culture (2018)

We continue our study of the lifespan by exploring adolescence, a stage of solidifying identity, completing many aspects of physical growth, and moving toward greater independence. In this chapter, we define adolescence as the years between the ages of 13 and 18. These years encompass what is referred to as early adolescence—roughly, the middle school years—and middle adolescence—roughly, the high school years. Late adolescence—the traditional college years—will be included in the next chapter on emerging adults.

Like all age groups, adolescents are not a homogenous group and, therefore, we must resist sweeping summarizations. They are a diverse group in many ways, including their cultural backgrounds, religious beliefs, uses of technology, and approaches to friendships and academics. The goal in this chapter, however, is to explore factors that universally pertain to adolescent development. That said, there will always be a need to learn about individual adolescents by coming close enough to understand their unique areas of giftedness, personalities, hopes for the future, and deepest fears. The hope is that understanding some fundamental things about this age group also encourages such micro-level interactions.

Our emphasis as Christians in social work remains on developing young people with the *telos*, or ultimate goal, of healthy connections with God, themselves, and other people. This overarching goal becomes more specific in the adolescent years as young people begin processing what they have learned about the world and formulating their own belief systems. Their relationships become more sophisticated. Notably, over time, their personal identities are moving from the developmentally normal state of fragmentation to a fully solidified self. Each of these processes will continue into the emerging adult stage and beyond, but adolescence represents a uniquely formative period as identity exploration assumes a central role.

As indicated by the Yale quote above, adolescents inhabit a world that responds to their deep questions in ways that can direct their development in unhelpful and unsatisfying directions. Their search for identity and belonging make them particularly vulnerable to the broader culture's answers to these questions. These answers, however, often do not result in their flourishing. Encouraging young people toward actual means of flourishing requires, among other things, adults who engage adolescents, guiding them in the right direction.

We will illustrate a way of looking at adolescence by examining a case and exploring some fundamental aspects of this exciting time period. Social workers will be guided toward important things to assess and consider when working with adolescents and their parents.

Let's keep these thoughts in mind as we look into the life of an adolescent, Jamiyah, and her family.

The Case of Jamiyah

Jamiyah is a 16 year-old, African-American adolescent who lives with her family in Baltimore. She is a high school sophomore who receives average grades in school. Jamiyah is the youngest child and only daughter with three older brothers—Akeil (22), Shameel (20), and Marcus (19). Jamiyah's two oldest brothers have the same father, but Marcus and Jamiyah each have different fathers. Jamiyah's father, Troy, has been absent for the majority of her life. Troy had a two-year romantic relationship with Jamiyah's mother, Jacquie, but the relationship ended when Jamiyah was a toddler. Troy has had no contact with Jamiyah for the past thirteen years. She has been raised entirely by her mother and older brothers. Jamiyah is close to all three of her brothers and they are protective of her as the only girl and youngest child in the family.

Jamiyah is an attractive, athletic young woman who plays the guard position on her high school women's basketball team. She has a moderately wide circle of friends, but is especially close to her "BFF"—a girl she has known since kindergarten. She has had several boyfriends in the past and is currently dating a high school senior named Bryan. The relationship is unstable as they have broken up and reconciled multiple times during the three months they have been dating. Bryan and Jamiyah are sexually active, but this is unsurprising as Jamiyah has been sexually active with other boyfriends since middle school. Jamiyah has little free time due to her basketball schedule, but when she does, she texts her friends and watches movies. She also enjoys drawing and has been told that she has considerable artistic talent.

Jamiyah has been told by several teachers over the years that she has far more academic potential than she realizes or actualizes. She has little motivation for school work and spends very little time on homework. She currently receives B's and C's, but this is with minimal effort. Her teachers believe she has significant, but untapped, academic ability.

Jamiyah's relationship with her mother is currently poor. As a single mother, Jacquie works many overtime hours as a certified nursing assistant in order to support her family. She works in a local nursing home where she has been employed for the past thirteen years. While she cares about her daughter and feels they had a good relationship during Jamiyah's younger years, the past several years have been difficult. Jamiyah's mother is often too busy, tired, and stressed to enforce healthy restrictions on her daughter. Jamiyah has no curfew and often comes in late at night or early in the morning, long after her mother is asleep. Jacquie is aware that her daughter is out late, but feels powerless to change the situation. She feels that she has steadily lost control over her daughter's behavior and often just ignores the situation.

On top of her fatigue, Jacquie struggles with chronic pain related to a back injury. She has been prescribed pain killers and takes these regularly, but they make her drowsy. Her drug tolerance has also increased so that the medications no longer manage her pain. Frequently in pain, especially after work, Jacquie is often irritable and has little patience with any of the children.

The family lives in an urban area of Baltimore in a modest two-bedroom home which they rent. They have lived there for the past five years. The home is organized and tidy, but needs numerous repairs and the landlord is unresponsive to maintenance requests. The neighborhood had a relatively high crime rate when they moved in, but has deteriorated considerably during the past five years. A heroin dealer rents the home next door and there are people pursuing drugs next door at all hours of the day and night. There is also active gang involvement in the neighborhood, although at this point the family has not been the victims of any crime.

Jamiyah takes the public bus everywhere she goes, including school, as it is unsafe to walk in her neighborhood. She is old enough to obtain a driver's license, but no one in the family owns a car for her to practice driving. Jamiyah rarely thinks about her life in the future; her focus is exclusively on her life in the present. She may attend community college, but has no idea what her vocational interests are at this point.

Jacquie identifies as Baptist because she was raised in the church, but she now works most Sundays and has not attended church in several years. Her children have never attended church outside of attendance at a summer Bible school program when they were young. Jacquie and her two sisters were raised in a nearby neighborhood in Baltimore by a single mother. Unfortunately, Jacquie did not know her father and her mother is now deceased. Her sisters moved from the area many years ago and they have not maintained relationships with each other. Outside of a few work acquaintances, Jacquie lacks social connections as she has no relationships with family or friends.

Jacquie struggles with depression and has little hope for the future. She had great expectations for her children at one time, but feels disappointed at their choices. Akeil, her oldest son, is currently incarcerated in a state prison two hours away for armed robbery. Akeil became involved with a gang during middle school and, despite Jacquie's warnings, began using drugs and stealing to support his habit. He has been in prison for one year and has four more years to complete his sentence. Jacquie visits him every few months and tries to write letters, but is deeply disappointed in her son and struggles to find the emotional energy to stay connected to him.

The two younger brothers finished high school, not wanting to follow in Akeil's footsteps. Neither of them, however, has pursued any college classes. They live at home and work odd, part-time jobs to make money. They have both been encouraged to go to a technical school and to identify a vocation, but they lack the motivation to pursue specific vocational goals. Jacquie suspects that Shameel may be using drugs, but lacks clear evidence. She has warned all of her children about drugs and attempted to set limits when they were younger, but feels discouraged by their choices. Ultimately, she feels that her parenting is to blame for their poor life choices, not to mention the absence of their fathers. In her frustration and guilt, Jacquie has withdrawn from the parenting role at this point.

Jamiyah enjoys playing basketball, but struggles to feel content in about every other area of her life. She tries not to think about her father, but feels great anger when she does. Without her mother's knowledge, she has tried to locate her father several times in the past, but has been unable to find him. She is angry that he abandoned his responsibility to her and her mother and wishes she could confront him in person.

Although it makes her feel guilty, Jamiyah is also angry with her mother. Jamiyah knows that her mother has given up as a parent and that she is discouraged about the way the family is turning out. However, Jamiyah wants her mother to be active in her life and doesn't feel she should be blamed for her brothers' poor choices. The nature of their relationship makes her feel sad, guilty, and angry.

At times, Jamiyah also feels depressed and hopeless, although she hides her feelings from everyone. She does not see the point of school as she has little optimism for the future. Jamiyah would like to marry and have children someday, but does not have any future goals beyond these. Jamiyah knows that she can easily attract guys with her good looks. She enjoys new boyfriends in the beginning, but eventually gets tired of the related drama. Jamiyah has friends, but they know little about her true self as she keeps that hidden from everyone. Her friends see her as carefree and confident because this is what she portrays on the outside, but most of the time she feels angry, sad and hopeless on the inside.

Despite their problems, Jamiyah remains closely connected with her brothers. They tell Jamiyah they are concerned about her poor motivation for school, sexual activity, and drinking habits, but she does not listen to their advice. They want her to make good decisions and to have a positive future, but do not know how to get through to her.

Jamiyah has been offered drugs at school, but has refused them, not wanting the problems of her older brother. She does drink regularly, however, often coming home drunk. She attends parties at the homes of people who are out of high school two or three times per week, including school nights. Jamiyah is sexually active because it is an expectation of relationships in her school.

We will return to the case of Jamiyah and her family after considering some important aspects of adolescence.

Agency + Boundaries

We begin with concepts of importance in work with adolescents and their families. During the adolescent years, young people need appropriate levels of agency and boundaries in order to develop in the right direction. To understand this point, we need to first review the nature of agency and boundaries and then consider their application to this life stage.

Agency, as indicated earlier in this text, is a critical aspect of God's design for humanity. There are many decisions that God does not make for us, leaving space for our unique and independent choices. He elevates human agency by giving us the ability to make decisions, such as whether or not to marry, where to live, and a host of other major and minor decisions. Agency refers to the ability of a person to make their own choices within a given environment. The elements of an environment that restrain the range of an individual's choices such as socioeconomic status or ethnicity are often referred to as social structures (Giddens, 1979).

Many researchers and practitioners believe that an additional psychological component of agency is the belief that one's choices actually have the power to influence the course of one's life (Bandura, 2008; Barker, 2005; Watts & Guessous, 2006). From this perspective, agency entails not solely the freedom to make choices, but the accompanying belief that one's choices *matter*. Some scholars refer to this dynamic as internal locus of control, the sense that control lies within one's self and not solely in outside factors (Jackson & Coursey, 1988). They are not meaningless choices, but choices that serve a particular purpose. Indeed, a critical component of agency is its connection to the belief that one's choices have relevance in the grander scheme. Agency loses its potency when disconnected from the belief that one's choices have any power to produce their desired effect. A true sense of agency then encompasses the freedom to act, as well as the belief that one's choices can actually produce change.

Self-determination theory provides additional insight into the nature of agency. The theory—widely emphasized in social work—contends that individuals have an innate psychological need to make choices for themselves. This is especially important among populations whose agency is routinely circumvented, such as children, disabled persons, and the elderly. The theory argues that an individual is far more motivated and engaged to work toward goals when the goals have been chosen by them. Selecting one's own goals implies an ownership that is distinct from goals that are mandated or chosen by someone else (Deci & Ryan, 2012). Expectedly, persons "buy into" their own goals more deeply and purposefully.

However, a counterbalance to self-determination theory—rarely highlighted in social work—is the need for agency and autonomy to be contained within proper boundaries. As a discipline, social work rightly focuses on the ways in which social structures, such as poverty or racism, unjustly limit the range of human choices. It is unjust, for example, for an adolescent to experience limitations in their vocational options simply because they have received poor schooling. Removing the barriers imposed by social structures is highly important, but misses another aspect of agency. Although choices can be unjustly limited, all limitations on agency should not be removed. Some limits on choices are healthy and necessary.

Agency is best experienced within healthy limits and boundaries. This is beautifully illustrated in the human-divine relationship. For Christians, true freedom is not simply the freedom to do whatever one wishes. True freedom comes paradoxically through obedience and submission to God's laws. This type of submission does not diminish or inhibit our humanness or our inherent agency. It actually benefits us, as following God's commands distances us from the destructive power of sin. Submission becomes the path to freedom.

Adolescents + Agency + Boundaries

Parents and social institutions that display a healthy respect for adolescent freedom *and* boundaries enable the highest levels of positive youth development (Roehlkepartain, Syvertsen, & Wu, 2017). The message of freedom within limits, however, runs counter to the present cultural moment when personal autonomy and individual choice are often prioritized. A cultural emphasis on freedom is communicated in subtle and not-so-subtle ways to contemporary young people. Adolescents, for example, are encouraged to make their own choices in major areas such as gender and sexuality. While personal thoughts and feelings rightly enter such decisions, they ought not necessarily be the top priority. Our choices are best made within a broader context of theological, biological, and social realities.

Finding the balance between autonomy and boundaries is not easy. This struggle is illustrated in churches. Some churches overemphasize obedience to God's law which results in a lack of understanding of the totality of grace. Other churches emphasize grace without an emphasis on obedience which results in weak discipleship. The same danger applies to adolescent development. Emphasizing freedom over boundaries creates an imbalanced environment in which the adolescent's personal autonomy, not their character and virtue formation, is prized. Conversely, setting and enforcing boundaries without a respect for adolescent freedom fosters an authoritarian environment where compliance is often underscored by resentment.

Balance between these variables is particularly important during the adolescent stage. Problems can be created by an overemphasis in either direction. Emphasizing agency and autonomy over boundaries carries risk for those in this developmental stage for two reasons. First, we cannot trust that adolescents have developed the wisdom to make healthy independent choices. The high stakes nature of adolescent decisions, coupled with their inexperience, implies the need for healthy limits around the young person. In most cases, they simply have not had enough experiences to draw upon in making current decisions. With good adult modeling and instruction, adolescents are certainly capable of making wise and beneficial decisions. To varying degrees, adolescents may display mature cognitive functioning such as self-regulation and logical thinking that facilitate good choices. But even in cases such as these, limitations at some level are still needed due to the adolescent's lack of experience.

Secondly, adolescents need boundaries not only for their protection, but also for their formation. It is critical that they learn submission to boundaries, not only as young children, but also at this stage of life. Submitting to something or someone beyond themselves lays the important groundwork for healthy submission to God and other people. Too much emphasis on freedom can nurture selfishness as one's own desires are prioritized above all other demands. We are all predisposed to self-centered decisions, those that revolve around our own sense of what is best for us. Healthy limits, in other words, contribute to the development of young people whose worlds do not entirely revolve around the fulfillment of their own desires and wishes.

From the other side, emphasizing boundaries over freedom creates a restrictive and unhealthy developmental environment. Adolescents grow from making decisions. The learning they gain from experiences creates templates for future decision-making. Making independent decisions also facilitates growth in self-confidence, self-efficacy, and understanding about how the world works. Adolescents need the space to make choices because this facilitates growth in the psychological and cognitive areas that support good decision-making (Roehlkepartain, Pekel, Syvertsen, Sethi, Sullivan, & Scales, 2017). This is critical preparation for the future when they will be routinely making more independent decisions.

As indicated earlier, restricting agency can produce anger and resentment within adolescents. For many young people, the strength of these emotions can trigger internalizing and/or externalizing responses (Buschgens, van Aken, Swinkels, Ormel, Verhulst, & Buitelaar 2010; Galambos, Barker, & Almeida, 2003). Acting-out behaviors may result where adolescents forcefully push against restrictions. Withdrawal can also occur as young people feel so disheartened by boundaries that they internalize their negative emotions in order to cope. A friend who is an adolescent psychotherapist describes withdrawal as "making one's self smaller" in order to survive. Some adolescents do not have the temperament for rebellion, but will try to survive a harsh or overly restrictive home environment by "disappearing into the woodwork." Both internalizing and externalizing responses, or some combination of each, are problematic for adolescents. In these cases, actions become the means of expressing emotions. Adopting such patterns not only produces serious consequences in the present, they often create problematic lifelong patterns of coping.

A large body of research has looked at authoritative, permissive, and authoritarian parenting styles over time (Baumrind, 1991, 1996). The findings, which overwhelmingly favor an authoritative style that balances freedom and boundaries, provide further support for the balance of agency and boundaries. Adolescents need freedom, but they do not flourish under conditions of unbridled freedom. Conversely, they need boundaries, but do not flourish under boundaries that extinguish autonomy and decision-making.

It is important to additionally state that adolescents benefit most from boundaries that are undergirded by love. These types of boundaries have a distinct quality. They are oriented for the formation and protection of the young person more than the parent or institution's need for control. They are oriented more "for" something, the well-being of the adolescent, than "against" something, danger in the world. This does imply that adolescents will always welcome boundaries given in love, but they are typically better received than those given for other reasons.

A balance of agency and boundaries is important for all of us, but particularly for adolescents. To flourish developmentally, teenagers need room to make independent decisions as well as boundaries to limit those decisions. They are growing in decision-making abilities and in their understanding of the world, yet still require the guidance and protection of caring adults. A healthy combination of both elements encourages the formation of young people who can make thoughtful independent decisions that take others into account. This provides the groundwork for what we hope to nurture in adolescents—a life characterized by freedom within boundaries.

It Feels Warm in Here

The second point about adolescence relates to the nature of contexts that encourage development in the right direction. We focus on a descriptive factor that applies broadly to adolescent development—the *level of warmth* within their various relationships and environments. Suggesting that contexts, particularly home environments, should be warm may seem obvious to Christians in social work. Warmth implies unconditional love and positivity, factors that feel instinctively right when it comes to successful relationships. There may be facets of "warmth," however, that have not been given enough attention. Warmth, after all, is a quality that can be nurtured anywhere, at any time, and requires no particular intelligence level or material resources.

First, we need to define "warm" relationships and environments. One author describes warm relationships as those that include "attentive listening and a mutual sharing of lives and life stories. . . an openness of heart, a willingness to make one's life visible to others, and a generosity of time and resources" (Pohl, 1999, p. 13). Warmth additionally entails the degree to which the adolescent feels loved and accepted. This characteristic has been measured in research studies by questions about how often the other person listens to the teen's point of view and how often they help the teen with important issues (Hoskins, 2014; Maccoby and Martin, 1983). In one large study looking at churches that were ministering to adolescents, "warmth" was the top quality identified by adolescents when asked about a church where they would voluntarily chose to stay involved. The adolescents defined a warm church as one that was "welcoming, accepting, authentic, hospitable, and caring" (Powell, Mulder, Griffin, 2016). The teens frequently used the metaphor of "like family" to describe the relationships and ethos of warm churches.

Warm parenting is often contrasted in the research literature with harsh parenting (Cicchetti & Toth, 2005; sarıta atalar, Dilek, Grusec & Gencoz, 2013). Warm parenting is characterized by verbal approval, demonstrations of tenderness, and expression of support, while harsh parenting entails clear disapproval, inconsistent behavior, and the frequent expression of negative emotions, including anger and hostility (Tuttle, Knudson-Martin, & Kim, 2012). Descriptions of warm parents also focus on affect and describe those parents as being able to openly and frequently express affection for their children (Pekel, Roehlkepartain, Syvertsen, & Scales, 2015). Such parents are additionally interested in their children's activities, excited about their accomplishments, and empathic when their children encounter struggle.

As we might expect, warm parenting is correlated with a long list of desirable adolescent outcomes including academic motivation, socio-emotional skills, responsibility, avoidance of high-risk behaviors, making and keeping plans, and finding purpose in life (Roehlkepartain, Pekel, Syvertsen, Sethi, Sullivan, & Scales, 2017). In one interesting study of parenting styles and early adolescent brain development, a warm parenting style was shown to contribute to structural growth in the amygdala and prefrontal cortex—areas of the brain linked to emotional regulation and cognitive functioning (Whittle et al., 2014).

In sum, warm relationships—whether with parents, teachers, youth workers, or other adults (Benson, 2010)—are characterized by a posture of listening and the demonstration of authentic interest. A clear component of warm relationships also includes the ability to respond appropriately and consistently to one's own emotions, even when displeased by the adolescent's behavior. A warm relationship is characterized by positive verbal affirmation and clear and consistent displays of care, compassion, and love (Caughlin & Huston, 2010).

Warm relationships are beneficial in general, but why are they particularly important for adolescents? The answer relates to the primary developmental tasks undertaken during adolescence. One of the chief tasks of adolescence famously identified by theorist, Erik Erikson (1963), was identity development. Erikson believed that one of the primary goals of the stage was determining who one is in relationship to others and the wider world. Erikson's theory has been expanded upon by a research team who summarized the developmental tasks of adolescence in three questions: who am I (identity), where do I fit (belonging), and what difference do I make (purpose) (Powell, Mulder, & Griffin, 2016).

How do the questions of adolescence relate to a warm environment? To use a scientific metaphor, warm environments create the right laboratory conditions for these questions to be successfully wrestled with and responded to during this time period. If exploring and solidifying identity ("who am I?") is a primary task of this stage, warm environments provide the context for tipping fragile identities in a positive direction. In other words, if the external environments of the adolescent affirm them as individuals inherently worth loving and being heard, the teen will be far more inclined to eventually adopt healthy self-acceptance. When the identity question is consistently answered through relationships that indicate "someone worth loving," the potential for the teen adopting a positive view of themselves increases greatly. It is key that a warm environment that communicates unconditional love persists even when the child makes poor decisions. In this way, a warm environment mirrors grace— undeserved favor despite one's behavior. There may be no greater gift we can give young people than the gift of warm, unconditionally loving relationships that incarnate grace. We all need warm relationships, but those in the midst of identity formation particularly benefit from a context of unconditional love and grace.

The belonging question, "where do I fit," is also best answered in the context of warm environments and relationships. Warm relationships answer the belonging question with a resounding, "with us, that's where!" Such relationships communicate belonging and safety even when teens are in an atmosphere of hostility. A warm relationship with a teacher, for example, in the midst of a difficult school environment can represent a safe place for a struggling adolescent (Center for Promise, 2015). Perhaps, like me, you have had the blessing of having one caring adult relationship during your adolescence that served to reinforce your worth and provide a sense of hope for the future. Throughout my years as an adolescent psychotherapist, I heard testimony after testimony about the transformative power of warm and timely relationships.

The psychological safety that comes from warm parenting or other adult relationships gives adolescents a "home base" from which to address hostile external environments (Laursen & Collins, 2009; National Scientific Council on the Developing Child, 2015). If an adolescent knows they can return to a safe home base, they are better equipped to address questions of belonging in other contexts of their lives. Ultimately, we all carry an innate sense of longing for our Creator and we want adolescents to find their "home base" there. While warm relationships do not ensure this outcome (nor does their absence preclude it), they create healthy structures within the adolescent, including self-acceptance and a sense of belonging that can facilitate future openness toward God and other people.

The third major question relates to purpose ("what difference do I make?"). Warm environments allow adolescents to explore their many questions related to purpose. These include questions about vocation, areas of giftedness and interest, and areas of present and future service. This area also includes questions about spirituality and faith. A warm environment enables the adolescent—whatever their communication style, temperament, or personality—to deeply explore their potential interests and callings.

Being known by another person is helpful in understanding one's self. A significant part of understanding one's purpose is learning about one's areas of interests and giftedness, a process supported by close and loving relationships. For some young people, self-insight is minimal as they regularly withhold, or distance themselves from, their thoughts and feelings. Warm relationships help adolescents to gain self-insight by providing reflections from the outside. They also allow for healthy experimentation as adolescents may try various activities in pursuit of their purpose. When relationships lack warmth, however, a sense of safety is absent and the potential for their healthy self-exploration by the adolescent can be thwarted.

It is important to note that while warm environments properly assist adolescents with these important questions, hostile or cold environments frequently shut down exploration. In these cases, adolescents will look to other sources for answers to their deep questions including peers, school, and media. While this is expected to some degree, unfortunately these sources often provide false answers to the adolescent's deep questions. Revised accounts of the good life are substituted for true flourishing. Indeed, the ways that sources of media answer questions about who they are and where they belong often steer young people in harmful directions. All adolescents are susceptible to the counterfeit messages of the good life offered by broader culture, but warm relationships help to steer adolescents toward the right answers to their questions.

With these observations in mind, let us return to the case of Jamiyah and her family.

Jamiyah Revisited

Jamiyah displays many strengths, but there are also numerous concerns related to her current situation. Her personal strengths include her athleticism and sports involvement, her academic aptitude, artistic ability, and the presence of friends in her life. The relationship with her older brothers has historically been strong, another positive factor in her life. Jamiyah has made the deliberate choice to stay away from drugs which is also highly positive, especially in light of the modeling from her older brothers.

When we evaluate Jamiyah's environment in terms of agency and boundaries, we note an environment that is dominated by agency, but not balanced by healthy expectations or boundaries. A permissive style of parenting—largely the result of her mother's current physical and mental health—is in place which permits Jamiyah to make her own choices about things like homework, curfew, and sexual activity. While she is making some healthy decisions such as choosing to be involved in sports and avoiding drugs, Jamiyah also makes decisions that may prove harmful to her in the long-term. Her avoidance of school work, for example, will likely limit her academic and vocational choices in the future.

Jamiyah's frequent and heavy drinking, particularly in the homes of strangers, places her at significant risk for alcohol-related injuries, as well as crimes such as sexual assault. There are numerous risks present as she is a young woman who is drinking late at night in a dangerous neighborhood. The choice to be sexually active is not surprising as it is a normal expectation within her environment, but it also has potential for future harm. As is the case with other adolescents, sexual activity outside of marriage initiates a physical relationship without the commitment or psychological maturity to sustain it.

At this point, Jamiyah needs not only boundaries, but higher expectations. She needs someone to *expect* more from her, someone to identify her gifts and abilities and to encourage her to explore them. Her two brothers try to encourage her, but Jamiyah clearly needs more adult involvement in her life. Because of the circumstances, Jamiyah has far too much agency, more than her maturity and level of judgement can handle. In terms of the future, she is making decisions regarding school work and the future that may have long-term implications. Because she is not being held to higher expectations, Jamiyah accepts mediocrity in areas of her life and is unmotivated to explore her God-given gifts and potential.

As mentioned previously, true agency also entails the belief that one's actions impact the future. In this respect, Jamiyah seems to be lacking in true agency. There is a disconnect between her present actions and her belief that they are connected to her future. This is due in part to feelings of depression and hopelessness, but also may be the product of scarcity in her adult relationships. For adolescents, these connections come partly through the influence of adults who both model this type of agency and guide adolescents in this process.

The lack of boundaries is additionally problematic because in addition to heavy drinking, an externalizing behavior, Jamiyah is also internalizing her emotions, an approach that will not serve her well in the future. Unsurprisingly, she has anger at her absent father, but is not verbalizing or acknowledging her emotions in a healthy manner. She has adopted a pattern of withdrawal as she is internalizing feelings of depression, hopelessness, anger, and guilt. This is noteworthy because an ongoing pattern of internalizing her negative emotions will likely only result in more depression or more drinking.

There are concerns related to Jamiyah's relationships. While there are some relationships in her life, there are also gaps that potentially affect her development. The first relates to her father. On one hand, while her father's absence has prevented Jamiyah from a potentially inconsistent and painful paternal relationship, on the other hand she lacks the nurture and support that could come from a relationship with her father.

The absence of her father might be offset by her relationship with her mother, but there are many weaknesses present in this relationship also. Jacquie's depression and her disillusionment with parenting, both of which appear to have been present for some time, have created emotional neglect toward her daughter. This has not been the case always, however, as there is positive mother-daughter history. While the current situation is not based on a core lack of concern for her daughter, Jacquie is not functionally active in Jamiyah's life. This means that despite the vulnerability of adolescence, Jamiyah has nearly no parental involvement in her life.

At this point, Jacquie's own mental and physical health are an additional concern. She is able to complete her job responsibilities, but is clearly suffering in many ways. Her social isolation and the guilt and hopelessness she feels as a mother only place her at risk for increased depression if she does not receive assistance.

As we have discussed in previous chapters, the lack of parental connection can contribute to many problems in Jamiyah's development. Warm parental relationships potentially facilitate confidence, identity formation, and self-understanding. The lack of parental involvement leaves Jamiyah vulnerable when answering big questions about identity, purpose, and belonging. This seems to be reflected in her ambivalence about her future, her many short-term boyfriends, and her lack of academic motivation. Outside of the sense of belonging Jamiyah experiences in sports, she seems to be floundering. Additionally, Jamiyah lacks warm relationships with other adults who might fill some of the gaps in her life. There is no church, extended family, or social service involvement to supplement the relational gaps in her life.

As Christians in social work, these relational gaps garner our attention because Jamiyah needs to be surrounded by warm relationships in which she is encouraged to discover herself and to grow. Jamiyah needs her mother and other caring adults to affirm her gifts and potential, and most importantly, to communicate that she is worthy of love. The lack of these items is concerning because the future hope is that Jamiyah will see herself as beloved by God.

The lack of affirming relationships, not to mention the lack of a father and the inattention of her mother, likely play a role in Jamiyah's decisions related to dating and sexual involvement. Dating relationships are typical places for adolescents to find affirmation and a sense of belonging. While it may not be unhealthy for her to be dating at her age, the lack of parental input and supervision mean that Jamiyah's decisions are not life-giving and ultimately may cause her additional problems.

Finally, we will revisit the three questions of adolescence—identity, purpose, and belonging—in Jamiyah's life. While we do not know exactly how she would currently answer these questions, Jamiyah's life in the present lacks the structures to answer her identity and belonging needs in healthy ways. She identifies a sense of belonging in sports, which is positive, but she needs to experience belonging in other healthy places as well. While she does not need to know her specific future plans, Jamiyah is floundering, lacking even minimal direction for her future. What is worrisome is not that she is rooted in the present, but that she doesn't seem to have a vision of what her future could entail. At this point, we can also reasonably conclude that Jamiyah is searching, but lacks a strong sense of identity. While many adolescents share her search to define themselves and to feel a sense of belonging, Jamiyah lacks relationships that will direct her toward positive answers to these questions. She looks to romantic relationships to define herself, but already finds these to be unsatisfying.

The role of Christians in social work is intervening in ways that facilitate positive and hopeful developmental pathways for adolescents like Jamiyah who are loaded with potential, yet need help to flourish beyond their current circumstances. Jamiyah is not being solidly pointed in the direction of the *telos* for which she was created. There is hope for Jamiyah's healthy growth toward God and others, but changes are needed in order for her to develop in the right direction. Her key means of developing well—the relationships around her—lack the consistency, warmth, and affirmation she needs to experience the world as reliable and emotionally safe. Jamiyah also desperately needs engagement, attention, and boundaries from her mother. Because she is hardwired to survive, Jamiyah will continue to find ways to adapt to her environment, but those are already taking maladaptive forms as she is dangerously internalizing her emotions as well as engaging in externalizing behaviors.

Chapter Summary

Adolescence is an exciting stage when identity formation takes center stage and young people begin to form their own beliefs about themselves and the world. It is also a stage of developmental vulnerability as young people attempt to answer deep questions about their purpose and identity. The culture around them answers their questions with an attractive vision of life that ultimately lacks the ability to satisfy their deepest needs. For example, self-centered freedom is valued over mutually submissive relationships. To weather this challenging cultural terrain, adolescents need warm relationships with loving and grace-filled adults who respect their need for freedom and boundaries and direct their development in the right direction.

Discussion Questions

1. Identify some characteristics of harsh parenting and warm parenting. Now think about factors that influence parents to adopt one general style over the other.

2. Think about adolescents who have a weak sense of agency or internal locus of control. What interventions may specifically target this struggle by empowering young people?

3. How does contemporary North American culture define the good life for adolescents?

4. If you were working with Jamiyah and her family, what would be your primary goals? Identify the rationale for your approach.

5. In 2-3 sentences, identify a telos or purpose for Jamiyah's development.

References

Bandura, A. (2008). An agentic perspective on positive psychology. In S.J. Lopez (Ed.), *Positive psychology: Exploring the best in people* (pp. 167-196). Westport, CT: Praeger Publishers/Greenwood Publishing Group.

Barker, C. (2005). *Cultural studies: Theory and practice.* London: Sage.

Baumrind, D. (1991). Effective parenting during the early adolescent transition. In P.A. Cowen & H. Hetherington (Eds.). *Family transitions* (pp. 111-164). Hillsdale, NJ: Eribaum.

Baumrind, D. (1996). The discipline controversy revisited. *Family Relations, 45,* 405–414.

Benson, P. L. (2010). *Parent, teacher, mentor, friend: How every adult can change kids' lives.* Minneapolis, MN: Search Institute.

Buschgens, C.J., Swinkels S.H., Ormel J., Verhulst, F.C., Buitelaar, J.K. (2010). Externalizing behaviors in preadolescents: Familial risk to externalizing behaviors and perceived parenting styles. *European Child Adolescent Psychiatry, 19,* 567-575.

Caughlin, J. P., & Huston, T. L. (2010). The flourishing literature on flourishing relationships. *Journal of Family Theory & Review, 2,* 25–35.

Center for Promise (2015). *Don't quit on me: What young people who left school say about the power of relationships.* Washington, DC: America's Promise Alliance.

Cicchetti, D., & Toth, S. L. (2005). Child maltreatment. *Annual Review of Clinical Psychology, 1,* 409–438.

Deci, E.L. & Ryan, R.M. (2012). Self-determination theory. In P.A.M. Van Lange, A.W. Kruglanski, & E.T. Higgins (Eds.). *Handbook of theories of social psychology* (pp. 416-437). Thousand Oaks, CA: Sage.

Erikson, E.H. (1963). *Childhood and society* (2nd ed.). New York: W.W. Norton and Company.

Galambos, N.L., Barker, E.T., & Almeida, D.M. (2003). Parents *do* matter: Trajectories of change in externalizing and internalizing problems in early adolescence. *Child Development, 74,* 578-594.

Giddens, A. (1979). *Central problems in social theory.* London: Palgrave.Hoskins, D.H. (2014). Consequences of parenting on adolescent outcomes, *Societies, 4,* 506–531.

Jackson, L.E., & Coursey, R.D. (1988). The relationship of god control and internal locus of control to intrinsic religious motivation, coping, and purpose in life. *Journal for the Scientific Study of Religion, 27*, 399-410.

Laursen, B., & Collins, W. A. (2009). Parent-child relationships during adolescence. In R. M. Lerner & L. Steinberg (Eds.), *Handbook of adolescent psychology: Vol. 2: Contextual influences on adolescent development* (pp. 3–16). Hoboken, NJ: Wiley.

Maccoby, E.E. & Martin, J.A. (1983). Socialization in the context of the family: Parent-child interaction. In P.H. Mussen (Ed.), *Handbook of Child Psychology* (pp. 1-103). New York: Wiley.

National Scientific Council on the Developing Child (2015). Supportive relationships and active skill-building strengthen the foundations of resilience (Working Paper 13). Cambridge, MA: Center on the Developing Child at Harvard University. Retrieved from www.developingchild.harvard.edu.

Pekel, K., Roehlkepartain, E. C., Syvertsen, A. K., & Scales, P. C. (2015). *Don't forget the families: The missing piece in America's effort to help all children succeed.* Minneapolis, MN: Search Institute. Retrieved from www.search-institute.org/dff.

Pohl, C.D. (1999). *Making room: Recovering hospitality as a christian tradition.* Grand Rapids, MI: Eerdmans.

Powell, K., Mulder, J., Griffin, B.M. (2016). *Growing young.* Grand Rapids, MI: Baker Publishing Group.

Roehlkepartain, E. C., Syvertsen, A. K., & Wu, C.-Y. (2017). *A snapshot of developmental relationships between parents and youth.* Minneapolis, MN: Search Institute.

Roehlkepartain, E.C., Pekel, K., Syvertsen, A. K., Sethi, J., Sullivan, T. K., & Scales, P. C.(2017). *Relationships first: Creating connections that help young people thrive.* Minneapolis, MN: Search Institute.

Sarıta, D., Grusec, J.E., & Gencoz, T. (2013). Warm and harsh parenting as mediators of the relation between maternal and adolescent emotion regulation. *Journal of Adolescence. 36*, 1093-2101.

Tuttle, A., Knudson-Martin, C., & Kim, L. (2012). Parenting as relationship: A framework for assessment and practice. *Family Process, 51*, 73-89.

Watts, R. & Guessous, O. (2006). Sociopolitical development: The missing link in research and policy on adolescents. In S. Ginwright, P. Noguera, & J. Cammarota (Eds.), *Beyond resistance! Youth activism and community change* (pp. 59-80). New York: Routledge.

Whittle, S., Simmons, J.G., Dennison, M., Vijayakumar, N., Schwartz, O., Yap, M.B., Sheeber, L., & Allen, N.B. (2014). Positive parenting predicts the development of adolescent brain structure: A longitudinal study. *Developmental Cognitive Neuroscience, 8*, 7-17.

Yale Center for Faith and Culture (2018). *Adolescent faith and flourishing.* Retrieved from https://faith.yale.edu/adolescent-faith-flourishing/adolescent-faith-flourishing.

Chapter Ten

Emerging Adulthood: Feeling In-Between

I'm not lost for I know where I am. But however, where I am may be lost.

A.A. Milne *from* Winnie-the-Pooh

Winnie-the-Pooh captures the emotions that often accompany the next stage of life—feeling slightly lost, even though you are moving in a particular direction. Emerging adults may be doing what they are "supposed to" by attending college, getting a job, or "settling down." Yet they often lack a sense of the big picture and the trajectory of their future. Concrete plans and preparation may be undertaken, but the end goal can be frustratingly fuzzy. Despite the challenges they face, as an undergraduate college professor, I can testify that emerging adults are remarkably creative and engaging persons who enrich my life greatly.

We continue our study of the lifespan by exploring emerging adulthood, a formative life stage situated between the early and middle adolescent years and "full" adult years. A term first coined by researcher, Jeffrey Arnett (2000), *emerging adulthood* has become widely used in North American culture as the particular tasks and challenges of this stage have become more clear. Importantly, Arnett (1994, 2015) has identified the emerging adulthood stage as characterized by five dynamics: identity exploration, instability, self-focus, feeling in-between, and possibility. When emerging adults were asked about the events that would signify them as adults, they identified three things: accepting personality responsibility, making decisions apart from other influences, and financial independence from parents. Many scholars now believe that, during the past few decades, emerging adulthood has surfaced as a separate developmental stage in response to cultural changes, especially social and economic factors (Brown, 2006; Bynner, 2005; Swanson, 2016).

Similar to adolescence a century ago, cultural shifts impact the way we experience human development. In the case of emerging adults, the developmental markers that historically signified one's launch into "adulthood" have been delayed, creating a need to look specifically at the needs and realities of this newly formed group. Many social and economic changes in recent decades have contributed to the formation of this distinct life stage. Good-paying industrial or agricultural jobs that previously required little or no higher education have largely disappeared from the current work force and economy. Technical schools remain good options for many young adults, but are increasingly selective and expensive. More professions require graduate education, some necessitating many years of costly schooling. This means that many more young adults are students, often for long periods of time. The dramatic rise in college costs has also markedly increased student debt, making it difficult for many emerging adults to afford living independently of their families (National Center for Education Statistics, 2017). The average age of marriage has also been delayed to the late twenties (U.S. Census Bureau, 2018; Vespa, 2017). This means that some of the "settling down" and responsibilities that are historically initiated by marriage have also been delayed (Arnett, Zukauskiene, & Sugimura, 2014).

Like all age groups, emerging adults are highly diverse and, therefore, cannot be easily summarized or described. While many of the struggles identified by emerging adults persist across socioeconomic classes (Arnett, 2016), the group remains complex in multiple ways. Their cultural backgrounds, hopes and dreams, religious beliefs, and approaches to friendships and vocation vary. Some will marry young and others will choose not to marry, favoring cohabitation or singleness instead. Some will attend technical school or community college, beginning their work lives at relatively young ages while others will not finish advanced training for their vocation until their late twenties or early thirties. Some will not attend college, entering the work force directly after high school. Our goal is to explore factors that pertain broadly to emerging adults while acknowledging that innumerable individual particularities exist.

Our specific emphasis remains on developing emerging adults in the direction of healthy connections with God and other people. The process becomes more specific during this stage as emerging adults process and respond to the world around them in increasingly sophisticated ways. Relationships become more complex and identity exploration and solidification continues.

We will illustrate a way of viewing emerging adulthood by examining the case of Robert and exploring some fundamental aspects of this time period.

The Case of Robert

Robert is a 26-year old White male who lives in an urban neighborhood in Los Angeles. Robert is the only child born to his parents, Kala (51) and Michael (53). His parents had a brief romantic relationship when Robert was born, but have not been together for many years. Kala and Michael met through a mutual friend and both live in the same neighborhood where they were raised. Robert lived with his single mother throughout his growing up years. They currently live together in the small home she purchased many years ago. Michael moved around when Robert was young, living with friends at times and renting apartments on his own at other times. The family's working class neighborhood, once safe and thriving, has unfortunately declined in recent years. Crime rates are now high. Several gangs are present and drug dealing is commonplace, despite heavy police presence.

Robert is highly gifted intellectually, a reality which became clear to his parents and teachers early in his life. He began speaking and reading at an early age and, throughout his childhood, demonstrated a keen interest in learning and a nagging desire to "figure things out," whether scientifically, mechanically, or interpersonally. Recognizing his potential early, Kala strictly limited Robert's exposure to TV and video games, supplying him with a steady stream of library books instead. Throughout his childhood and adolescence, Robert devoured books from a wide range of subjects, but was especially interested in biology and astronomy.

In his giftedness and inquisitive nature, Robert resembles his father. Though Michael was not formally educated beyond high school, he possesses a deep curiosity about life and a love for learning. Michael is also interpersonally skilled, demonstrating a masterful ability to talk to and make others feel at ease. He has always been generous, offering to help individuals financially and in other ways whenever possible. Despite his intelligence and remarkable ability to make and nurture friendships, however, Michael's lack of education made it difficult for him to succeed vocationally. He held intermittent jobs over the years, but was more often unemployed, at times relying on "hustling" or drug dealing to support himself. Michael is well-known and loved in the neighborhood for his generosity and "big" personality.

Kala is a hardworking, stern woman with high expectations of herself and those around her, particularly her son. While she is not emotionally warm toward others or as a mother, she is a highly driven and strong-willed person. Kala has been employed since before Robert's birth at a local nursing home where she supervises the food service. Her pay and benefits are low, but the job is steady and predictable and she excels in it. Kala has few friends or connections with her extended family. Most of her life has been focused on her job and parenting her son. Because she recognized Robert's potential early in his life, she has always had high academic standards for him, insisting on good grades.

Also recognizing that Robert benefited from interaction with his father, both intellectually and emotionally, Kala has always been supportive of their relationship. Kala and Michael are friendly and caring toward one another despite the fact that Michael has not consistently provided child support. Although his role modeling has not always been positive, Michael is a loving father who maintains a close relationship with his son. He has always hoped that Robert would take advantage of his gifts in ways that Michael never could. He stopped by the home two or three times per week during Michael's early years to help with homework and "hang out" with his son.

Despite its strain on her income and Michael's inconsistent financial support, Kala sent Robert to a private Catholic school from first grade on. Robert received a significantly better education at this school than he would have in the local public school. He benefited in this setting from the academic rigor and the nurture of numerous caring priests and teachers. Robert excelled academically and in sports—football and basketball—throughout his schooling years.

The defining event of Robert's life, however, occurred when he was seven years old. To the family and neighborhood's astonishment, one night Michael was arrested and accused of murdering two young women from the neighborhood. A witness tied Michael to the shooting, the by-product of a drug deal gone bad, leading to a highly traumatic period for Robert, Kala, and Michael's many friends in the neighborhood. Although Michael was actually innocent of the crimes, to everyone's horror, he was convicted and sentenced to life in prison. His case was repeatedly appealed and, for many years, the family truly believed the case would be overturned. Despite their hope and belief that justice would prevail and Michael would be released, appeal after appeal have been lost during the past nineteen years.

Michael's incarceration abruptly changed the course of Robert's life as communication with his father instantly became more difficult. Though devastated by the situation, Robert and Kala faithfully visited Michael every weekend, an hour-long bus ride each way. Kala stubbornly refused to let the father-son relationship die, knowing its positive impact on her son's life. Robert and Michael defied odds for several years, maintaining a close relationship in spite of nearly impossible circumstances. Michael even helped Robert with homework during their weekly visits. But over time, physical separation and the time taken up by visits took their toll. By high school, Robert and Kala stopped visiting altogether. It became increasingly difficult for Michael to relate to Robert's life and his interest in "life on the outside" steadily declined. It also became harder for Robert to explain the events of his life. Robert has channeled his hopelessness and frustration into legal efforts, becoming a self-taught legal expert as he continues to research possible avenues for overturning his father's conviction. Despite occasional glimmers of legal hope, however, this has not occurred.

In addition to Robert's academics and sports, he gravitated toward high-risk behavior in high school. He began selling drugs at school and in the neighborhood, flying completely under the radar of school authorities and the police during this time. He was able to manage extensive drug dealing while also excelling in other areas. As a high school senior, Robert received numerous academic and sports awards. While Robert could get into almost any college, most of them were out of reach financially. He fixed his sights on a local state college due to its reasonable tuition costs. During his senior year, however, a multi-millionaire alumni of Robert's school learned of his aptitude and generously pledged to cover tuition costs at any school of his choosing. This expanded Robert's options and, ultimately, he chose to attend Yale University, double majoring in biology and physics.

Robert excelled academically and interpersonally at Yale, but struggled to reconcile the dynamics of his "rough" family background with the economically and socially privileged status of most of his classmates. He made frequent trips home to Los Angeles. Robert made many friends and dated numerous different women during college, but carefully hid the truth about his father's incarceration and the poverty of his upbringing. Early in his college career, struggling to reconcile his past life with his present, he returned to a familiar behavior from high school years and began selling marijuana to his Yale classmates. Despite being high on marijuana most of the time himself, Robert astonishingly rose to the top of his class and graduated from college with honors.

Armed with a prized degree from Yale, Robert's vocational possibilities were endless. Most of his classmates moved into lucrative positions in New York City and internationally. Robert, however, felt a strong emotional tie to Los Angeles and decided to return to his mother's home while determining his next steps after college. Back at home, Robert quickly reconnected with his childhood friends, most of whom were floundering vocationally and abusing and/or selling drugs. Confused about his future and struggling to integrate different "worlds," Robert returned to a familiar pattern three years ago, selling drugs in his old neighborhood and eventually expanding his drug sales beyond the neighborhood.

Despite the urging from his mother and Yale friends to settle down and establish himself in a respectable job, Robert continues to struggle. Meanwhile, he has made large amounts of money through his illegal activities. Robert utilizes his extensive knowledge of chemistry to manufacture a unique brand of marijuana known for its intense and consistent high, a reality that has substantially boosted his reputation, sales, and profits. He gave his mother $20,000 to pay off her mortgage and also bought her a new car. Like his father, he has a generous nature and often uses his income to buy things for friends and to assist others in need. Meanwhile, he continues to live with his mother and spend little money on himself, on some level knowing that money does not motivate him.

While Robert continues to have numerous friendships and romantic relationships, he consistently feels unmoored and uncertain about his purpose or goals in life. He devotes considerable energy and money to his friendships, always giving his friends whatever they need or request. Yet Robert cannot find his own footing in life, despite the gifts of a superior intellect and education. He misses his father, but does not try to reconnect with him. As his illegal activities expand, Robert knows that it is only a matter of time until he is arrested and likely faces jail time, considering the size of his drug operation. Despite these nagging realities, he continues to stumble through life, living mainly in the present and hoping that he does not get caught by the police. His hopelessness toward the future is high, but his own heavy drug use pushes away painful thoughts and feelings. At times, Robert thinks about pursuing a respectable job, but cannot bring himself to follow through with the application process.

Robert has had numerous caring adult relationships over the course of his life, especially from high school teachers and coaches. During his growing up years, throughout Yale, and in the present, he has had a large group of friends and acquaintances. Robert easily attracts women and has dated numerous people, but has kept most of these relationships short-term. Despite his Catholic education, Robert feels no personal connection to Catholicism. He has no problem with religion, but does not see its relevance to his life. Many of the stable adults in Robert's life, including his college benefactor, have distanced from him at this point, feeling that he disappointed them, wasting the precious opportunities he was given.

We will return to the case of Robert after considering some broad aspects of emerging adulthood.

Anxiety

While identity exploration and the sense of possibility continue to be exhilaratingly high during this stage, emerging adulthood can simultaneously be marked by feelings of stress and anxiety. Over half of emerging adults self-identify as anxious (Arnett, 2015; Arnett & Schwab, 2013). While previous generations have certainly faced their share of stressors during this time period, a marked increase in the amount of anxiety experienced by many emerging adults deserves our attention. In other words, the question is less about which generation has faced greater stresses and more about how those stressors are internalized and experienced differently.

As indicated previously in this text, some amount of stress is normal, even productive, but anxiety is another story altogether. Anxiety can contribute to high-risk behaviors, including substance abuse and risky sexual behaviors. In order to manage anxiety, many look to substances or to activities that provide, at least temporarily, respite. Others channel their anxiety into frenetic activity, attempting through performance to alleviate deep-seated fears about their worthiness, talent, intelligence, or ability to be loved and accepted. Neither avoiding anxiety through substance use nor through compensatory behaviors, such as striving for perfectionism, addresses the root issue. They often backfire, in fact, exacerbating the underlying problem.

A rise in emerging adult anxiety has been documented by college counseling centers across the country. Well over half of help-seeking students request assistance with "overwhelming anxiety" (Gallagher, 2015). We might conclude that the anxiety is mainly generated by academic stress because the problem is noted within college students. This seems plausible as the pressure to succeed academically can be high due to expensive college costs and greater competition from peers as more students attend college and graduate school. The problem, however, is similarly noted within emerging adults outside of academia (Blanco et al., 2008), suggesting stressors beyond solely academics.

What aspects of this stage of life or the surrounding culture trigger anxiety? A number of theories have been offered. Some point to familial factors, such as parental over-involvement in the lives of their children, which stifles young adult self-confidence and self-efficacy (Bradley-Geist, & Olson-Buchanan, 2014). Also related to parenting, some believe that emerging adults lack resiliency— the ability to grow from adversity— leading them to be easily overwhelmed by stressors. Some conclude that emerging adult anxiety is a response to longstanding problems which have increased over time (or are more readily identified), such as childhood neglect. Neglect, for example, increases overall anxiety as individuals internalize and have to manage the fear of rejection (Bifulco & Thomas, 2012; Schimmenti & Bifulco, 2015).

Some point to economic factors, such as high college costs, which contribute to internal and external pressure to perform in order to make college a "worthwhile investment." A flat labor market in many places has created stiff competition for jobs, again stimulating performance anxiety. Others point to relational stressors during emerging adulthood. Still others draw our attention to the ambivalence in romantic relationships during emerging adulthood as a source of anxiety (Halpern-Meekin, Manning, Giordano, & Longmore, 2013). Finally, social media have been shown to increase emerging adult anxiety. For some young adults, a fragile sense of self can lead them to make constant social comparisons, perpetually feeling inferior (Chen & Lee, 2013; Chou & Edge, 2012; Nesi and Prinstein, 2015).

Each of the theories mentioned are supported by empirical evidence, but most studies in this area explore relationships and not causes. It is difficult to pinpoint the causes of emerging adult anxiety, as individuals vary in terms of the things that are stressful for them. Some do not find academics anxiety-producing, but find other areas such as romantic or family relationships highly stressful. Others are highly stressed by academics, weighted by internal and external pressure to achieve.

If we cannot identify exact causes, what can we say about anxiety among emerging adults besides that it is common and risky? A one-two punch during emerging adulthood may explain the anxiety. One, identity formation is front-and-center. Although Erikson (1963) identified identity formation as the task of adolescence, scholars now believe the greater portion of identity work happens during emerging adulthood (Arnett, 2015). Two, the traditional roles of adulthood that defined people's identity, for example as a "wife," have been delayed. So the combination of the need to define one's self without the support of traditional roles equals anxiety and the feeling of being in-between.

The struggle to determine one's identity is compounded by the enormous range of choices available to emerging adults. Emerging adulthood has been described as a "shopping period in which to discern what life style best fits a young person's desired adult lifestyle" (McMillan, 2017, p. 5). Shopping implies shelves and shelves of attractive choices and the freedom to choose whatever one wants. In a previous chapter, however, we discussed the need for agency within boundaries. Too many options overwhelm. The range of options available to emerging adults, while gloriously broad, can also trigger anxiety. Many resist committing to things, fearing mistakes that limit their future options.

The problem is that not committing makes the anxiety worse. Commitment to things such as jobs, college majors, relationships, and/or religious belief systems actually *lowers* anxiety (Hardy et al., 2013). In other words, it is important for emerging adults to form commitments along the way because these help to define their identity. They learn about themselves through commitments, even those that alter the directions they thought they were moving. For example, one of my students who recently transferred her major to social work described a difficult past year of taking college courses without a sense of direction. This led her to feel unmotivated academically and highly anxious, uncertain that she would ever find an area of study that fit her.

The practical implications for Christians in social work serving emerging adults are multiple. First, we must not minimize the anxiety of young adults or imply that it represents individual or generational weakness. A better explanation for the problem relates to timing; they are piecing together an identity at the same time that cultural and economic realities make that more challenging. As in every case, compassion and careful listening, not judgement, are needed to understand the core struggles of each individual.

Secondly, it is clear that individuals who can make solid decisions and commitments during this stage feel more positive and hopeful. Helping young adults to sort through their decisions carefully while also diffusing the need to make "perfect" decisions is important. Moving forward with what one understands at the present is important to clarity in the future. Conceptualizing this stage as a journey that involves exciting opportunities as well as disappointments and false starts is also helpful. At times, as practitioners, we are also responsible for challenging destructive habits, such as heavy alcohol use and sexual promiscuity. The goal is never to shame, but to assist young adults in seeing how such behaviors are counterproductive and destructive to their well-being.

Thirdly, we serve emerging adults well when we encourage them to make *healthy* identity commitments. Broader culture encourages young adults to pursue goals that are not ultimately life-giving such as earning and stockpiling large amounts of money, engaging as much recreational activity as possible, or dating as many people as possible before settling down in marriage. As Christians in social work, part of our responsibility is not just challenging faulty cultural perceptions, but pointing young people in the direction of true flourishing. This means, for example, encouraging service in civic institutions such as religious or secular non-profit organizations (King & Merola, 2017); encouraging dating relationships that encompass the whole person, not just casual physical relationships.

Those who locate sources of identity outside of things like vocation, finding a mate, or making money will fare considerably better during this stage (Nelson & Padilla-Walker, 2013). But this is not surprising as development in the right direction points beyond immediate gratification and self-centered pursuits in search of something far larger and richer.

A Morality of Self-Fulfillment

We need to briefly pause and consider the nature of the broader culture in which emerging adults are developing. Many writers and theologians have described contemporary American culture as "post-Christian," implying that while some may argue that the country was founded on Judeo-Christian principles, secularization is now its guiding force. For many years, Christian principles were the moral foundation for fundamental aspects of American culture, including its laws and policies. But if Christian moral roots have been uprooted, then we must ponder what has grown in their place.

Morality in early America was originally based on the objective moral authority of the Bible, but shifted over time toward universally agreed upon moral laws. The late twentieth century, however, brought further movement away from biblical absolutes as morality took on a therapeutic nature, largely driven by one's personal preferences. Morality became individualized, based on each person's likes and dislikes. Governed not primarily by external expectations, but by one's own inclinations and feelings, individual choices took center stage. Setran and Kiesling (2013) write of this shift that, "moral individualism is related to the 'thinning' of the communal moral fabric in emerging adulthood" (p. 142). Along with individualized morality came disdain for belief systems that seemingly limit individual choice. Many religious belief systems, including Christianity, are deemed judgmental by emerging adults, perceived as intruding on individual rights and choice-making.

In an effort to explore morality more deeply, Christian Smith and colleagues (2011) conducted detailed interviews with a diverse cross-section of emerging adults. Their findings were sobering. The research team highlighted aspects of contemporary American culture that influence the daily lives of emerging adults, including rampant consumerism, hyper-individualism, and moral relativism. From emerging adults themselves, they noted five major problems: routine intoxication, materialistic life goals, regrettable sexual experiences, disengagement from civic and political life, and confused moral reasoning. If we think of mainstream cultural values as the laboratory in which emerging adults are growing, their practices make sense. They conclude that emerging adults lack the ability to reason about morality because they have not been adequately taught to do so, not by parents or institutions such as schools, colleges, or churches. Certainly not by the culture around them.

In a similar vein, research group Barna Trends, (2017) describes a "morality of self-fulfillment" based on their emerging adult research. Self-fulfillment-driven morality was defined in the following ways: looking within to find one's self, not criticizing others' life choices, enjoying yourself as the highest goal in life, believing whatever you want as long as the beliefs don't negatively impact society, and permitting any sexual expression as long as the persons are consenting adults. Notably, self-identifying Christians responded similarly to the group that did not endorse faith, concluding, "the highest good, according to our society, is finding yourself and then living by what's right for you" (p 53). While Christians were four times more likely to identify moral truth as absolute, the same group endorsed five out of the six guiding principles of the morality of self-fulfillment. It seems that while Christians believe in biblical authority, that belief is disconnected from their lived practices.

What are the practical implications of this research for Christians in social work who interact with emerging adults? First, this research confirms the fact that a telos ordered toward individualism or consumerism represents development in entirely the wrong direction. Neither of these pursuits point toward flourishing, because they violate fundamental aspects of the created order, that we are created to be in loving relationship with God, others, and the world. Individual choices must be contained within boundaries and the material world is not to be idolized, but stewarded. Concerningly, individual morality points persons inward versus pointing them outward toward higher laws that benefit them. Consumerism keeps emerging adults perpetually spinning as accumulation of material goods never satisfies the deep needs of the soul.

Previously in this text, we have discussed the importance of safe and close relationships because they nudge us away from self-centered choices and desires. To maintain loving, communal relationships, our focus must tilt toward others. Further, we do not find ourselves solely by looking within, but by looking to God and other people. The most important role for social workers is forming relationships with young adults that provide moral role models, real-life examples of living wisely, with moral integrity and consistency. A core research finding is moral lostness because morality has not been properly taught at home or in civic institutions. Close, trusting relationships provide opportunities for modeling, not to mention challenge, in areas of emerging adults' lives that are sinful and therefore destructive to them. Loving relationships are not completely driven by consent and support; love also implies truth-telling and challenge. Relationships involving challenge can be tricky with emerging adults who are sensitive to individual freedom and judgmentalism, but nurturing safe relationships enables honest mutual dialogue.

Secondly, while many of our clients are not persons of faith, they can be encouraged to live wisely, to orient their lives toward flourishing. Assisting them in bringing health to their relationships and encouraging them to deeply ponder their choices are important. Many young adults are unconscious cultural participants, not considering the ways they are being shaped and directed by forces outside of themselves. For example, some engage in frequent sexual "hook-ups," more because it is commonly practiced than because they truly endorse the behavior. This also deeply challenges them to consider their character they are forming. Some young adults disconnect their present behaviors from their character or see this life stage as "not counting" as they intend to eventually settle down. This challenge —the reality that all of their choices, including those in the present, have relevance—is highly important.

Thirdly, we often have opportunities to work with families. Encouragingly, research indicates that the majority of emerging adults want to remain connected to their parents (Smith, Christofferson, Davidson, & Herzog, 2011). Despite some media-driven stereotypes, they are not interested in abandoning their families after leaving home. Many parents, however, abdicate responsibility for moral teaching and modeling after adolescence. We ought to empower parents to remain engaged and, at times, to challenge aspects of their young adult's lives. They ought not minimize activities, such as heavy drinking or sexual promiscuity, as normal parts of growing up. Nor should they minimize their influence in their children's lives. In their desire to stay connected with their parents, some emerging adults are actually longing for more (or continued) guidance from their parents. This does not imply the over-parenting represented by parental anxiety, but parents who provide loving, and sometimes painfully honest, guidance and feedback. We are not advocating for parents who control— agency is critical—but a removed, hands-off approach is not helpful either. As we have seen, emerging adults have struggles, and the last thing they need is to be left alone in those struggles.

Finally, a morality of self-fulfillment calls for churches to offer a compelling vision of a better way of living. In its emphasis on the individual over the collective, self-fulfillment morality creates real challenges to engaging emerging adults in church. Many distrust religious institutions as authoritarian and judgmental. On this point, emerging adults honestly describe some outposts of the body of Christ which have been far more focused on behaviors they are against than loving their neighbor. However, Christians in social work ought to take every viable opportunity to connect emerging adults to churches as within, they come into contact with deeply rooted beliefs and traditions that counterbalance the subjective individualized morality of the culture. They are exposed to ancient songs, words, and traditions that draw them toward something far richer and greater than themselves. They learn ways of being in the world that are transcendent, focused on service to God and others, rather than their own fleeting fulfillment.

Let's now return to the case of Robert, considering his situation in light of our observations related to emerging adults.

Robert Revisited

Robert's case illustrates some of the struggles of this life stage. Like many emerging adults, he is struggling with general aspects of emerging adulthood as well as his unique experiences. His case represents not a happy ending, at this point, but someone hurting and floundering. In these respects, he is the complex type of person often seen by social workers. These cases defy easy answers, pushing us to explore many variables.

Despite giftedness and educational opportunities, Robert is floundering. Despite many relationships, Robert feels disconnected. Despite the moral education of his religious schooling, Robert is morally lost. He lacks purpose beyond the meeting of his immediate needs. Ultimately, Robert is unable to transcend the limitations and traumatic events of his upbringing, despite his opportunities educationally and intellectually. At this point, we need to step back and ponder why Robert is developing this direction.

We look first at his family relationships. Robert's strongest attachment historically was to his father. His relationship with his mother as the only physically available parent, while not emotionally rich, also fills a highly important role in his life. Kala has been a steady presence in Robert's life, pushing him toward important goals and modeling faithfulness in her job and mothering. Robert's understanding of his mother's sacrifices for him have created a sense of love and loyalty to her, demonstrated by his desire to help her financially.

The relationship with his father, however, has clearly been fractured by his father's long-term incarceration. This traumatic separation occurred when Robert was just seven years old, before he had the ability to comprehend the complexity of the situation. Despite their visits and attempts to stay connected, such circumstances are difficult for a young boy to understand. Their attachment, once solid, eroded over time. Robert responded to his father's situation by pouring himself into studying and pursuing legal means of getting his father's case reversed. These efforts have been fruitless, however. He has not been able to fix the situation, despite his intellectual talent and hard work. Understandably, Robert has experienced the world as harsh and unjust.

While Robert's parents nurtured his intellectual development, his moral and psychological development were not a strong focus. Kala worked from early in the morning until late at night so Robert was either alone or with peers much of the time. Michael's situation limited his ability to impact Robert's life beyond the emotional support of their weekly visits. Robert was nurtured cognitively, but there is clear evidence of moral immaturity in college as he lived a dual existence with one foot in illegal activity and the other in academia. His current disregard for the law may be the product of his hopelessness. He may not care enough about his future to change his behavior. Related to this, his immoral behavior may be the product of disillusionment. This would be an understandable response to the injustice suffered by his father. It may also be a product of the morality of self-fulfillment, engaging in behaviors that make him feel good and appear, at least to him, harmless to others. We do not see Robert questioning his own illegal behavior or its consequences of his drug sales upon the lives of other people, including his customers, friends, and parents. Though Robert received strong moral instruction at school, this did not alter the course of his behavior as he realized he was easily able to outwit authorities and to sell drugs widely. Likely each of these dynamics has contributed to the breakdown in Robert's moral development.

The lack of moral modeling and guidance play into this case also. Despite the gift of a superior education, he relies upon familiar behaviors and ways of functioning in the world. While Robert's behavior is risky, in some ways, he takes few risks, relying on familiar behaviors to get by. In doing so, however, he exposes himself to the many consequences of his high-risk behavior including promiscuity and drug dealing and manufacturing.

Identity struggles are also evident in Robert's life. Understandably, during college, Robert wrestled with his life in the past and his life in the present. He was never fully able to feel at home at Yale and relied on "old" behaviors as a way of coping with the dissonance. Here we get the sense that Robert does not know who he is or where he truly belongs. He struggles to identify himself and seems lost in each setting.

Related to this, Robert does not have a strong sense of purpose beyond the present. Hopelessness is prevalent and he is unstable psychologically.

He uses drugs to manage his negative emotions, lacking the ability to work through them productively. In addition to moral lostness, Robert displays psychological immaturity. Significant trauma in his life has occurred and he needs help processing the complexity of the ongoing scenario with his father. While it is productive for him to pursue legal maneuvering, it may also be a way of avoiding deep pain related to the situation. Processing his trauma would help Robert to solidify his identity, clarify his purpose going forward, and assist him with future relationships. A related concern entails expectations. They have always been high for Robert, which can be positive, but can also be overwhelming. We get the impression that he is academically prepared for life, but not emotionally or morally prepared.

We also see the influence of cultural philosophies in Robert's life. The morality of self-fulfillment is reflected in his approach to substances and reliance on them to cope and feel good. Avoiding pain is a theme in his life, one that unfortunately moves him away from processes that might free him emotionally. Robert's casual, non-committal attitudes toward sexuality further reflect individualized morality. Finally, the priority of enjoying himself as much as possible, demonstrated by his drug use and sexuality, further contribute to shallow fulfillment.

Robert is not without hope, however. With help understanding his deep-seated emotions, especially hopelessness and anger, and connecting his emotions to his high-risk behaviors, he can change. Immediate changes are needed because his risky behaviors carry life-changing consequences. Fully processing the trauma of his father's imprisonment is central to decreasing his anger and distancing from risky avoidant behaviors. Understanding his relationship with his mother will also be important going forward.

Robert lacks healthy adult role models at this stage in his life, though he has had positive role models in the past. Most of his time is spent with peers who are also struggling and lack ability to speak truth and wisdom into his life. Robert also needs assistance solidifying a highly disjointed identity. He cannot seem to reconcile his potential and strong education with the other parts of his life—his upbringing, his hopes and dreams. Growth in this area would significantly decrease his hopelessness and likely help him to identify positive goals vocationally and relationally going forward. Without assistance, he may remain stuck in immature patterns of functioning that thwart his movement into adulthood.

Finally, while Robert had the benefit of a Catholic education and at least some exposure to religion through it, it was not formative enough to influence him as he moved through college and beyond. His high-risk behaviors suggest a lack of rootedness; he could find solid rooting in a church. Robert has many gifts and a remarkable story. But at this point, he lacks relationships that point his development in the right direction. With some help, however, he could locate goals and purposes that would transcend those currently driving his life.

Chapter Summary

Emerging adulthood is an exciting, formative stage. Young people are setting up their lives, making decisions that impact their lives going forward. Yet it also can be a time of challenge. Contemporary culture forms emerging adults in ways that work against their flourishing, making it necessary for families and churches to instead nurture countercultural ways of being in the world. Emerging adults increasingly feel anxious and they increasingly look to themselves, not authoritative external sources, for moral decisions. Finally, the developmental challenges of this time period intersect with innumerable other unique variables in the lives of young adults. Christians in social work are needed to form honest and trusting relationships, to nurture moral and psychological growth, to point young people toward wise decisions, to challenge sinful or inconsistent behavior, and to empower parents as mentors and guides.

Discussion Questions

1. What examples have you observed of a morality of self-fulfillment in, for example, media usage or dating patterns?

2. If you were working with Robert, what would be your primary treatment goal and why?

3. If you were working with Michael, what would be your primary treatment goal and why?

4. What are advantages of emerging adulthood? How can young adults utilize those advantages in healthy ways?

5. We mentioned the church as an important institution for reconnecting emerging adults with biblical moral authority and creating an alternative vision of the "good life." What obstacles exist to getting emerging adults engaged in church? What ideas do you have for overcoming these obstacles?

*case is based loosely on *The Short and Tragic Life of Robert Peace* by Jeff Hobbs (2014). New York: Scriber.

References

Arnett, J. J. (1994). Are college students adults? Their conceptions of the transition to adulthood. Journal of Adult Development, 1, 154-168

Arnett, J.J. (2000). Emerging adulthood: A theory of development from the late teens through the twenties. *American Psychologist, 55,* 469-480.

Arnett, J. J. (2015). *Emerging adulthood: The winding road from the late teens through the twenties* (2nd ed.). New York: Oxford University Press.

Arnett, J. J. (2016). Does emerging adulthood theory apply across social classes? National data on a persistent question. *Emerging Adulthood, 4,* 227–235.

Arnett, J. J., & Schwab, J. (2013). *The Clark University poll of parents of emerging adults.* Worchester, MA: Clark University.

Arnett, J.J., Zukauskiene, R., & Sugimura, K. (2014). The new life stage of emerging adulthood at ages 18-29 years: Implications for mental health. *Lancet Psychiatry, 1,* 569-576.

Barna Trends (2017). *Barna trends 2018: What's new and what's next at the intersection of faith and culture.* Grand Rapids, MI: Baker Books/Barna Group.

Bifulco, A., & Thomas, G. (2012). *Understanding adult attachment in family relationships: Research, assessment and intervention.* London: Routledge.

Blanco, C., Okuda, M., Wright, C., Hasin, D.S., Grant, B. F., Liu, S.-M., & Olfson, M. (2008).

Mental health of college students and their non-college-attending peers: Results from the National Epidemiologic Study on alcohol and related conditions. *Archives of General Psychiatry, 65,* 1429–1437.

Bradley-Geist, J. C., & Olson-Buchanan, J. B. (2014). Helicopter parents: An examination of the correlates of over-parenting of college students. *Education + Training, 56,* 314-428.

Brown, J. D. (2006). Emerging adults in a media-saturated world. In J. J.Arnett, J. L. Tanner, J. L. (Eds.), *Emerging adults in america: Coming of age in the 21st century* (pp. 279–299). Washington, DC: American Psychological Association.

Bynner, J. (2005). Rethinking the youth phase of the life-course: The case for emerging adulthood? *Journal of Youth Studies, 8,* 367–384.

Chen, W., Lee, K-H. (2013) Sharing, liking, commenting, and distressed? The pathway between facebook interaction and psychological distress. *Cyberpsychology. Behavior. Social Networking, 16,* 728-734.

Chou, H.-T.G., & Edge, N. (2012). They are happier and having better lives than i am: The impact of using Facebook on perceptions of others' lives. *Cyberpsychology, Behavior, Social Networking, 15,* 117-121.

Erikson, E.H. (1963). *Childhood and society* (2nd ed.). New York: W.W. Norton and Company.

Gallagher, R.P. (2015). *National survey of college counseling centers 2014.* Project Report. The International Association of Counseling Services (IACS).

Halpern-Meekin, S., Manning, W. D., Giordano, P. C., & Longmore, M. A. (2013). Relationship churning in emerging adulthood: On/off relationships and sex with an ex. *Journal of Adolescent Research, 28, 166-188.*

Hardy, S.A., Stephen W. F., Zamboanga, B.L., Kim, S.Y., Anderson, S.G., Forthun, L.F. (2013).

The roles of identity formation and moral identity in college student mental health, health-risk behaviors, and psychological well-being. *Journal of Clinical Psychology, 69,* 364-382.

Hobbs, J. (2014). *The short and tragic life of robert peace.* New York: Scriber.

King, P.E. & Merola, C.M. (2017). Crucibles of transformation. In L.M. Padilla-Walker & L.J. Nelson (Eds.). *Flourishing in emerging adulthood: Positive development during the third decade of life* (pp. 330-374). New York: Oxford University Press.

McMillan, J.L. (2017). The paradox of choice in emerging adulthood: Anxiety and ambivalence. Retrieved from https://etd.ohiolink.edu/!etd.send_file?accession=bgsu1499426843058909&disposition=inline.

Milne, A.A. (1926). *Winnie-the-Pooh.* London: Methuen & Co. Ltd.

Nelson, L.J., & Padilla-Walker, L.M. (2013). Flourishing and floundering in emerging adult college students. *Emerging Adulthood, 1,* 67-78.

Nesi, J., & Prinstein, M.J. (2015). Using social media for social comparison and feedback-seeking: gender and popularity moderate associations with depressive symptoms. *Journal of Abnormal Child Psychology, 43, 1427-1438.*

Schimmenti, A., Bifulco, A. (2015). Linking lack of care in childhood to anxiety disorders in emerging adulthood: The role of attachment styles. *Child and Adolescent Mental Health, 20,* 41-48.

Setran, D.P., & Kiesling, C.A. (2013). *Spiritual formation in emerging adulthood: A practical theology for college and young adult ministry.* Grand Rapids, MI: Baker Publishing Group.

Smith, C., Christofferson, K., Davidson, H. & Herzog, P.S. (2011). *Lost in transition.* New York: Oxford University Press.

Swanson, J.A. (2016). *Trends in literature about emerging adulthood, 4,* 391-402. Retrieved from http://journals.sagepub.com/doi/pdf/10.1177/2167696816630468.

U.S. Census Bureau, Decennial Censuses, 1890 to 1940, and Current Population Survey, Annual Social and Economic Supplements, 1947-2017. Retrieved from https://www.census.gov/content/dam/Census/library/visualizations/time-series/demo/families-and-households/ms-2.pdf.

U.S. Department of Education, National Center for Education Statistics (2017). *The condition of education2017. Retrieved from* https://nces.ed.gov/fastfacts/display.asp?id=40.

Vespa, J. (2017). The changing economics and demographics of young adulthood: 1975–2016. *Current Population Reports,* P20-579, Washington, DC: U.S. Census Bureau.

Zwier S., Araujo T., Boukes M., & Willemsen L. (2012). Boundaries to the articulation of possible selves through social networking sites. The case of Facebook profilers' social connectedness. *Cyberpsychology, Behavior, and Social Networking, 14,* 574-576.

Chapter Eleven

Middle Adulthood: At the Intersection of Growth and Decline

You said everywhere you look the world is changing,
Everywhere the water's closing in,
Something deeper still is always rearranging,
Something's lost, something new begins.

Patty Griffin (2015)

We continue our study of the lifespan by exploring middle adulthood, a stage of life situated in-between the emerging and older adult years. The song lyrics above reference the many changes, often experienced as losses, that can be associated with midlife. Children are being launched and parents are aging or dying. Referred to as the "sandwich" generation, middle adults frequently experience challenges as they are "sandwiched between" dependents who are younger and older—children, grandchildren, and parents. Some middle adults do not have family responsibilities, but have jobs that demand their time and energy. Others face health problems, financial strain, or marital and family conflict.

More positively, middle adults are often viewed as the central and stable core of the work force, providing guidance to younger workers while continuing to grow themselves in confidence, knowledge, and responsibility. They play a key role in society by simultaneously nurturing the next generation and responding to the needs of elderly family members. Indeed, middle adults fulfill central roles in numerous respects as they bridge the gap between youth and older adults and form the core of the work force. In various ways, middle adults help to stabilize society.

Middle adulthood is distinct as it represents a time of neither significant developmental gains nor significant developmental losses. In a broad sense, it represents a time characterized by developmental stability. How can this be the case if, as just described, middle adulthood entails multiple stressors and life changes? We do not mean that middle adults do not have *experiences* of gain or loss. By developmental stability, we mean that in a big-picture sense, middle adulthood is neither characterized by preparation nor by decline (Lachman, Teshale, & Agrigoroaei, 2015). The first half of the lifespan is typically dominated by preparation. Preparation for forming deep relationships and engaging a meaningful vocation. In contrast, older adulthood often represents a period of decline, not in value or worth, but in one's physical abilities and vocational contributions. When we view the entire lifespan from this perspective, middle adulthood represents a time of developmental stability when one draws on lessons learned during the first half of life and considers one's current self in relationship to the end of one's life.

Our focus as Christians in social work is on supporting middle adult development in the direction of healthy connections with God and other people. We will illustrate this perspective by looking at a case and exploring some of the fundamental aspects of this unique life stage. Keep this background in mind as we look into the life of Laura, a woman in middle adulthood.

The Case of Laura

Laura is a 53 year-old Caucasian female who resides with her husband, Brent (54), in a upper middle class suburb of Detroit. Laura and Brent have been married for thirty years and have three children—Samantha (26), Phoebe (23), and Michael (22). The couple met and began dating over thirty years ago during their junior and senior years at a large public university in Ohio. They had both dated other people casually during high school and college, but began dating one another in college and the relationship quickly became serious. They were engaged and married the year after Laura graduated.

The couple began their married life in Cleveland where Laura worked as a public accountant in a national accounting firm and Brent as an IT specialist for a corporate bank. While they have each changed places of employment over the years, they have continued to work in the same fields throughout their careers. The couple lived in the Cleveland area for the first eight years of their marriage, but moved to Denver for opportunities to advance in their jobs. They lived in Denver for nearly eighteen years. To continue to advance in her company, Laura was required to transfer to a company branch in Detroit four years ago. Laura works as an accounting manager where she supervises over forty employees. Her work requires long hours, including nights and weekends, as she has to address challenging human resource issues and monitor numerous departmental projects. She makes a large salary, but with her high salary are heavy performance expectations. Shortly after they moved, Brent found a satisfying job in his field working for a small start-up company. His work also entails long hours as his company is rapidly expanding into international markets. His job necessitates week-long business trips to London every month.

The couple's children are in various stages of schooling. Samantha is in her third year of a psychology doctoral program in Denver. Phoebe recently graduated from a Christian liberal arts college and is in her first year of a Master's degree in Accounting at a large university in Colorado. Michael is in his senior year at a Christian liberal arts college in northern Michigan where he is studying Computer Science. His school is a three-hour drive from his parents' home. The children were young when they moved to Denver and consider that part of the country to be their home. All three children graduated from high school there and have spent minimal time in the Detroit area since their parents' move. The two younger children have spent summers with their parents and have met a few people in the Detroit area, but all three children feel their closest friendships were formed during their years in Colorado.

Laura was born and raised in rural Ohio and is the oldest of two children. She has a brother who lives with his family in Washington, D.C. where he works as an attorney. Laura's mother, a retired elementary school teacher, died two years ago from an aggressive form of cancer. Her 80-year old father lives in the Ohio home where Laura was raised. He retired from a long and successful career in banking administration.

Laura struggles with some health problems, notably high blood pressure and arthritis and joint damage in her knee which causes her considerable pain. She will likely require knee replacement at some point in the future. She occasionally exercises by riding an elliptical bike, but does this inconsistently because of knee pain. Laura is in menopause and uses hormone replacement therapy to help with symptoms including hot flashes, insomnia, and mood swings. Her eating habits are relatively poor as she frequently skips breakfast and lunch. This leads to snacking throughout the day and often eating fast food dinner late in the evening. Laura smokes one cigarette in the morning and one in the evening. She drinks an average of two glasses of wine after work to help herself relax.

Following each of her pregnancies, Laura experienced post-partum depression which was successfully treated with anti-depressant medication. More than depression, however, Laura has struggled throughout her life with anxiety. She recalls severely biting her nails from the time she was a young girl. Laura has also struggled with anxious and racing thoughts since childhood. These have contributed to long-term difficulty falling and staying asleep. The onset of panic attacks during college led Laura to see her doctor. While she has consistently taken medication for generalized anxiety and panic attacks since college, she continues to experience low-level anxiety on a daily basis.

Laura's fear is often centered around disappointing others and deep feelings of insecurity and inadequacy. While anxiety runs in her family as her maternal grandmother had similar struggles, Laura's struggles additionally relate to her early experiences. Her parents remained married, but had a highly emotionally distant relationship throughout Laura's growing up years. Somewhat unusual for the time period, both her father and mother were highly invested in their careers. They felt that praising their children would lead to them being arrogant and cocky, so they withheld affirmation of any sort. While their physical needs were met, Laura and her brother learned to be independent and to care for themselves. As an emotionally sensitive and anxious child, Laura particularly needed adult assistance in calming and affirming herself. The lack of adult input and attention only exacerbated Laura's underlying fears. To gain her parents' attention and approval, she focused on academics, a place where she excelled. She was a diligent and excellent student throughout school, frequently at the top of her class. But these attempts to gain approval led to a cycle of using performance as a means of validating herself and her existence.

Laura is introverted by nature, needing considerable time alone to physically and emotionally recharge. Over the years, she has been more comfortable with a small group of friends than being at large parties or in large groups. Despite this tendency, Laura's hard work and professional skills have led to a steady string of job promotions. While she excels in her job, she often feels out of her comfort zone as she has to speak before groups and to confront employees with work or performance issues. She struggles with the constant fear of not "measuring up" or being judged negatively by her fellow employees or employers. This fear leads her to work harder, attempting to avoid situations where she is evaluated negatively. The few times this has happened in her work life have been devastating, leading to days of lying in bed, depressed, followed by a renewed determination to work harder.

Laura has a couple of female friends at work, but has no friends to whom she opens up completely. Her marriage has been a source of emotional support at times, but for many years, the couple has been more focused on their jobs than on their relationship. This has contributed to an awkward pattern of emotional and physical distance that they both would like to change, but do not really know how. They have been co-habiting and co-parenting for many years, but are now facing the "empty nest" years which only highlight the distance in their marriage. Brent has an easygoing personality and a commitment to the marriage, but his communication and social skills are poor, making it difficult for him to form authentic friendships and to connect with his wife and children.

While Laura enjoys being a mother and loves each of her children, she also feels inadequate and inferior as a mother. She struggles to communicate openly and honestly with her children in the same way that she struggles with her husband and friends. Often, she and Brent lack the interpersonal skills to have meaningful conversations with their young adult children. This has led to superficial parent-child relationships. Each of the children look primarily to their friends for support and advice. The superficial relationship has also contributed to some poor decisions on the parts of the children. Despite going to Christian colleges, all three kids drank (or drink) alcohol and partied heavily during college, establishing patterns that have persisted in graduate school for the older two children. Like their parents, they are all good students and have kept up their academic work and grades. But they strongly question their Christian upbringing, feeling that it is overly conservative and irrelevant to the contemporary world or daily lives. None of the children attend church and Samantha has been living with her boyfriend for the past year and a half. Laura feels responsible for these choices and views them as indications of her failings as a mother.

The death of Laura's mother was difficult because their relationship was never the one that Laura hoped for. Equally difficult is her current relationship with her father. Since her mother's death, he needs support and help from Laura more than ever, but they are not close and that makes conversations awkward and difficult. Laura feels a responsibility to be supportive, but feels this is an area in which she also fails. Her family of origin was not emotionally connected, a reality that made it difficult to cope during her mother's illness and death. Laura has a cordial relationship with her brother, but they are not close or connected.

Brent and Laura were each raised in nominal Christian homes. After marrying, they began attending mainline Protestant churches and brought their children to church fairly regularly, but faith was never discussed openly or explicitly in their home. Laura believes in God and prays on occasion, but experiences the same struggle to feel emotionally connected to

God as she does with interpersonal relationships. She does not feel close to God and often has doubts about the validity of faith in general.

We will return to the case of Laura and her family after considering some important aspects of middle adulthood.

Roles Meet Resources

As indicated in the introduction, middle adults balance numerous social roles,-such as spouse, parent, child, friend, neighbor, and employee. Middle adults often also belong to a number of organizations—civic, religious, and professional. Importantly, middle age seems to be a time of filling not only multiple roles, but filling *complex* roles (Antonucci, Akiyama, & Merline, 2001). For example, while parenting young children can be extraordinarily stressful, the demands of parenting adolescents and young adults add considerable complexity as higher order skills, such as negotiation and judgment, are required. Certainly not all middle adults are parents and some do not become parents until middle adulthood. But many in this stage are experiencing what can be the most demanding years of parenthood. Similarly, having been in their careers for some time, many middle adults have higher levels of job responsibility than they did as young adults.

Beyond the number and complexity of the roles they play, middle adults often experience more major life events, both positive and negative, than any other stage (Aneshensel & Pearlin, 1987). Significant life events can include children graduating from high school and college, leaving the family home, marrying, and having their own children. They may include career changes, promotions, and relocations. They can also include the death of one or both parents or dealing with one's own health problems. While there is clear variation by person, middle adulthood is a time period that requires ongoing adaptation to changing circumstances.

If middle adults have numerous and complex roles and face many major life events, how do they successfully meet the demands of their life stage? Beyond this, how can they not only survive and cope with the dynamics of their lives, but find ways to *thrive* during this time of life? Interestingly, by this stage of life, middle adults have many resources at their disposal. In His wisdom, God has seemingly matched a period of great demands with a period of great ability to cope with those demands. One author writes, "The resources of midlife are as outstanding as its challenges, and thus the key to successful development is the proper balance between stressors and coping resources" (Heckhausen, 2001, p. 353). Others describe middle adults as "...at the peak of their competence, ability to handle stress, sense of control, purpose in life, productivity, social responsibility, assertiveness, and authority" (Lachman, Lewkowicz, Marcus, & Peng, 1994, p. 201).

To break this down further, middle adults have resources in a few different areas. First, for the majority of people, their personalities are stable by middle adulthood (Allemand, Zimprich, & Hertzog, 2007; Lachman, Maier, & Budner, 2000). While there are exceptions, particularly for individuals with histories of neuroticism, the core components of most people's personalities are stable by this point in life (Bleidorn, Kandler, & Caspi, 2014). This reality implies that by this point, individuals have had time to grow in self-insight as experiences have revealed the ways their personalities are wired. Characteristics such as introversion, extroversion, or levels of one's flexibility are typically apparent by this time period. A stable personality and insight into one's natural wiring are resources because they strengthen problem-solving and coping capabilities. Energy is diverted from striving to understand one's self and directed toward the stressor or problem itself. Understanding yourself well means that energies can be primarily oriented toward responding to the problem. Middle adults can also adapt their environment and responses to better *fit* their core personality.

Related to a stable personality, middle adults have a good sense of their core gifts and weaknesses. This self-knowledge is a resource as a healthy sense of competence is experienced in some areas yet an acknowledgement of limitations occurs in other areas. A balance of self-competence and the willingness to honesty face one's limitations facilitates adaptation to stress. Persons draw upon both internal and external resources when facing stressors.

Secondly, middle adults have the advantage of applying the learning and competence from earlier experiences to those in the present. This is helpful in both a practical and psychological sense. Lessons and knowledge gained in one's work can be practically applied to present and future scenarios. In a similar sense, middle adults have already weathered and survived stressors in their lives. These experiences form the scaffolding for approaching stressors and problems in the present. They form the foundation on which middle adults approach problems in the present and future. As already indicated, middle adults often provide leadership in their social roles; the combination of learning from past experiences and high levels of self-insight and self-competence can be extraordinarily useful in roles requiring leadership.

Thirdly, middle adults are growing in wisdom, a tremendous resource in facing stress, changes, and difficulties. Scholars write, "In midlife, losses become more common: one loses parents and sometimes spouses, children grow up, and careers may pall. The stress from these events may have devastating effects…yet it is also through these losses that one may start to develop wisdom" (Aldwin & Levenson, 2001, p. 208). While middle adulthood makes stressful demands, stress also challenges one's assumptions about the world and can contribute to growth in wisdom.

In a psychological and spiritual sense, growth in wisdom leads to movement away from activities and striving that are increasingly viewed as invalid and unimportant. Some have referred to middle adulthood as a particularly rich time of shedding the "false self"—the part of one's self that is motivated by external approval and perfection—toward the "true self"—the part of one's self that is motivated to embrace one's core creational self. For Christians, movement toward the true self is movement away from preoccupation with the broader culture's view of success as physical beauty or monetary gain. Moving toward one's true self can produce a richer sense of self-acceptance, dependency on God, and acceptance of the mystery that lies beyond comprehension. Christians who leave behind a preoccupation with external approval are freed to more authentically accept themselves. This posture opens one more fully to the expansiveness of God and his love.

Movement away from the false self also shifts energy away from the self and onto the needs of others. This other-centered movement interestingly coincides with a time of life that often entails caretaking of a physical and/or emotional nature. For example, emerging adult children look to their parents for guidance, and aging parents increasingly need emotional support, particularly if widowed or alone. In Christian terms, we are able to more faithfully love our neighbor when, as middle adults, our own psychological needs demand less attention.

In sum, middle adults may be uniquely prepared for the roles they often play—as caretakers and leaders. Their stable personalities, experience, and other-centered movement create resources for meeting the stressors of their lives. Another important aspect of middle adulthood relates its unique vantage point toward the past and the future.

The Benefits and Pitfalls of Time

Middle adults not only demonstrate resources, they benefit from an increasing sense of the limited amount of time they have left or, to put it another way, their mortality. Unlike earlier stages, middle adults measure their lives less in terms of the life already lived, but in terms of the time left (Lang & Carstensen, 2002). Popular media emphasize midlife "crises" prompted by a panicked awareness of one's age and limited time through behaviors such as impulsive sports car purchases or extramarital affairs. Research, however, indicates that crises as popularly portrayed occur in just a minority of cases and are far more nuanced than popular media would suggest (Arnett, 2018; Freund & Ritter, 2009; Lachman, 2015). Indeed, while many middle adults endorse concerns about getting older, reappraising one's life in relationship to the "time left" is healthy and adaptive for most people (Lang & Carstensen, 2002; Nurmi, 1994). While some individuals with rigid personalities and particularly poor levels of adaptability may be thrown into crisis by a sense of their mortality (Putney & Bengtson, 2001), the majority of middle adults find their way to an enriched understanding of life by facing their mortality.

That said, the unique vantage point from the "middle" can create questions that *feel* like crises as persons measure what they have done in their lives against the amount of time they have left. In many cases, people envisioned themselves doing more in their areas of vocation, for example, than they have actually accomplished. But instead of initiating a crisis, the disconnect between vision and reality often facilitates a richer, more realistic expectation of one's self, others, and the world. Indeed, a sense of mortality can prompt midlife individuals to focus on the things that really matter. Among these are investing in relationships. Some middle adults will focus on growing deeper friendships. For others, there is a desire to instill wisdom in younger generations, preventing others from the mistakes of youth (McKee & Barber, 1999). Many middle adults shift from idealistic hopes of changing the world to enriching their present relationships and responsibilities. Future plans are made, but they are increasingly tempered by realism. Middle adults are adopting more grounded views of what they can control. At the same time, they are releasing adolescent or young adult dreams about ways of life that have proven to be unrealistic and/or unobtainable.

Although crisis is not universally characteristic of middle adulthood, social workers will encounter middle adults responding to stressors and major events in their lives in ways that are self-destructive or avoidant. Significant struggles often surface in response to highly destabilizing events such as job losses, unexpected deaths, divorce, forced relocation, or severe difficulties with children (Wethington, Cooper, & Holmes, 1997). Destabilization is compounded further by co-occurring losses. Additionally, individuals may experience high levels of social isolation as events such as divorce or relocation alter their social networks. Circumstances may force middle adults to "start all over" as they are forced to make new friendships after a move or to date again following a death or divorce.

Similarly, unexpected job losses can cause middle adults to regress to the feelings of insecurity and anxiety that are more characteristic of young, inexperienced employees.

In some cases—depending on variables such as an individual's personality, coping abilities, and history—life events and changes produce crises. Some individuals, for example, experience depression as they question the choices of their earlier lives, feeling deep regret or shame for their former decisions or patterns of behavior. Some experience anxiety, feeling trapped in their roles as spouses, parents, or breadwinners. Others are overwhelmed by the fact that their achievements do not come close to their hopes and dreams.

When middle adults are unable to cope, assistance in coming to terms with the events, choices, and consequences of their lives is needed. At times, our clients have histories involving activities that have painful and ongoing consequences. At other times, our clients cannot move beyond the anger and disappointment of being unable to bridge barriers to meaningful employment or to move into higher levels of economic stability. Experiencing the impact of their choices, some wish they could turn back the clock and be better parents, spouses, or friends. Experiencing the harshness of a fallen world, some feel disillusionment to the point of despair.

Demonstrating and applying God's forgiveness and the need for self-forgiveness are important components of meaningful work with mid-life adults who are stuck and unable to cope or move forward. Emphasizing the importance of confession and avoiding the pitfalls of shame are important themes as individuals take stock of their lives. Identifying signs of redemption in the midst of the darkest situations is critical. Middle adults will need to fully grieve losses—relational or otherwise. But healing will come as they are able to trust God's loving and redemptive purposes for their lives, despite mistakes or disappointments.

With these observations in mind, let's return to the case of Laura. Laura's case can be evaluated through the lens of healthy development and middle adult developmental themes. Specifically, we need to consider how Laura can be encouraged to develop in the right direction, forming healthier relationships with herself, others, and God.

Laura Revisited

There are many areas to affirm in Laura's life. She has been married for over thirty years. She is a loving and devoted mother to her three children. Admirably, Laura feels a sense of responsibility to her father and tries to support him. Laura's long faithfulness in these roles attests to the fact that she believes marriage and family are important commitments. Her behaviors also belie underlying emotional attachments to her husband, parents, and children.

Beyond familial roles, Laura is a gifted accountant. She exhibits considerable intellectual ability, a strong work ethic, and vocational talent. The fact that she has been promoted steadily in her jobs over the years is a testimony to both her hard work and giftedness. Additionally, although faith was not discussed in their home, Laura and Brent have taken their children to church regularly, demonstrating a desire, on some level, to incorporate faith and worship into their lives and the lives of their children.

There are also areas of struggle in Laura's life, however. She deals with the ongoing challenge of managing multiple roles simultaneously. She is balancing the needs of her marriage, young adult children, father, employees, and employer. Her roles are certainly also complex ones. Laura has considerable experience in juggling multiple roles as she has been doing so for many years. She has worked full-time and been a parent for over two decades. Her years of experience suggest a well-honed ability to successfully manage her time and the requirements of home and work. However, we can also see areas in which Laura is less competent, a reality that interferes with her thriving as a middle adult.

While she is intelligent and able to multi-task well, Laura demonstrates weaknesses in the emotional or psychological realm that have negatives consequences in her life. So while Laura has many resources to bring to bear on her stressors, she also demonstrates important gaps. Her family of origin was not characterized by warmth, a pattern that Laura has replicated in her own family and adult life. Her poor ability to communicate with emotional depth and honesty have negatively impacted her own life and her relationships. Her relationships have remained on relatively superficial levels which have also prevented her from gaining the wisdom, encouragement, and insight that could come from deep relational connections.

It seems that despite her intellectual giftedness, Laura lacks healthy self-insight, one of the resources of middle adulthood. It may be that Laura keeps herself so focused on tasks and performance that she does not fully consider the fears and insecurities that drive her. A pattern of emotional distance and avoidance, while well entrenched by midlife, is not unchangeable, however. Laura could be encouraged to identify her core emotions and to address them with honesty and openness. Laura's deep fears, particularly her struggles with insecurity and not measuring up, likely have their origins in her early history also. As an emotionally vulnerable child in a home lacking parental affirmation, she understandably looked to performance as a way of validating herself.

As an intelligent and capable woman, a pattern of reliance on performance has likely "worked" for Laura. Yet her long-term struggle with anxiety also suggests that the pattern has been maladaptive and needs to change to facilitate Laura's future well-being. Gaining self-insight and the ability to communicate openly has the potential for drawing her closer and connecting her more deeply to her spouse and children, outcomes that would richly benefit her life in the present. At this stage of life, emotionally reconnecting with her husband and children remains highly possible. Shifting her priorities will also better prepare her for the next stage of life as eventually her performance will show signs of decline. Laura is an introvert, but she needs social support and lacks it currently. It is critical that she strengthen her social supports with family members, friends, and her church.

There are implications of the pattern of emotional distancing in her human relationships, but also in her approach to God which is decidedly more cognitive than affective. She believes in God and attends church, but lacks a sense of emotional connection with God. While behavioral patterns are critical in the spiritual realm, Laura could benefit spiritually from increased emotional openness to God and His love, grace, and acceptance. As a woman who has struggled for many years with anxiety and deep insecurities, she could benefit greatly from an assurance that she is loved and accepted entirely apart from her abilities.

Middle adults may struggle with a growing sense that aspects of the world lie entirely out of their control. This is a healthy realization which can lead to more realistic and accurate views of one's role and place in the world. It can be particularly difficult, however, for individuals who rely on personal control as a means of coping and managing their anxiety and fears. For Laura, accepting areas of life where she has little control, including the actions of her children and the death of her mother, will likely be difficult because she demonstrates a strong need for control. Maintaining a sense of self-efficacy while acknowledging aspects of life outside of her control is important to her emotional health and coping going forward. Facing past regrets related to parenting is another important task. That said, it is not too late to work on strengthening relationships in the present.

Laura demonstrates internal struggles with self-acceptance, self-doubt, and anxiety related to her performance. Such emotions are undoubtedly incongruent with the way others see her and the competence she projects externally. However, growth in the right direction implies a growing sense of peace within herself. We want to see Laura moving away from her false self and toward her true self. For some people, this shift starts when their performance eventually comes up short or they receive negative feedback from others. In Laura's case, this rarely occurs. At this stage, there are few places in her life where she experiences the limits of her performance. Therefore, she will need steady encouragement to make behavioral changes such as decreasing her work hours and increasing her self-care practices. It is hopeful that rebalancing her time will also produce positive internal outcomes.

Laura's approach to work seems problematic in the sense that it assumes a significant part of her overall identity. Because she has historically experienced success in her work, this pattern has worked well for her. However, the imbalance between her work life and the rest of her life creates vulnerability. Her work roles could change, but more importantly, the imbalance leads to shortchanging relationships. Such patterns can create deficits that are more acutely felt in middle adulthood as the nest empties and friendships are not adequately maintained. Holding her work in proper balance with the rest of her life is important for Laura as it creates habits that facilitate healthy movement into the next stage of her life. Laura has to recognize the limits of work success and see it as just one component of a multi-layered and multi-dimensional life.

Laura also demonstrates poor self-care in the way she cares for herself physically. Smoking, poor eating habits, and minimal exercise are all poor habits that can carry long-term consequences into old age. Shifting priorities away from work would facilitate more time for self-care as well as more openness to the needs of other people in her life.

The death of Laura's mother two years ago, while not a major crisis in her life, has impacted her, nonetheless. The death of a parent can lead to confronting one's own mortality. For many, the death of a parent or parents often leads to psychological growth and the sense of finally "becoming an adult." These dynamics could produce growth in Laura's life, however she also has regrets related to the relationship with her mother as it was not of the quality she desired. Laura's response to her feelings has been to avoid thinking about the loss by burying herself in work responsibilities. A more helpful response would be to allow her regrets from this relationship to influence her present relationships by adding emotional depth. Additionally, Laura should be encouraged to fully process this loss and its meaning for her own life and mortality.

Finally, Laura has grown in competence in her many roles, but we might question if she is growing in wisdom. Wisdom implies, among other things, focusing one's energies on the things that truly matter. It also implies learning from your mistakes and turning from a self-centered to an other-centered orientation. Viewed from this perspective, Laura lacks some of the resources and good gifts that can be obtained during midlife. With encouragement to reflect more deeply on her emotions and experiences, Laura would likely grow in wisdom. She would steadily rely less upon her own performance. This would free her to focus on investing emotionally in her marriage, children, and other people.

In sum, Laura needs to develop patterns that will sustain her during old age, including stronger social supports, increased wisdom and self-insight, and healthy self-care practices. Engaging in individual and corporate spiritual disciplines is highly important to her well-being and development. Reorienting her life around the things that matter is also important. These changes will help her to draw upon the resources of midlife, prepare for the next stage of life, and develop in the right direction.

Chapter Summary

Middle adulthood represents a unique time period when the focus is neither on preparation nor decline. Viewed from a perspective of the entire lifespan, it is a period of developmental stability. Yet it is simultaneously a time of major life events and multiple roles, many of them complex in nature. At times, crises disrupt the equilibrium of middle adulthood, and help is needed to grow and to restore stability.

In many respects, middle adults benefit from their position in the middle, drawing lessons from their past experiences. They also draw wisdom from the reality that they are mortal beings with limits. They are shedding unrealistic views of what can be accomplished during the course of their lives, freeing them to focus on forging meaning and depth in relationships and future goals.

These developmental dynamics create rich opportunities for development in the right direction. The natural midlife turn toward richer relationships and meaningful goals can move persons closer to God and other people. Movement away from the false self and toward the true self can align individuals more closely with the persons they were created to be. Ultimately, it is important to harness these natural by-products of middle age as we assist people in developing in the right direction. In cases where individuals are thwarted or moving in destructive directions, however, our goal is always to realign their path through compassionate and competent challenge.

Discussion Questions

1. The Bible speaks often of wisdom. How can we assist middle adults in growing in wisdom, or is this something that must develop organically?

2. Many people experience the consequences of poor decisions and choices by midlife. How can we hold people accountable while also responding with compassion, knowing that we are all fallen?

3. Think of an example of a person in middle adulthood who models wisdom. What aspects of their life would you like to emulate?

4. Are there implications for middle adults who carry unresolved issues into older adulthood? Why or why not?

5. Middle adults were described as having stable personalities. How might this be a resource for them in coping with stress?

Resources

Aldwin, C.M. & Levenson, M.R. (2001). Stress, coping, and health at midlife: a developmental perspective. In M.E. Lachman (Ed.), *Handbook of Midlife Development* (pp. 188-214). New York: John Wiley & Sons, Inc.

Allemand, M., Zimprich, D., & Hertzog, C. (2007). Cross-sectional age differences and longitudinal age changes of personality of middle adulthood and old age. *Journal of Personality, 75*, 323-358.

Aneshensel, C. & Pearlin, L. (1987). Structural contexts of sex differences in stress. In R. Barnett, L. Biener, & G. Baruch (Eds.), *Gender and stress* (pp. 75-95). New York: Free Press.

Antonucci, T.C., Akiyama, H., & Merline, A. (2001). Dynamics of social relationships in midlife. In M.E. Lachman (Ed.), *Handbook of Midlife Development* (pp. 571-598). New York: John Wiley & Sons, Inc.

Arnett, J.J. (2018). Happily stressed: The complexity of well-being in midlife. *Journal of Adult Development, 20*, 10.1007/s10804-018-9291-3.

Bleidorn, W., Kandler, C., Caspi, A. (2014). The behavioral genetics of personality development in adulthood—classic, contemporary, and future trends. *European Journal of Personality, 28*, 244–255.

Freund, A. M., & Ritter, J. O. (2009). Midlife crisis: a debate. *Gerontology, 55*, 582–591.

Griffin, P. (2015). Made of the sun. On *Servant of Love* [CD]. Nashville: Thirty Tigers.

Heckhausen, J. (2001). Adaptation and resilience in midlife. In M.E. Lachman (Ed.), *Handbook of Midlife Development* (pp. 345-394). New York: John Wiley & Sons, Inc.

Lachman, M.E. (2015). Mind the gap in the middle: A call to study midlife. *Research in Human Development, 12,* 327-334.

Lachman, M.E., Lewkowicz, C., Marcus, A., & Peng, Y. (1994). Images of midlife development among young, middle-aged, and elderly adults. *Journal of Adult Development, 1,* 201-211.

Lachman, M.E., Maier, H., & Budner, R. (2000). *A portrait of midlife.* Unpublished manuscript, Brandeis University, Waltham, MA.

Lachman, M. E., Teshale, S., & Agrigoroaei, S. (2015). Midlife as a pivotal period in the life course: Balancing growth and decline at the crossroads of youth and old age. *International Journal of Behavioral Development, 39,* 20–31.

Lang, F.R. & Carstensen, L.L. (2002). Time counts: Future time perspective, goals, and social relationships. *Psychology and Aging, 17,* 125-139.

McKee, P. & Barber, C. (1999). On defining wisdom. *International Journal of Aging and Human Development, 49,* 149-164.

Nurmi, J.E. (1994). Age differences in adult life goals, concerns, and their temporal extension: a life course approach to future-oriented motivation. *International Journal of Behavioral Development, 15,* 487-508.

Putney & Bengtson, (2001). Families, intergenerational relationships, and kinkeeping in midlife. In M.E. Lachman (Ed.), *Handbook of Midlife Development* (pp. 528-570). New York: John Wiley & Sons, Inc.

Wethington, E., Cooper, H., & Holmes, C. S. (1997). Turning points in midlife. In I. H. Gotlib & B. Wheaton (Eds.), *Stress and adversity over the life course: Trajectories and turning points* (pp. 215-231). New York: Cambridge University Press.

Chapter Twelve

Older Adulthood: Finishing Well

Even to your old age and gray hairs, I am he, I am he who will sustain you.

Isaiah 46:4 (NIV)

...every individual lifetime is a creative act of divine love, and what seems like ordinary life, even in the most common sense, is the ultimate love of God seeking ever fuller expression.

Loder (1998, p. 326)

Last, but far from least, we consider older adulthood, the final stage of the lifespan. In a culture obsessed with youth and the first half of life, the marks of aging on our physical bodies are a frequent topic of discussion. The scientific search for the origins of aging at the genetic level has been underway for some time. While aging is inevitable, there is hope of slowing the process which would extend the lifespan and the life quality of many older adults. The physical process of aging is far-reaching as changes are noted all the way down to our very molecular level where cells increasingly lose their capacity to function and divide (Levine, 2004).

Even with technological advances, however, aging is a universal process. While its rate differs by individual due to lifestyle or genetic variation, aging is a normal phenomenon, programmed into our physical bodies by our Creator. Factors that accelerate aging have been identified such as smoking, alcohol abuse, obesity, a sedentary lifestyle, and poor nutrition. However, despite individual variation, there are unalterable physical changes that unfold over time. A decrease in brain size, for instance, contributes to slower abilities in processing new information, recalling short-term details, and responding to stimuli. Decreases across each of the senses—vision, hearing, smell, taste, and touch—are also noted.

In addition to the normal physiological changes associated with aging, many older adults struggle with short-term illnesses as well as chronic diseases. Contrary to popular belief, death is not actually caused by old age, but by serious conditions that disproportionately impact older adults, such as heart disease, cancer, strokes, or chronic respiratory diseases (Murphy, Xu, Kochanek, & Arias (2017).). Additionally, there are many older adult conditions that are not life-threatening, but impact one's quality of life, such as arthritis, diabetes, and hearing and vision problems.

Older adulthoods are a far from homogenous group. In fact, in the U.S., they are an increasingly ethnically and racially diverse group (World Health Organization, 2011).). The average lifespans of Americans and many older adults around the world are increasing with the improved knowledge about health and the ability to successfully treat conditions such as heart disease and cancer. Older adults represent a large and increasingly complex group. To better understand within-group differences, researchers have made various age-related distinctions. For example, some categorize the "young-old" as those between ages 60-69, the "middle old" as those between 70-79, and the "old-old" as those over 80 (Cohen-Mansfield, Shmotkin, Blumstein, Shorek, Hazan, 2013). We will broadly consider this group while acknowledging the great diversity by age and other important factors.

Unfortunately, although older adults carry the knowledge and wisdom of experience, in Western cultures they are often devalued as a group. In a fast-paced world characterized by ever-changing technological advances and a 24-hour news cycle, the contributions of older adults can be seen as irrelevant or outdated. Their limitations are often highlighted over their potential contributions. It is within this general context that we must thoughtfully consider older adulthood. As Christians in social work, we must ask ourselves how we can honor and uphold both the contributions and the needs of older adulthoods. We must consider the biblical themes of humanity—embodiment, fallenness, relationality, the need for redemption, and agency—as they intersect with the unique realities of older adulthood. We will illustrate this perspective as we look at the case of William.

The Case of William

William is 82-year-old African-American widower who lives in a neighborhood in Pittsburgh. He has been living alone since his wife of twenty-seven years died of lung cancer eight months ago. William worked for a large railroad for forty-four years—his entire career—before retiring.

He worked his way up over time from a maintenance position at a yard in Pittsburgh to an engineering position, a position he held for the last twenty years. During his twenty years as a locomotive engineer, William rode the train for seven days straight followed by seven days off. He greatly enjoyed this schedule and the work. He liked the challenge of needing to stay current with technological advances.

William has been retired for sixteen years. Initially he struggled with retirement, finding the lifestyle change very difficult because he so enjoyed his work and schedule. But after many years, he has adapted to retirement. In fact, William often feels relieved because technological advances have continued at such a rapid rate that he now wonders if he would have been able to keep up.

Financially, William is stable as he receives a monthly pension from his former employer and Social Security benefits as well as Medicare health insurance. He has additional money in savings for emergencies and owns his home and several vehicles. William's hobby is restoring cars, so he has a pick-up truck that he drives, but several older cars he has purchased and is steadily restoring. His lifestyle is not extravagant, but he has enough money to live comfortably.

William grew up just two miles from where he lives currently. He was born and raised in a working-class neighborhood on the south side of the city. William was the oldest of three sons born to his parents, Elaine and Thomas. Each of the boys are two years apart in age. William's brothers are both living and live in the same neighborhood as where they were raised. Thomas was employed by a factory that produced commercial heating systems. Elaine was a full-time homemaker who was a talented cook and seamstress. Thomas died suddenly forty years ago from a heart attack and Elaine died twenty-two years ago from leukemia, a disease she struggled with for nearly three years.

William does not recall much about his childhood, but remembers it as a generally happy time in his life. He had a circle of friends in the neighborhood with amusing nicknames like Hook, Beef, and Guff. Together they had many adventures, getting into occasional trouble, but mostly just having good fun. None of the boys came from particularly warm or happy homes, but they weren't especially aware of it at the time. William played with his brothers when his friends weren't available. They engaged in typical roughhousing and fighting, but had a fairly good relationship overall. As the oldest son, William was protective of his brothers and would defend them (with his fists) if needed.

Like many other men of his generation, Thomas was a stern and demanding father. The family structure was highly traditional. His role as the male was the breadwinner and his wife's responsibility was the parenting and homemaking. He was infrequently engaged with his sons, generally interacting with them only when discipline was needed. Thomas was a harsh disciplinarian, spanking the boys with a belt when they got into trouble. The only other time he talked to the boys was when handing out household chores. Thomas had a strong personal work ethic and expected the same of his children.

Elaine was a good homemaker who prepared wonderful meals and maintained a structured and organized household. As a mother, she was as stern as her husband. She required regular chores, completed homework, and obedience from the boys. When the boys did not comply, she informed her husband who issued the discipline. Elaine came from a poor family who experienced many hardships. She adopted a practical, no-nonsense approach to life which she passed along to her sons. Elaine was not an emotionally warm or nurturing mother. She loved her sons, but worried that she would "spoil" them if she was overly tender. Not wanting them to be arrogant or prideful, she withheld praise or affirmation, even when they demonstrated academic or sports accomplishments.

William was an average student during school. He excelled, however, in mechanics and enjoyed taking apart his bicycles and, as a teen, working on his beat-up car. In high school, William had several friends and he also played on the basketball team. He wasn't a popular student, but he wasn't a social outcast either. He briefly dated a few girls during high school.

After high school, William had a couple friends who entered the military. Not sure about what to do with his life, this option seemed attractive, so William joined the Navy. He completed his basic training in South Carolina and then was stationed on ships on and off for the next four years. He spent most of his time near Japan. William was trained as a ship mechanic.

William says that his years in the military were the most formative of his life. When he entered the military, he was an immature young man with a short temper. He often got into fist fights with fellow crewmen and was severely disciplined several times. It was during those years on a ship, however, that he first came into contact with people who were Christians.

Growing up, William's family attended a Baptist church on occasion, but were not highly religious. Most of the crewmen were similar to William—immature and self-centered. Also like him, they liked to drink and party whenever they were off-duty. But on the ship, William met a small group of people who were interested in getting to know him more deeply. They asked questions about his beliefs, family history, and feelings about the future. This impressed William as no one had asked him deep questions like these before. They invited him to a weekly Bible study which William started attending. Shortly thereafter, William converted to Christianity. This group of men became close friends and they began learning and growing together.

When his four years were completed, William moved back to Pittsburgh where he began his career. He struggled to adjust to civilian life and missed the Christian fellowship he had experienced in the Navy. William attended a local Baptist church for about a year, but steadily began to drift away from the church and the Christian practices he had learned in the Navy. Without the encouragement and direction of a church, William returned to the friends and the lifestyle of his youth.

After returning from the Navy, William married Dedra, a woman he knew from high school. They were married for eight years and had two children together—Randall (58) and Janet (56). While the marriage started out well, within a year, the couple were fighting regularly. Some of their conflicts were heated and physical. They separated a couple of times and eventually divorced. William's parents were ashamed to have divorce in the family and, for several years, discontinued contact with him and their grandchildren. Dedra was the primary parent for the children. Because of his atypical work schedule, William saw the children one weekend a month.

A year after the divorce, William remarried Jacquie, a divorced woman he met through a friend. She had two daughters, ages four and six, from her first marriage. Although they saw their biological father on alternate weekends, Jacquie was the primary parent and so William became the stepfather to two young children. Like his own father, William was a stern, authoritarian father and stepfather. He saw his biological children so infrequently that the relationship became very distant. He felt awkward around his children, not really knowing how to communicate with them. Eventually, both sides lost interest in spending time together and the children stopped visiting him altogether when they were teenagers. William also struggled as a stepfather. He imitated his father by taking a stern and authoritarian approach, but this created animosity between him and his stepdaughters. Their relationship was highly conflictual during their teen years when the girls resented him and challenged his authority. Both girls began rebelling by using drugs, drinking heavily, and even running away on occasion. The issues between William and his stepdaughters created great tension in his marriage. The couple remained married during the girls' growing up years, but the conflict only intensified when they left the home. William moved out and the couple divorced after twenty years of marriage.

William remained single for a couple of years, but became lonely and interested in dating again. He began dating a divorced woman he met in the neighborhood bar. At age 55, William married for the third time to Mary. Both William's and Mary's children were grown and the couple settled into a stable lifestyle. They had been married for 27 years when Mary died. William has five grandchildren who range in age from adolescents to young adults. Unfortunately, he has not cultivated a close relationship with any of his grandchildren.

William has been struggling greatly since Mary's death eight months ago. He sees their relationship was the one and only truly successful one in his life; he feels lost without her. William now lives alone. He has a distant relationship with his children and is completely estranged from his ex-wives and stepchildren. All but one of his long-term friends have died in the past decade. His social support is now entirely gone. He belongs to a local VFW and goes there on occasion, but winds up drinking heavily and not having any meaningful conversation.

William feels depressed most of the time, reporting symptoms of hopelessness, poor sleep, erratic eating, and occasional suicidal thinking. His physical health is also poor. He has been diagnosed with Type 2 diabetes and had a heart attack four years ago. He did cardiac rehabilitation following the heart attack, but has resumed poor eating habits and he also smokes ½ pack of cigarettes per day. He needs a hip replacement, but does not want to have surgery so he experiences pain whenever he walks.

Since his wife died, William has been thinking more about his own mortality and about the faith of his youth. He still believes in God, but has not been in a church or practiced his faith for many years. He imagines that God is angry at him for leaving the faith and for the life he has lived. He tries to avoid thinking about his life in the past or the future, but this is difficult as he knows that his life will not go on indefinitely.

We will return to the case of William after considering some important aspects of older adulthood.

Loss and the Resurrection

The individual experiences of older adults vary greatly. Some suffer from conditions like dementia where their bodies slowly and agonizingly decline. Others enjoy physical health for the majority of their lives, experiencing sudden or short-term deterioration prior to death. As indicated earlier, however, physical decline is a universal component of aging. As embodied persons, we cannot escape the ways that our bodies, impacted by the fall, are moving toward diminishment and ultimately, toward death. On the other hand, our embodiment also implies that we are to live fully and faithfully in the present, looking forward to the future, but not disengaging from daily life either. A holistic perspective means that we are neither to ignore the realities of aging nor be entirely defined by them either.

Long-time Quaker author and educator, Parker Palmer, now in his eighties, wrote,

> I would be lying if I said that I am awed by all that comes with old age ... and yet it is because of the diminishments of age, not in spite of them, that I often find myself in awe as I stand on the brink of everything (2018. p.18).

In this brief quote, Palmer captures perhaps the most important tension faced in older adulthood—adapting to limitations in the present while looking to the future with expectation and hope. Like other wise Christians before him, Palmer is further pointing out how the late stages of the life journey create an advantageous perspective. His use of the word "awe" suggests that the growth of old age is not simply learning in the way we usually think of it—the traditional, cognitive sense. It is multidimensional learning that engages beauty, wonder, and mystery.

Of older adulthood, Richard Rohr (2011) describes a life stage that seems to be moving downward yet which is actually moving upward. By this, he implies, like Palmer, that physical diminishment can facilitate an understanding of what truly matters in life. Rohr rightly suggests that as we are less "productive" in a worldly sense, our lives are simplified and we are more able to see the beauty and importance of relationships with God and other people. Our energy shifts from proving our worth through production to experiencing our worth in the context of relationships. As we become more dependent, Rohr argues, a healthy sense of our dependence on God and others emerges. In other words, old age can, if we allow it, produce what Jesus speaks of as "dying to ourselves" or releasing the grip on performance and self-sufficiency. This counterintuitive perspective, Rohr argues, is consistent with the message of the Gospel in which suffering produces deep growth, the last wind up first, and the weak are strong. Such messages contradict a broader culture which emphasizes power and productivity.

Accepting the reality of diminishment is one of the greatest challenges for older adults. An important role of Christians in social work is helping older adults to cope with losses. We often think of losses in concrete terms, such as the death of a spouse or the end of one's formal career. Older adults certainly experience losses of this nature, but they additionally experience ongoing losses associated with the diminishment of their physical selves. In other words, loss impacts older adults in highly identifiable ways and in ways that are far more subtle. Therefore, thriving in older adulthood implies an ability to face decline without denial or avoidance, to maintain agency wherever possible, and perhaps most importantly, to hold the hope of the resurrection.

The Denial Trap

A significant challenge of older adulthood is facing reality openly and honestly. Social workers are well aware of the psychological defense mechanisms—mechanisms for avoiding negative emotions and experiences—first identified by Freud. Denial is a powerful defense that can be relied upon throughout the lifespan; older adulthood is no exception. Some older adults, in an attempt to avoid facing the difficulties of their declining physical health or cognitive acuity, will distance themselves from these realities by simply denying their existence or minimizing their severity. In these cases, it is helpful to understand denial less as willful "stubbornness" and more as the manifestation of deep emotions, such as fear or anger. This does not mean that older adults are not responsible for their behaviors and responses, but that it is important to explore the emotions underlying their actions.

The decline in physical, socioemotional, and cognitive capacities can understandably trigger anxiety and fear about the future. There are often many unanswerable questions about the speed and progression of decline due to disease or the aging process. Some older adults lack the ability to process these emotions in a healthy manner and fall back upon denial as a means of coping. People may have short periods of denial, especially when coping with a crisis, but long-term denial becomes problematic and even dangerous for older adults. If, for example, older adults take physical risks beyond their capacity or refuse to comply with necessary medical recommendations, their behaviors may be communicating a deeper struggle with the fear and anxiety of loss (Loder, 1998).

Another area where loss may be experienced is in the sense of control (Beckett & Taylor, 2010). As mentioned earlier in this book, God gives all persons agency and we thrive when we can make independent choices within appropriate boundaries. The importance of agency extends throughout the lifespan. Older adults often experience reduced control over their environments as their limitations increase and their range of choices decreases.

Adaptation is, of course, needed to successfully cope with loss. When losses are great or cumulative in nature, adapting is not a singular or short-term event, but an ongoing process. The process of adaptation involves fully exploring one's emotions, including sadness, fear, and anger, and coping with present realities. The grieving process requires letting go of what has been lost, exploring the new circumstances, searching for meaning by looking back, and feeling at home in the new reality (Lyon, 2004). Grief means, however, that the intensity and nature of one's emotions change frequently. Interestingly, most older adults will cope with losses in ways that are similar to their coping styles earlier in life. Individuals who have grown in wisdom from life experiences will adapt to the changes of old age. In fact, as indicated above, they will be enriched by the experiences of old age and grow from them. At times, however, individuals focus so much on their losses that they miss the gains that come from a simpler life with the freedom to invest in others with less self-interest (Loder, 1998).

Developmental theorist Erik Erikson (1963) referred to the primary older adult task as "ego integration vs despair." This dichotomy provides a useful way of thinking about work with older adults. Individuals who review their lives and feel a deep sense of gratitude, despite mistakes they have made along the way, will experience a strengthened sense of self (Butler, 1998). But individuals who have not developed healthy relationships in their lives—with God and other people—may struggle with "despair" or depression as the end of their life comes closer. These individuals may exhibit high levels of guilt, regret, and hopelessness about the future. They may be characterized by resigned passivity or internalized hostility. Loder (1998) writes, "In the face of death, the despairing person can only express fear and attack life with disgust, regret, and demand" (p. 321).

The consequences of estranged or untended relationships loom large for older adults, who lack the physical and emotional support of friends and family at a time when increasing support is needed. This has practical, but also psychological implications. Individuals who enter older adulthood with unresolved issues and regrets are more likely to struggle internally with the experiences of older adulthood. It will be harder for them to feel peaceful about the end of their lives (Lyon, 2004).

This is an important place for social work intervention. Assisting older adults in finding peace with their mistakes, especially their relational ones, is important as unresolved issues contribute to despair. In some cases, it may be realistic and appropriate to encourage reconciliation in broken relationships or nurture in emotionally distant ones. Christians in social work can play a vital role in assisting older adults in finding peace with their past and their present as God's grace and forgiveness reach across the lifespan. Even in situations where relationships cannot be repaired or actions undone, the message of forgiveness can bring peace to the most troubled heart. One author writes, "We need not be crushed under the weight of the shortcomings of our past, for it is God's compassion, and not our effort, that authors the final word about our lives" (Lyon, 2004, p. 283). In many cases, the body of Christ becomes family, visiting older adults who need to be reminded that they have not been abandoned or left alone. Our visible presence can be a reminder that there is no period of life without God's nourishing presence.

Perhaps the greatest contribution of Christians in social work is holding out the hope of the resurrection. This applies to all age groups, but has particular relevance to those closer to the end of their lives. At times, professional ethics and agency policies may prohibit us from explicitly speaking of resurrection hope, but we carry it with us wherever we go. Older adults, even those of deep faith, need to be reminded that they have a future hope. Ultimately, we can embrace death as we will be with Christ. Lyon writes,

> The experience of old age has been contextualized by belief in the resurrection. Although our life in this world ends with death, our death is not the final thing about us. God redeems our lives from final meaninglessness, and our present experience is nurtured through hope in the resurrection of our bodies in Jesus Christ (Lyon, 2004, pp. 283-284)

Agency and Scaffolding

Earlier in the book, we referenced the work of Russian psychologist, Vygotsky (1978), who identified the zone of proximal development and the need for scaffolding that challenges children to learn, but simultaneously supports them. This concept has relevance during older adulthood. In this case, however, children are moving toward increased capacity (less scaffolding) and older adults are moving toward decline (more scaffolding). Scaffolding needs to increase as downward development outpaces upward development (Balswick, King, & Reimer, 2016).

There are two ways to err in providing scaffolding for older adults— providing too much and providing too little. They both create dangers, as too much scaffolding creates frustration or hostility as the older adult feels infantilized. Their sense of agency is restricted, which can also lead to passivity or learned helplessness (Beckett & Taylor, 2010). On the other hand, too little scaffolding is dangerous because harm can occur if older adults attempt more than they should. Harm can occur when others wrongly assume that they can comply with medications or medical instructions.

Scaffolding is a core place of challenge when working with older adults as needs can change quickly. It is important not to degrade older adults through infantilization, but it is equally important not to provide supports as needed. Balancing agency and scaffolding requires honest questioning and dialogue. Practitioners will also need to be sensitive to older adults with a pattern of either under- or over-estimating their abilities, taking a directive approach when needed.

Importantly, it has been pointed out that older adults need not only scaffolding in a physical sense, but also in a relational sense (Balswick, King, & Reimer, 2016). Relationality is not lost in old age. In some cases, such as dementia or severe strokes, the capacity for reciprocity in relationships may be lost. But older adults, like persons of every stage, need loving and affirming social interactions. These are not only key to their daily well-being and life satisfaction, but to their ongoing adaptation to loss and preparation for the future.

Older adults, particularly, benefit from multigenerational relationships. They benefit from the companionship and similar experiences of other adults, but also from relationships with younger people. Beautiful relationships can be built across generations as older adults can provide non-judgmental listening and accepting and, in return, young people can educate older adults about their experiences in the contemporary world. One author notes,

> It is often grandparents, who do not fear death, who most adequately inspire a love of life in their grandchildren…it may be that from points closest to death, we are most able to affirm life. From points in the midst of old age, we can most effectively encourage youth (Loder, 1998, pp. 320-321).

Interestingly, while social isolation is well-documented among older adults due to the death of friends, decreased opportunities, and social withdrawal (Cornwell, Schumm, & Laumann, 2008), many older adults are actually demonstrating more selectivity in their relationships. Some authors report a "pruning" process whereby they demonstrate agency by pursuing relationships of value to them. In light of the totality of their lives, many older adults recognize the importance of relationships of quality. They only maintain relationships worth keeping, demonstrating in this manner a new manifestation of agency (Lang & Carstensen, 1994). The size of their network may decrease, but older adults seek out people who provide emotional support. The sense of limited time creates an urgency that leads many to reconnect more deeply in current relationships, including with grandchildren and those of younger generations.

Let's keep these observations in mind as we return to the case of William.

William Revisited

William's case clearly illustrates some of the challenges of older adulthood. We note a pattern of loss across William's life. He displays physical decline in his struggles with chronic disease, pain, and limitation. His wife of 27 years has been gone for only a short time. And William is acutely experiencing the consequences of failing to nurture close relationships with friends and family throughout his life.

That said, there are several areas of strength in William's life. His ability to build and maintain a satisfying, long-term career and to stay current with technological changes is a testimony to his intelligence, giftedness, work ethic, and faithfulness. Not surprisingly, with his enjoyable career, William struggled initially with retirement, but adapted over time. His long-term interest in car restoration is another positive in his life. Financial security is additionally a strong protective factor at this stage of his life.

In many respects, William's life story contains many strengths as well. Although his family of origin was emotionally disengaged, William remembers his early life as fun and carefree. He recalls many friends and brothers who were playmates. He looks back on his Navy years as among the best of his life. While he unfortunately distanced himself from the church after the Navy, a spiritual foundation was formed during this time in his life. Finally, William clearly had a strong and healthy attachment to his third wife, Mary. This speaks positively to his ability to form relational connections with others when he avails himself of the opportunity.

Despite his strengths, however, William has had many struggles in his life. These center around his poor history of relationships. Like many people, William became the same type of parent and stepparent that he experienced in his family of origin. His disengagement with his spouses and children has unfortunately produced consequences that contribute to William's current struggle. These behaviors had previous consequences as well, especially in his marriages. At this stage of his life, we would like to see William learn and grow from his past experiences rather than be overwhelmed by regret. This level of self-insight and growth may not be possible until William's mental health is more stable. But his high level of intelligence and motivation suggest that this type of growth is very possible.

William is not currently functioning well. Perhaps his most immediate need is assistance in coping with the recent loss of his wife. William needs help exploring and processing his emotions about this major loss. Unfortunately, he lacks any current relationships that are close enough for this level of communication to happen. This suggests a two-fold goal of processing his loss individually, but steadily increasing his social circle, perhaps through a grief support group or local church.

In a broader sense, William expresses many regrets. It is important for him to process these regrets in order to face his future with hope and not despair. There is time for him to come to terms with his past and to experience peace in the present. First, William could take small steps to communicate with his children and grandchildren. He will likely need coaching about how to engage them, but the possibility of reconnecting with them may still be viable. William seems to be experiencing many fears, yet there also seems to be potential for tenderness in relationships. He would likely benefit greatly from listening to the activities and experiences of his grandchildren. Much of William's life has seemed to be self-focused; shifting to an other-focused shift would be extremely healthy.

William's spiritual history remains an important resource in his life, even though he has not practiced his faith for many years. Reconnecting him with the faith of his youth would likely help William to experience God's forgiveness and, related to that, an ability to forgive himself. Now in older adulthood, William needs the hope of the resurrection that he had so many years ago. A community of faith would further enrich William's life by affirming the message of future hope and providing social support.

We must additionally consider the level of scaffolding in William's life. His serious mental health symptoms, particularly his suicidal ideation, suggest that increased scaffolding is urgently needed. His social isolation makes this situation dangerous and it is imperative that William reach out for professional help, sharing his internal struggle honestly and openly. William's self-care is also concerning as he is smoking and eating poorly despite a history of serious heart disease. This reckless behavior may be a product of his depression or his social isolation, but his future health is being jeopardized, regardless. At this point, William has far too little relational scaffolding for his well-being and safety. Indeed, we cannot consider William's ability to thrive as an older adult until his mental health is stable.

Considering Erikson's (1963) ego integrity vs. despair dichotomy, William's current life leans toward despair. He needs help processing and adapting to many layers of loss. His fears are understandable, but they only contribute to his depression and hopelessness because they are entirely internalized. Reconnection with his early faith is important if he is to turn from regrets in the past and look forward to the future with hope. William is not currently growing or thriving in older adulthood; his development at this point is not in the right direction. It is not too late, however, to respond to William's core human needs—for loving relationships, support with his medical and mental health needs, and connection with his loving Father. Pointing William in the direction of reconnection with God and other people will help him to reposition his life toward hope and peacefulness, both in the present and future.

Chapter Summary

Old age is unique in many ways. Notably, as individuals near the end of their lives, their vantage point closer to death can produce unprecedented growth. Indeed, older adulthood can be an extraordinarily rich time for relationships with God and others. One author writes, "Growing old can literally be a *growing* process in which a human rises above temporal concerns by growing closer to God" (Lyon, 2004, p. 280). But adaptation to loss is a necessary aspect of growing older. Some persons look back on their lives and, instead of feeling gratitude, they are overwhelmed by feelings of regret. Faced with their mortality, some experience panic rather than hope and expectation toward the future.

Christians in social work carry resurrection hope to individuals in both categories, affirming God's love, forgiveness, and our future hope. We affirm our core human needs for life-giving relationships throughout the lifespan. It is clear that God nurtures his beloved creation from our beginning in the womb to our ending at death. Therefore, nothing, not old age, dementia, nor the most egregious of past mistakes, can separate us from his love.

Discussion Questions

1. How can we help older adults to avoid despair and to embrace old age as a rich stage of life?

2. In two or three sentences, identify a telos or purpose for William's development.

3. There are situations for which people need additional scaffolding, but firmly resist it. How can we respect the agency of such individuals while protecting them from harm?

4. What does it mean to live well and, as the Apostle Paul writes, to "finish the race well?"

5. This chapter discussed the importance of coming to peace with one's regrets. What about situations for which those regrets are overwhelming?

References

Balswick, J.O., King, P.E. & Reimer, K.S. (2016). *The reciprocating self: human development in theological perspective.* Downers Grove, IL: InterVarsity Press.

Beckett C. & Taylor, H. (2010). *Human growth and development.* Thousand Oaks, CA: Sage.

Butler, R.N. (1998). *Aging and mental health: positive psychosocial and biomedical approaches.* Boston: Allyn & Bacon.

Cohen-Mansfield, J., Shmotkin, D., Blumstein, Z., Shorek, A., Eyal, N., Hazan, H., CALAS Team (2013). The old, old-old, and the oldest old: continuation or distinct categories? An examination of the relationship between age and changes in health, function, and well-being. *International Journal of Aging and Human Development, 77,* 37-57.

Cornwell, B., Schumm, L. P., & Laumann, E. O. (2008). The social connectedness of older adults: A national profile. *American Sociological Review, 73,* 185-203.

Erikson, E. (1963). *Childhood and society* (2nd ed.). New York: Norton.

Lang, F. R., & Carstensen, L. L. (1994). Close emotional relationships in late life: Further support for proactive aging in the social domain. *Psychology and Aging, 9,* 315-324.

Levine, R.A. (2004). *Aging with attitude: growing older with dignity and vitality.* Westport, CT: Praeger Publishers.

Loder, J.E. (1998). *The logic of the spirit: human development in theological perspective.* San Francisco: Jossey Bass.

Lyon, K.B. (2004). Faith and development in late adulthood. In F.B. Kelcourse (Ed.), *Human development and faith* (pp. 269-284). St Louis: Chalice Press.

Murphy, S.L., Xu, J.Q., Kochanek, K.D., Arias, E. (2017). *Mortality in the united states.* NCHS Data Brief, no 328. Hyattsville, MD: National Center for Health Statistics.

Palmer, P. (2018). *On the brink of everything: grace, gravity, and getting old.* Oakland, CA: Berrett-Koehler Publishers.

Rohr, R. (2011). *Falling upward: a spirituality for the two halves of life.* San Francisco: Jossey Bass.

Vygotsky, L. S. (1978). *Mind in society: The development of higher psychological processes.* Cambridge, MA: Harvard University Press.

World Health Organization (2011). Global health and aging. Retrieved from https://www.who.int/ageing/publications/global_health.pdf?ua=1.